SCOTLAND YARD'S
HISTORY OF
CRIME
IN 100
OBJECTS

ALAN MOSS AND KEITH SKINNER

The
History
Press

Front cover images left to right: an undamaged version of Charlotte Bryant's weedkiller tin (see p. 141); Ruth Ellis' Smith & Wesson .38 revolver (see pp. 145–6).
Back cover images left to right: timing device used by the IRA (see pp. 229–30); Florence Maybrick's bottle of Valentine's Meat Juice (see pp. 129–31).
Images reproduced by kind permission of the Metropolitan Police Service.

First published 2015
This paperback edition first published 2022

The History Press
97 St George's Place, Cheltenham,
Gloucestershire, GL50 3QB
www.thehistorypress.co.uk

Typesetting and origination by The History Press
Printed in Turkey by IMAK

Trees for Life

Contents

Introduction

THE OBJECTS FEATURED in this book come from Scotland Yard's Crime Museum. They illustrate the history of crime and how methods of investigation have developed over the years. Some objects are courtroom sketches from the collection of William Hartley, a reporter who attended many of the high-profile trials between 1893 and 1919; his drawings give an insight into some of the characters involved. Some are everyday objects that became vital clues, whilst other objects are interesting curiosities. This book features some weapons, but the authors do not wish to risk concentrating unduly on violence. They have tried to provide a range of exhibits, and to avoid putting into the public domain any previously unknown details that might give improper inspiration. They have also taken into account Scotland Yard's own judgements about what items should or should not be featured.

The Crime Museum at New Scotland Yard has accumulated an intriguing and fascinating variety of exhibits from crime scenes since the collection was established in 1875. The police have always needed to store property belonging to prisoners and evidence that might be relevant to court cases. Some of those objects could never be returned to their criminal owners when the court cases were concluded. They were sometimes examples of criminal ingenuity that illustrated the very essence of those crimes, so they were very much an educational resource for police officers.

The officer in charge of the property store, Inspector Percy Neame, and his assistant, PC Randall, started exhibiting some of the tools of the criminal trade so that their colleagues could see first-hand the housebreaking implements, forgery equipment and disguised weapons that might be found on suspects on the streets of London. As the collection expanded, the attraction of the museum increased, not only to police officers, but also to judges, lawyers, forensic scientists and many others who were intrigued by the prospect of seeing for themselves the infamous details that they had read about in newspaper accounts of the high-profile cases dealt with by Scotland Yard detectives. Sometimes the exhibits have passed through the private hands of police officers and even judges, who unofficially retained souvenirs of the famous cases in which they played a part. As with many museums, the precise circumstances of each item's acquisition have not always been recorded with precise detail, but Bill Waddell, curator from 1981 to 1993, deserves great credit for establishing the modern catalogue.

The nature of some of the exhibits, and concern for the victims of crime, has always dictated that the museum could not be open to the general public. Demand for opportunities to visit the museum, even amongst police officers, has invariably outstripped the available visiting times, and this, over the years, has created a premium on the chance to see the museum's contents. A journalist wrote a description of the museum in *The Observer* of 8 April 1877, and his comments about the appropriateness of the title 'Black Museum', by which the collection became known, was the first record of the name that was used for many years.

In 1889, Charles Clarkson and J. Hall Richardson described the museum in their book, *Police! A General Account of the Work of the Police in England & Wales*, at a time when it had not been properly organised:

There remains to be mentioned an extraordinary feature of the Convict Office. What becomes of all the property, 'portable' or otherwise, taken from prisoners at the time of their committal? Most of it is of a trivial character, but some of it is valuable. Since 1869 it has not been forfeited to the Crown in the same way that the pence of a pauper are forfeited to the common treasury of a workhouse. Every article has to be restored to its rightful owner, and it may happen that, even after an interval of a long term of years, the rightful owner has a memory so retentive as to place a purely fictitious value upon his chattels, should any portion of them be missing or damaged. It is a strange collection of miscellaneous wares, a musty mass of odds and ends, which is stored in the cellars and garrets of the Convict Office in Scotland Yard. But every pocket-knife, bonnet-box, packing-case, or whatever it may be, has to be duly docketed, so that it may be produced when wanted. The dust of years falls upon these relics, and gives a black coating to the contents of the bins in which they are kept; they are mute witnesses that their owners are yet living, though dead to the world. Periodically all the unclaimed goods are sold, but there is always a large stock on hand, and amongst it may be noted many articles which have been produced in evidence in the course of celebrated trials.

There are five chief inspectors, but one of these, Mr Neame, is in charge of the Convict Supervision Office ... the Black Museum is allotted a room in the basement of the Convict Office in Great Scotland Yard, which is in reality a private house, ill adapted for the purposes required. In fact, the museum is in a cellar, and it is a collection, displayed in amateurish fashion, of relics which recall certain causes célèbres. Therein is the chief interest, and perhaps the grimness of the show is not lessened by the bareness of the boards upon which the array of knives, pistols, revolvers, and criminal curios is laid out. There is no attempt at cataloguing the items, and the museum, as at present arranged, serves no useful object.

This book features 100 objects from the museum as a method of illustrating the development of crime and its detection over nearly two centuries. We hope that the stories behind these objects will create a better public understanding of the museum and about crime itself.

This updated edition has enabled us to include some exhibits that have been added to the museum in the last few years to reflect recent trends in policing. Techniques for extracting DNA from crime scenes have continued to advance. Body-worn video cameras have produced graphic evidence of the violent situations faced by police officers on the streets. Firearms can now be constructed from 3-D printers. Cybercrime equipment gives an insight into the world of criminals who can defraud victims of enormous sums of money. And yet old-fashioned policing methods, supported by CCTV, can be crucial in bringing prolific burglars like the Wimbledon Prowler to justice.

The Crime Museum is now accommodated in the basement of the New Scotland Yard building on Victoria Embankment (SW1A 2JL), the fourth location in its life, and we are pleased to note that its standard of presentation and explanation about the exhibits is better than has ever been achieved before.

We have undertaken the project with a profound appreciation of the work of the countless detectives who have combatted criminals indulging their dreadful cruelty, greed and violence. Those officers have contributed to the world-wide reputation of Scotland Yard as a centre of excellence in the investigation of crime.

Many of the crimes described in this book can be regarded, at best, as distasteful, but there will have been a traumatic effect on those involved – including the officers investigating them. Ultimatley, our respect must primarily be owed to the victims, and their relatives, some of whom have suffered unspeakable torments of pain and suffering at the hands of criminals. We hope that the efforts of Scotland Yard, police officers elsewhere, and the legal system will always give the public the protection that they deserve.

Alan Moss and Keith Skinner
2022

100
Objects

John Sheppard

J. Thornhill Eques delin:

G. White fecit.

Sold by T. Bowles in St. Pauls Church Yard, J. Bowles against Stocks Market, & Geo. White in Hart Street between ye Church & Bloomsbury Markt pric. 1s.

Portrait of Jack Sheppard

THE PICTURE WAS donated to the museum by Sir Howard Vincent, who was appointed as the director of Criminal Intelligence at Scotland Yard in November 1883. A note to Percy Neame in November 1883 records Vincent's remarks about confirming the authenticity of the picture and states 'if genuine, we might have it for the museum'. Vincent resigned from Scotland Yard in 1885 and then became the Conservative MP for Sheffield from 1885 to 1905. He made a study of the French police's detection methods and compiled a report that he sent to a committee that was investigating the implications of the Turf Fraud trial – a corruption scandal in which many of the senior members of the Detective Branch had become embroiled. Vincent's carefully planned report led to his appointment to the Scotland Yard role, where he expanded and reorganised detectives into the Criminal Investigation Department.

The portrait shows notorious gaol-breaker Jack (or John) Sheppard in Newgate's condemned hold, wearing the handcuffs – reputedly held at the museum – from which he escaped, probably by using a knife blade to undo the screw-type mechanism that locked the device.

A century before the formation of the Metropolitan Police, Jack Sheppard, a 22-year-old failed carpenter's apprentice, turned to crime and became known more for his ability to escape from custody than his criminal exploits in theft, burglary and highway robbery. He lived with Elizabeth Lyon (a prostitute known as

DATE:
1724

EXHIBIT:
Mezzotint of Jack (or John) Sheppard in Newgate prison

'Edgworth Bess') and broke into St Giles roundhouse to release her from custody after she was arrested. Jonathan 'Thief-Taker General' Wild tried to gain a share of the profits from Sheppard's crimes, but Sheppard refused to collaborate, so James Sykes, a member of Wild's gang, lured Sheppard to a game of skittles where Constable Price of St Giles parish arrested him. Whilst being detained at St Giles roundhouse, Sheppard broke through the roof and escaped, despite still wearing his irons. He was later arrested for pickpocketing near Leicester Square and was held at St Ann's roundhouse, where Elizabeth Lyon visited him, only to be detained herself. They later escaped from their joint cell in Clerkenwell prison by filing through their manacles and a bar in the window, and then climbing down a rope made from bedclothes.

Wild, still anxious to be rid of his competitor, plied Elizabeth Lyon with drink and convinced her to disclose Sheppard's whereabouts. This led to Sheppard's arrest, detention in Newgate prison and conviction for burglary, for which he was sentenced to death. However, he managed to remove a bar from his cell and, after a visit from Elizabeth, escaped from the prison precincts disguised in women's clothing. At this point, both the authorities and Wild's men were hunting him, and he was eventually recaptured on Finchley Common by constables from Newgate. Sheppard was then placed in chains and held in a special room high up in Newgate prison. During a prison disturbance, Sheppard unlocked the handcuffs, climbed up a chimney, broke through to the roof of the prison and across to a neighbouring house from which he escaped into the street. His manacles were later found in the room of Kate Cook, one of his mistresses. The handcuffs held in the museum illustrate the unsatisfactory technology of the time.

On 10 November 1724, Sheppard, in a state of drunkenness, was arrested once again and sent to Newgate, but this time he did not escape and was publicly hanged a few days later at Tyburn in front of a crowd of 200,000 people.

Sheppard's involvement with highway robbery was a brief career carried out near Hampstead on 19 and 20 July 1724 with Joseph 'Blueskin' Blake. This was prior to one of his arrests that had taken place in Blake's mother's brandy shop in Rosemary Lane near the Tower of London (near the modern Royal Mint Street).

The management of prisons and the criminal justice system was very different in those days. Before the introduction of adequate salaries, it was quite common for public servants to purchase their offices, and to then set about recouping their investment by using opportunities to extract bribes from the unfortunate people who came into their jurisdiction. In 1739, Colonel Thomas de Veil was known as the first notably honest magistrate at Bow Street, for instance, in an era of 'trading justices' who routinely accepted bribes. Bow Street officers were often paid rewards directly by victims of the crimes they investigated, and in many cases deals were brokered between thieves and victims for the return of stolen property, the formal prosecution process often being avoided. Jonathan Wild, known as the 'Thief-Taker General', exploited the absence of a police force by manipulating a gang of thieves and the payment of rewards for return of stolen goods, before he himself was executed in 1725. Wild would often bribe prison guards to release his associates.

Thomas Bambridge became warden of Fleet prison in 1728, taking over from a John Huggins who had paid no less than £5,000 for the office. Many of the inmates had been imprisoned for debt, and were therefore likely to remain incarcerated until their families or friends paid off those debts. Bambridge became notorious for extorting money from prisoners for privileges and comforts, and his tenure was marked by sadistic and arbitrary punishments which became a blight on the reputation of the prison service.

The Parliamentary Gaols Committee of 1729 under James Oglethorpe MP famously set about trying to remedy the situation that saw many respectable people imprisoned for debt, and publicised the abuses within the prison system. They found that Bambridge had taken bribes to permit escapes as well as indulging in extortion, torture and murder. One prisoner, Jacob Solas, was placed in irons and held for two months in a windowless dungeon that also housed the dead bodies of prisoners prior to their burial. The committee took an interest in the prosecution of the wardens of both Fleet and Marshalsea prisons but were surprised both by light sentences and acquittals, and also by the conduct of the trial judge Sir Robert Eyre, who had allegedly visited Bambridge in Newgate prison before his trial. Bambridge was acquitted of the murder of Robert Castell who had been deliberately exposed to smallpox that was rife in a sponging house (a temporary prison for debtors). Huggins also faced trial for the murder of another inmate, Edward Arne, because he had left the prisoner in the death trap dungeon and knew about the dangers, but had done nothing. The Old Bailey jury brought in a special verdict after Huggins blamed a deputy warden Gibbon, who had died by the time of the trial, for the incident. Bambridge was also acquitted of theft of property of a Mrs Elizabeth Barkley in December, also arising from his stewardship of the prison. The implication that Sir Robert Eyre might have been willing to show improper favour to Bambridge created fresh complications for the momentum of the committee's noble attempts at prison reform.

Another early set of handcuffs, presented to the museum by Superintendent Digby of V Division in April 1882, had come from Mr W. Herrick of Kingston upon Thames whose family had owned them since 1795. The handcuffs were worn by a notorious highwayman, Louis Jeremiah Avershaw, commonly known as Jerry Avershaw, who was tried at Croydon for the murder of David Price, an officer from Union Hall, Southwark, who undertook a role similar to officers from Bow Street court. Avershaw was also tried for feloniously shooting at Barnaby Turner, another officer from Union Hall, for which he was executed, being hung in chains on 3 August 1795 on Wimbledon Common where the offence was committed. The location became known as Jerry's Hill. Avershaw and his associates made highway robbery a common hazard on Kennington Common, Hounslow Heath and Bagshot Heath at the time, and their activities were a major preoccupation for those concerned with combatting crime.

Dick Turpin, who had once been a butcher, was a more famous highwayman, but he had also been involved in deer poaching and in violent robberies as part of a gang that included John Fielder, Samuel Gregory, Joseph Rose and John Wheeler. These became known as the Essex Gang, most of whom were caught and executed for various burglary and robbery offences around 1735. Turpin, who had lodged in Whitechapel and Millbank, moved around frequently to escape the attention of parish constables, and would rob travellers on the approaches to London such as Barnes, Hounslow Heath, Kingston Hill and Epping. He then moved to Yorkshire under the name of John Palmer and was in custody for horse theft when he wrote from prison to his brother-in-law Pompr Rivernall at Hempstead, Essex. Rivernall would not pay the postage to receive the letter, which was eventually opened by a teacher, James Smith, who recognised Turpin's handwriting, informed the local JP, and then travelled to York to claim a £200 reward that had been offered for Turpin's arrest. Turpin was convicted of horse theft and was hanged at York on 7 April 1739. His grave can be found in a cemetery opposite St George's church in York.

One highwayman, John Popham, later turned to good, and apparently even became Lord Chief Justice from 1592 to 1607.

Highway robbery was a serious problem on the outskirts of London. It was the main reason for the re-establishment of the Bow Street mounted patrol in 1805 when the chief magistrate, Richard Ford, recruited fifty-two men to patrol the approaches of London on horseback. They wore blue greatcoats and trousers with spurred Wellington boots and red waistcoats. These patrols were stationed at various points on main roads into London. In Kent, for instance, patrols were stationed at Shooters Hill, Welling and on Bexley Heath. Ten years after its foundation, the boundaries of the Metropolitan Police were extended by an 1839 Parliamentary Act, partly to meet the need for the protection of travellers, and the horse patrols were incorporated into the Metropolitan Police.

2

Loving Cup

THE SILVER LOVING cup, used for shared drinking, is reputed, according to museum records, to have originated in the early nineteenth century from a young Irish titled lady who had become attached to a man from a lower social class, and was then thrown out of her home by her family. She had become pregnant and was then deserted by her lover, who went on to marry another woman who was independently wealthy. In a reflection of the fate suffered by many disgraced young women in those days, she became a prostitute and then the madam of a brothel in Edinburgh.

About twenty years afterwards, she welcomed a party of students into the brothel, recognised one of them as the son of her former lover and murdered him out of revenge. The records state that she was hanged, her body donated for the benefit of medical science, and, subsequently, it was her skull that was mounted in silver in the form of the loving cup.

In 1982, curator Bill Waddell had the cup examined by a scanning electron microscope at the Metropolitan Police Forensic Science Laboratory. This showed that stains inside the female skull were the sediment of red wine rather than blood. Marks on the front of the skull, previously believed to have been made by a saw used by a surgeon, or indeed by the woman while mutilating her murder victim, were in fact compression marks consistent with a blow from a heavy blunt instrument.

DATE:
c. 1807/8

EXHIBIT:
Silver-mounted loving cup made from a human cranium

—— 183?——
...ion to M.r Charles Figg...
...emorable Calthorpe S.r Inquest...
...r Justifiable Homicide...
...who was Slain while...
...ly Assembled on...

Culley Cup

SILVER CUPS GIVEN to members of a jury in 1834 represented public opinion about the verdict at an inquest that ruled that the killing of PC Robert Culley in a demonstration in 1833 was justifiable homicide.

Following the Reform Act 1832, which reallocated unrepresentative parliamentary constituencies and changed voting qualifications, an organisation called the National Union of the Working Classes was formed in London. The organisation called for a demonstration on 13 May 1833 at Coldbath Fields, Clerkenwell, to protest about the many working-class men still being debarred from voting. It was probably the first major demonstration that the Metropolitan Police had to control.

Lord Melbourne, the Home Secretary, was concerned about the republican sympathies of the organisation, and ordered the two joint Metropolitan Police commissioners, Sir Charles Rowan and Richard Mayne, to stop the meeting, but without any directions being put into writing. A decision was made that the assembly would become illegal once speakers started to address the meeting or flags were exhibited. At 1.30 p.m. about 300–500 people had gathered at the meeting ground, located near the present-day Mount Pleasant mail sorting office, and at about 2.45 p.m. a wagon left the Union Tavern carrying six speakers who intended to address the meeting. An activist by the name of Mee started to speak to the crowd and requested those displaying banners to remove them. They refused and Mee

DATE:
1834

EXHIBIT:
Silver cup presented to inquest jury members

fled the scene when he saw police officers approaching. There was a period of five to ten minutes of violent disorder before the meeting place was cleared. Police officers used truncheons and there were some doubts about whether there was any easy way of peaceably breaking up the crowd.

During the melee, PC Robert Culley became separated from his colleagues Tom Flack, James McReath and Samuel Acourt, and disappeared into the stone-throwing mob. Culley then emerged, clutching his chest and complaining that he had been stabbed. He staggered to the Calthorpe Arms public house where he collapsed and died in the arms of a bartender.

The incident is famous for the fact that the jury insisted, against the coroner's warnings, that a verdict of justifiable homicide be recorded on the basis that the actions of the police were 'ferocious, brutal and unprovoked', the Riot Act had not been read and the government had not taken proper precautions to prevent the incident. The court of the King's Bench Division overturned the verdict, but did not substitute an alternative, leaving the matter to a parliamentary select committee investigating the riot. The jury were feted by the public and were each awarded one of these inscribed goblets. The jury's decision was cruel in relation to the fate of Robert Culley and definitely not in the interests of keeping public order, but it was consistent with another jury's decision to acquit a demonstrator, George Fursey, who had seriously assaulted Robert Culley's colleague, Sergeant Brooks. The verdicts reflected public opinion about the police, concern for civil rights and the criticism of the level of force used by the police notwithstanding that the officers may privately have sympathised with the demonstrators' views. The verdict was an illustration of the independence of juries despite directions that they might receive from a judge or coroner. It followed the precedent of the 1670 trial of William Penn and William Mead, two Quakers who had been prosecuted for addressing a religious assembly that was not part of the Church of England, who were acquitted despite the jury being threatened by the judge and imprisoned for contempt of court.

Robert Culley's widow did become the centre of much public sympathy, however, and the subsequent reflection about the role of police officers did mark a positive turning point in police–public relations. Due to the violent situation and confusion of events, nobody was identified or prosecuted for killing PC Culley.

Although Britain is noted for valuing the right of free speech and for adopting a liberal attitude towards political demonstrations when the authority of the government is being challenged, this reputation took many years to acquire. In the early days of the Metropolitan Police, there was no expectation that contentious demonstrations could pass off peacefully, and experience at crowd control was still largely based on military attitudes. In 1819, for instance, fifteen demonstrators were killed and more than 400 injured by soldiers at St Peter's Field, Manchester ('Peterloo'). This followed the pattern where the numbers of rioters killed by the military far exceeded other riot deaths.

Nowadays, damage to property and looting tend to be the most dramatic effect of riots, together with a communal fear about the consequences of a breakdown in public order. In political demonstrations, the passionate beliefs of a crowd can easily be triggered into violence, and when this occurs, arrests of individuals may well be impracticable. The gathering of clear evidence against individuals for the crimes they commit in a mob rule situation can be very difficult. The legal offences of riot, violent disorder and affray no longer require a magistrate to read the Riot Act as a public warning, and are framed so that individuals are guilty if they are part of a group using or threatening unlawful violence in a manner that would cause a bystander to fear for their safety.

Riot Shield

PURPOSE-BUILT RIOT SHIELDS were introduced after the 1976 Notting Hill Carnival ended in violence, with stones and bricks being launched at the police. The public-order tactics until then had largely consisted of police officers engaging with crowds on a face-to-face basis. The full-length shields were made of perspex, allowing the officers to see ahead whilst sheltering behind groups of three shields that could be locked together as they moved forward. They were first used at a riot in Lewisham in 1977 after a series of clashes on London streets between the National Front and Socialist Workers' Party activists culminated in a National Front demonstration on 17 August 1977. In their efforts to keep the opposing factions apart, the police were pelted with missiles from both sides and sprayed with water pistols filled with ammonia. The commissioner, Sir David McNee, imposed a legal ban on demonstrations for two months, and the tension subsided.

The shield pictured was used in the Broadwater Farm riot of 1985. It shows not only smoke staining created by petrol bombs, but it also has a bullet hole caused by a gun fired against the police in the middle of the rioting.

On 28 September 1985, the police raided a house in Normandy Road, Brixton, in an attempt to arrest Michael Groce, a suspect in an armed robbery. Despite

DATE:
1985

EXHIBIT:
Riot shield used at Broadwater Farm

nobody in the house having a firearm, Groce's mother Cherry was shot in the chest by an armed police officer. She was taken to hospital and survived, but suffered paralysis until she died in 2011. Fuelled by false rumours of Mrs Groce's immediate death, spontaneous disorder broke out and, over the next two days, 200 arrests were made. Cars were overturned and set alight, petrol bombs were thrown and shops were looted. In various locations affected by rioting, one photojournalist suffered an aneurysm and died, and fifty people were injured. Disturbances also occurred in other communities with strong Afro-Caribbean links.

A week later, on 6 October 1985, and with tensions running high, the police in Tottenham arrested a young black man, Floyd Jarrett, in connection with a suspicious car tax disc, and went to his mother's home to search for further evidence. During the police search of the premises, his mother, Cynthia Jarrett, collapsed and subsequently died from a heart attack. A demonstration then took place outside Tottenham police station, but this did not resolve the tension. Gangs of black youths started to take over the Broadwater Farm estate, a relatively modern housing development with overhead concrete walkways and tower blocks. The police formed a cordon around the estate but it took a long time before there were sufficient numbers of

A close-up of the bullet hole from the 1985 Broadwater Farm riot

trained senior officers and other resources on hand to penetrate the upper walkways to deal with the situation. The police lines, protected by riot shields, were bombarded with petrol bombs and some were shot at with firearms. Fires were started and the fire service was unable to gain access to extinguish them.

One group of officers formed a squad to gain access to Tangmere House where a shop was on fire, but they were overwhelmed by rioters and forced to withdraw. In the process, PC Keith Blakelock was set upon by rioters, attacked with knives and a machete, and killed. His colleague, PC Richard Coombes, was severely injured. Arrests were impossible at the time due to limited resources and the volatile situation. Subsequent inquiries led to the arrest, trial and convictions of murder for Winston Silcott, Engin Raghip and Mark Braithwaite. The convictions were overturned by the Court of Appeal on 25 November 1991 on the basis of forensic tests indicating that interview notes might have been tampered with, an issue on which the two detectives concerned were later acquitted. (An electrostatic detection apparatus (ESDA) test was run, which allows impressions of writing to be discovered several layers of paper below that on which the original impression was made.)

The 1985 riots were the catalyst for reviews and improvements in tactics and equipment, police firearms training and deployment, senior officer public order training, and methods of evidence gathering in riot situations. The police then adopted smaller protective shields that enabled them to advance more quickly and to maintain the initiative in fast-moving situations. Armoured Land Rovers were made available to specialist firearms officers to counter the threat of gunfire, but employing effective tactics to deal with firearms incidents in riot situations remains a great challenge.

Personal protective equipment for police officers was introduced in the mid-1990s after a series of deaths of police officers from knife and gun attacks. Considerable effort was made to develop a protective vest made from material that could counter both knives and bullets, whilst also allowing reasonable freedom of movement and comfort for the police officer.

LIFE, TRIAL, CONFESSION, & EXECUTION

OF

JAMES GREENACRE,

FOR THE

EDGEWARE ROAD MURDER.

On the 22nd of April, James Greenacre was found guilty of the wilful murder of Hannah Brown, and Sarah Gale with being accessary after the fact. A long and connected chain of evidence was produced, which showed, that the sack in which the body was found was the property of Mr. Ward; that it was usually deposited in a part of the premises which led to the workshop, and could without observation have been carried away by him; that the said sack contained several fragments of shavings of mahogany, such as were made in the course of business by Ward; and it contained some pieces of linen cloth, which had been patched with nankeen; that this linen cloth matched exactly with a frock which was found on Greenacre's premises, and which belonged to the female prisoner. Feltham, a police-officer, deposed, that on the 25th of March he apprehended the prisoners at the lodgings of Greenacre; that on searching the trowsers pockets of that person, he took therefrom a pawnbroker's duplicate for two silk gowns, and from the fingers of the female prisoner two rings, and also a similar duplicate for two veils, and an old-fashioned silver watch, which she was endeavouring to conceal; and it was further proved that these articles were pledged by the prisoners, and that they had been the property of the deceased woman.—Two surgeons were examined, whose evidence was most important, and whose depositions were of the greatest consequence in throwing a clear light on the manner in which the female, Hannah Brown, met with her death. Mr. Birtwhistle deposed, that he had carefully examined the head; that the right eye had been knocked out by a blow inflicted while the person was living; there was also a cut on the cheek, and the jaw was fractured, these two last wounds were, in his opinion, produced after death; there was also a bruise on the head, which had occurred after death; the head had been separated by cutting, and the *bone sawed nearly through*, and then broken off; there were the marks of a saw, which fitted with a saw which was found in Greenacre's box. Mr. Girdlwood, a surgeon, very minutely and skilfully described the appearances presented on the head, and showed incontestibly, that the head had been severed from the body *while the person was yet alive ;* that this was proved by the retraction, or drawing back, of the muscles at the parts where they were separated by the knife, and further, by the blood-vessels being empty, the body was drained of blood. This part of the evidence produced a thrill of horror throughout the court, but Greenacre remained quite unmoved.

After a most impressive and impartial summing up by the learned Judge, the jury retired, and, after the absence of a quarter of an hour, returned into court, and pronounced a verdict of "Guilty" against both the prisoners.

The prisoners heard the verdict without evincing the least emotion, or the slightest change of countenance. After an awful silence of a few minutes, the Lord Chief Justice said they might retire, as they would be remanded until the end of the session.

They were then conducted from the bar, and on going down the steps, the unfortunate female prisoner kissed Greenacre with every mark of tenderness and affection.

The crowd outside the court on this day was even greater than on either of the preceding; and when the result of the trial was made known in the street, a sudden and general shout succeeded, and continued huzzas were heard for several minutes.

THE EXECUTION.

At half past seven the sheriff arrived in his carriage, and in a short time the press-yard was thronged with gentlemen who had been admitted by tickets. The unhappy convict was now led from his cell. When he arrived in the press-yard, his whole appearance pourtrayed the utmost misery and spirit-broken dejection; his countenance haggard, and his whole frame agitated ; all that self-possesion and fortitude which he displayed in the early part of his imprisonment, had utterly forsaken him, and had left him a victim of hopelessness and despair. He requested the executioner to give him as little pain as possible in the process of pinioning his arms and wrists; he uttered not a word in allusion to his crime; neither did he make any dying request, except that his spectacles might be given to Sarah Gale ; he exhibited no sign of hope ; he showed no symptom of reconciliation with his offended God! When the venerable ordinary preceded him in the solemn procession through the vaulted passage to the fatal drop, he was so overcome and unmanned, that he could not support himself without the aid of the assistant executioner. At the moment he ascended the faithless floor, from which he was to be launched into eternity, the most terrific yells, groans, and cheers were vociferated by the immense multitude surrounding the place of execution. Greenacre bowed to the sheriff, and begged he might not be allowed to remain long in the concourse ; and almost immediately the fatal bolt was withdrawn, and, without a struggle, he became a lifeless corse.—Thus ended the days of Greenacre, a man endowed with more than ordinary talents, respectably connected, and desirably placed in society ; but a want of probity, an absolute dearth of principle, led him on from one crime to another, until at length he perpetrated the sanguinary deed which brought his career to an awful and disgraceful period, and which has enrolled his name among the most notorious of those who have expiated their crime on the gallows.

On hearing the death-bell toll, Gale became dreadfully agitated ; and when she heard the brutal shouts of the crowd of spectators, she fainted, and remained in a state of alternate mental agony and insensibility throughout the whole day.

After having been suspended the usual time, his body was cut down, and buried in a hole dug in one of the passages of the prison, near the spot where Thistlewood and his associates were deposited.

T. Catnach, Printer, 2 and 3, Monmouth Court.

Pamphlet on James Greenacre

JAMES GREENACRE'S CASE was recounted in a pamphlet that would have been printed in large numbers to meet the public's thirst for knowledge about the murder of Hannah Brown. His death mask is held at the Crime Museum. Casts used to be taken of the heads of executed prisoners with the apparent aim of assisting research into crime in a period when phrenology (measuring skulls to ascertain details of parts of the mind) was fashionable.

PC Samuel Pegler was patrolling Edgware Road three days after Christmas in 1836 when he was called to a flagstone that had been covering a large sack, inside which was the nude torso of a woman, inclusive of arms, but without legs or a head. There were no detectives in the Metropolitan Police at that time, so Local Inspector George Feltham, who had once been in the Bow Street horse patrol, took over investigating.

Crime scene investigation was virtually non-existent in those days as the scientific developments had not yet been made. The police loaded the torso on to a wheelbarrow from a local building site and took it to Paddington Workhouse where the parish surgeon concluded that the victim was above average height, middle-aged and had no signs of disease. He also noted the mark of a wedding ring on one of her fingers and mentioned in his notes that the victim had an unusual malformation that would have left her incapable of having a child. Identification of the victim is always

DATE:
1837

EXHIBIT:
Contemporary pamphlet on James Greenacre

29

crucial to an investigation and, in the absence of a report of a missing person fitting the woman's description, the inquiries were likely to be difficult.

Samuel Pegler noted that there had been no impacted snow under the sack, indicating that the body could have been left there, according to the weather pattern, perhaps on Christmas Eve, when he remembered seeing a cart near the scene. He recovered a cord, some cloth and bloodstained wood shavings that seemed to be connected to the sack.

Ten days later, a lock-keeper in Stepney found a human head blocking one of the sluice gates of Regent's Canal, 7 miles away. It had apparently been sawn from its body and belonged to a woman aged 40–50 years. There was bruising over one eye and a torn earlobe, but finding this head did not answer the question of identity. It was before the age of photography, so her head was preserved in spirits and put on display for members of the public to attempt to identify her. This became a popular attraction, but aroused morbid curiosity rather than the evidence needed to prove her identity.

Two months later, an ostler (a man employed to look after horses) found a sack containing a pair of legs in a water-filled ditch in Camberwell, and they appeared to fit the trunk of the victim. So, the body was complete but still unidentified, until William Gay from Goodge Street became concerned that he had not heard anything from his sister, Hannah Brown. He was uncertain about identifying her from her head, but his sister had an ear injury from an earring being pulled out, and this was consistent with the head found by Pegler.

Brown had been due to marry James Greenacre, from Camberwell, the previous Christmas, but the wedding had been called off by Greenacre, who had accused Brown of misleading him by stating that she had savings. (At that time, a husband normally assumed rights over his wife's property.)

The identification of the body was a breakthrough in the investigation. When Greenacre was traced and arrested, his new girlfriend, Sarah Gale, was found to be in possession of Brown's earrings, whilst one of Gale's children's dresses was patched with material matching the cloth found in Edgware Road. The wood shavings helped to identify one of the sacks as coming from a local cabinetmaker known to James Greenacre and Sarah Gale. After initially denying knowing Hannah Brown at all, Greenacre then claimed to have killed her accidentally in an argument when they were both drunk. Medical evidence was used in the trial to show that the various parts of the body fitted together, and to rebut several aspects of Greenacre's defence about where he had struck her on the head. The evidence confirmed that her throat had been cut before, and not after, death, and that her stomach had contained no alcohol. Greenacre was hanged at Newgate on 2 May 1837.

It was a complicated inquiry that was solved before the introduction of the Detective Branch in 1842 and without modern crime scene examination techniques. Examination of the body is always a crucial part of a murder inquiry and normally the starting point of the police investigation. So murderers sometimes try to conceal the body or dismember it to make it easier to transport and more difficult to identify. Undertaking this grisly task after the murder itself reflects the state of mind of the killer.

Trying to dispose of a murder victim's body in this way may reflect a belief, widespread for many years, that it is impossible to be placed on trial for a murder without the body being found. This originated from the Campden Wonder case in the 1660s, when three men were hanged for murder of William Harrison from Gloucestershire, who later arrived back in the area alive and well, recounting a story of having been abducted abroad by pirates.

6 Edward Oxford's Gun

THE 18-YEAR-OLD EDWARD Oxford was the first of seven assailants to attack Queen Victoria. On 10 June 1840, from a range of 10yds or so, he fired with two pistols – one of which is pictured – at the pregnant queen whilst she was riding in a horse-drawn carriage with Prince Albert along Constitution Hill. Oxford was immediately overpowered by a member of the public, Joshua Lowe. At the same time Lowe's nephew, Albert Lowe, seized the pistols. PC Charles Brown then took Oxford into custody. No bullets were found at the scene and there were some doubts as to whether the pistols had been loaded. Oxford was tried for high treason, but there was a good deal of evidence about mental health issues suffered by his family. He was acquitted on the grounds of insanity and sent to Bethlem Hospital. In 1864 the patients there were transferred to Broadmoor, and three years later Oxford was offered release if he agreed to leave the country. He was last heard of on his way to Australia.

DATE:
1840

EXHIBIT:
Percussion pistol of the 'commonest kind possible' made in Birmingham, used against Queen Victoria

This was not the first time that the security surrounding Queen Victoria had been breached. In December 1838, 14-year-old Edward Jones, disguised as a chimney sweep, was caught in Buckingham Palace's Marble Hall, but ran from the building. He was caught by the police in St James's Street with items of the queen's underwear stuffed down his trousers. He became known as the 'Boy Jones' in newspapers, and is an early example of an intruder making his way into the grounds of a royal palace. He climbed over the wall from Constitution Hill and entered Buckingham Palace on 30 November 1840, and repeated his exploit the following night, on 1 December, when he was found hiding under a sofa in the queen's dressing room, ten days after she had given birth to her first child, Princess Victoria. Jones was sentenced to three months' detention, but was found again by police officers in a royal apartment on 15 March 1841, just under a fortnight after his release from prison. The Boy Jones was the inspiration for the film *The Mudlark* starring Alec Guinness who played Prime Minister Benjamin Disraeli in a story of a waif who entered Windsor Castle to meet Queen Victoria.

Another example from 1838 involved a man who wanted to meet Queen Victoria and who managed to get into Buckingham Palace and wait for her outside her bedroom. He fell into a drunken sleep in an adjoining room.

On 30 May 1842, John Francis fired a pistol at Queen Victoria when she was riding in a carriage returning to Buckingham Palace, at about 6 p.m., after her daily drive. Francis was immediately arrested by PC William Trounce from A Division and had in fact been seen the previous day threatening the queen at the same spot, but no further action had been taken, apart from excusing ladies-in-waiting from accompanying the queen. Security arrangements were very different in those days! Francis was convicted of high treason, but his death sentence was commuted to transportation for life. Prince Albert considered that the way in which Edward Oxford had been acquitted had, perhaps, encouraged a further attempt against the queen. This second attempt on the queen's life was one of the issues that influenced the formation of the Detective Branch.

On Sunday, 3 July 1842, soon after John Francis' death sentence had been commuted, Queen Victoria was riding in a procession of three carriages along The Mall from Buckingham Palace to the Chapel Royal at St James's Palace when 17-year-old John Bean held out a pistol at arm's length, pointed it at the queen's carriage and pulled the trigger. The pistol was old and did not fire. Bean had been holding it in his hand for some minutes beforehand with no attempt to conceal it. Charles Dassett, a member of the public, seized Bean and handed him into the custody of police officers, but they expressed their doubts about whether Bean could be charged with any offence as the gun had not fired, and the incident was not generally treated seriously by onlookers. The gun was loaded with a relatively small amount of powder, and Bean was charged with a misdemeanour rather than treason. The court heard evidence of his good character and then awarded a sentence of eighteen months. Prince Albert encouraged Parliament to pass a law against aiming a firearm at the sovereign, striking her, throwing anything at her or producing any weapon with intent to alarm her.

After a seven-year period without further incident, 23-year-old William Hamilton swore at the queen and discharged a gun, loaded only with powder, on 19 May 1849 in Green Park. He pleaded guilty under the new law and was transported for a period of seven years.

The most serious incident affecting Queen Victoria occurred on 27 June 1850, when she was starting her return journey from Cambridge House, Piccadilly, to Buckingham Palace. Robert Pate, a former lieutenant in the 10th Hussars, who had become mentally unstable, stepped out from the crowd of 200 or so people, and struck the queen with a cane, causing a bruise and bleeding to her forehead despite her bonnet taking most of the force of the blow. The senior footman, Robert Fenwick, grabbed Pate by the collar, and Sergeant James Silver then arrested Pate, who needed protection from the angry crowd. At Vine Street police station, Pate, who lived in Duke Street, St James's, was charged with assault. He was found guilty and transported for seven years.

On 29 February 1872, Arthur O'Connor, a 17-year-old Irishman, climbed over Buckingham Palace's wall and rushed at Queen Victoria's carriage with an empty pistol in one hand and a petition to free Irish prisoners in the other. O'Connor was the great nephew of Irish MP Fergus O'Connor. Queen Victoria's servant, John Brown, knocked the assailant to the ground before the queen could see the pistol, and was rewarded with a gold medal for his bravery. O'Connor was sentenced to twelve months' imprisonment, but the queen remitted another part of his sentence that involved twelve strokes of the birch, and he was later sent to Australia. The museum has a note from the then Prince of Wales asking to see the gun involved.

The last assailant to attack Queen Victoria actually fired a bullet at her, at Windsor railway station on 2 March 1882, as she was seated in her horse-drawn carriage on her way to Windsor Castle. Roderick MacLean was apparently aggrieved that a poem he had sent to Buckingham Palace was not being fully appreciated. The firing of the bullet was from a range of about 30yds, and missed its target. A number of Eton schoolboys tackled MacLean, who was then taken into custody by Chief Superintendent Hayes of the Windsor Borough Police. MacLean was tried for treason, his Belgian pistol being more effective than the firearms used by some of his predecessors, but the death sentence was avoided because he was found 'not guilty, but insane'.

On 5 April 1900, 15-year-old Jean-Baptiste Sipido attacked the Prince of Wales (later Edward VII) at Brussels whilst the royal party was on its way to Denmark. The young man leapt on to the footboard of the train carriage and fired four shots into the royal compartment – each of them missing its target – before Sipido was seized, shouting of his intention to kill the prince because of the casualties of the Boer War. Sipido was acquitted by the Belgian court, apparently because of his young age, and later became a director of the General Society of Belgian Socialist Cooperatives.

On 16 July 1936, as King Edward VIII was riding on horseback in a ceremonial procession down Constitution Hill after presenting new colours to the Brigade of Guards in Hyde Park, George MacMahon lowered a newspaper that concealed a gun and aimed at the king. A Mrs Lawrence, standing next to MacMahon in the crowd, grabbed his arm and Special Constable Anthony Dick then knocked the gun from his hand and arrested him. MacMahon, whose real name was Jerome Bannigan, was a publicity-seeking fantasist and claimed at one stage that he had not intended to harm the king, but that he had been paid £150 by a foreign power for the assassination, had been in contact with MI5 immediately before the incident, and had deliberately bungled the attempt. His revolver was brand new and had probably never been fired. It was later proved to be inaccurate for distances over 10yds; the king was about twice that distance away from him. MacMahon's story was rejected by the court and he was sentenced to twelve months' hard labour; King Edward had abdicated before his sentence was completed.

On 5 June 1939, Princess Marina, Duchess of Kent, was leaving her residence in Belgrave Square and was about to get into her car when a man named Vincent Lawlor fired a gun at her. The firearm, retained in the Crime Museum, had a barrel that had been shortened to the point where it had become a very inaccurate weapon and he missed his target. Lawlor was arrested and appeared in court, where he was bound over to keep the peace for one month on condition that he returned to his native Australia.

In 1974, a ransom note found in the possession of Ian Ball indicated his motive for intercepting and attacking the royal Rolls-Royce carrying Princess Anne back to Buckingham Palace after an official function. Ball's intention was to kidnap the princess and ask for a ransom of £3 million. Bizarrely, his note indicated that he had wanted the queen herself, accompanied by two solicitors to vouch for her identity, to personally bring the money to a jumbo jet at Heathrow Airport, to travel to Switzerland with him and then to write him a free pardon both for his crime of kidnapping and for a parking ticket he had incurred. Ball overtook the royal car, forced it to stop, jumped out of his Ford Escort and attacked the vehicle – intending to kidnap the princess – and managed to open the door, something that was then possible from the outside but is not now.

During the ensuing violent scuffle, protection officer James Beaton, whose own firearm jammed, shielded Princess Anne and was shot three times. The chauffeur, PC Michael Hills, and a member of the public who came to assist, were also shot and wounded. Princess Anne and her husband were taken on to the safety of Buckingham Palace in a police car.

Ball himself was chased, overpowered and arrested by PC Peter Edmonds as he fled from the scene. Ian Ball pleaded guilty to attempted murder and attempted kidnap, and was ordered to be detained under the Mental Health Act 1959 for a period 'without limit of time' on the grounds of criminal insanity.

The incident caused a major review of royalty protection methods and tactics, including driver training. The queen made a number of gallantry awards, including the George Cross to Inspector Beaton.

A starting pistol was used by an unemployed youth, Marcus Simon Sarjeant (b. 1964), on Saturday, 13 June 1981, as he stood in the crowd watching the procession for the Queen's Birthday Parade, the annual high point of London's ceremonial occasions. As Queen Elizabeth II passed from The Mall into Horseguards Road, mounted side-saddle on her police horse, Burmese, Sarjeant suddenly produced a gun and fired six shots in rapid succession towards her. The queen rapidly reassured the frightened horse and continued her ceremonial duties, without apparently turning a hair, whilst Sarjeant was overpowered by a special constable and a guardsman. A starting pistol actually fires blank ammunition to begin a race, but the true nature of the gun was only apparent afterwards.

The incident was investigated by Ian Blair, who later became the commissioner of the Metropolitan Police. Sarjeant had a framed portrait of Queen Elizabeth, on the back of which he had written various threats against her, and he indicated that he had intended at one stage to kill her, but had not been able to find a more effective weapon. He was charged under the 1842 Treason Act and was sent to prison for five years.

Just over a year later, there was an even more serious incident when, on 7 July 1982, Michael Fagan managed to scale the railings at a vulnerable corner of

Buckingham Palace, at about 6.40 a.m., then climb into the queen's private apartments and reach her bedroom, where he was able to spend almost ten minutes talking to her. The queen, a non-smoker, raised the alarm by telephoning for cigarettes, and Fagan was detained by a footman until a police officer arrived. Fagan apparently had no intention of injuring the queen and had legally committed no offence (apart from civil trespass), but was prosecuted for stealing a bottle of wine, a matter on which he was later acquitted. The obvious and embarrassing security lapses included part of the perimeter wall that could easily be climbed, a window left open, the night duty police officer in the queen's corridor not having been properly relieved and a failure to implement effective security in a manner that was also compatible with the privacy, comfort and unobtrusiveness required in the queen's own home. Fagan was committed under Section 60 of the Mental Health Act 1959.

Aaron Barschak was an interloper at a fancy dress party held at Windsor Castle to celebrate Prince William's 21st birthday on 21 June 2003. The self-styled 'comedy terrorist' infiltrated the guests and interrupted a speech by Prince William in which he thanked the queen and his father, the Prince of Wales, for organising the party. Barschak was rapidly arrested and taken away as he claimed to be the terrorist Osama bin Laden, but the implications of his ability to pose as a party guest was a concern and a scandal (notwithstanding the fancy dress costumes of many of the guests). Aaron Barschak was apparently trying to gain publicity for his unsuccessful career as a comedian, but escaped prosecution because of the lack of a specific law against trespassing on royal premises.

The 32-year-old Jason Hatch was the centre of a stunt, on 13 September 2004, when he climbed on to an exterior ledge of the facade of Buckingham Palace as part of a protest about the rights of fathers to gain access to their children in disputed child custody cases. Other protesters had created a diversion, and Hatch's colleague was detained by armed police and prevented from following him on to the ledge. In a climate of high security over terrorism, the armed officers considered, but did not use, their guns against him.

7 Death Mask of Daniel Good

DANIEL GOOD UNWITTINGLY caused a change of organisation that meant murders were no longer investigated by ordinary uniformed officers.

PC William Gardner from V Division was patrolling Wandsworth High Street on Wednesday, 6 April 1842, when he was called to a shop where a pair of trousers had been stolen. A shop boy had seen the theft committed by Daniel Good, known to be a coachman in

DATE:
1842

EXHIBIT:
Death mask of
Daniel Good,
executed at
Newgate on
23 May

the Roehampton residence of a Mr Shiel. Gardner took two shop boys to the big house and started to make a thorough search of the stables where Daniel Good worked. Their task was nearly finished and it was getting dark when Gardner shone his lantern for closer examination of what he thought was a plucked goose. As Gardner discovered that the plucked goose was in fact human flesh, he heard the sound of the stable door being bolted as Daniel Good escaped, locking the officer, the shop boys, the estate factor and Good's own son in the stable. After the hapless party managed to escape, inquiries were started to trace Good, whilst a bloodstained axe and various bones found in the harness room confirmed the case as one of murder.

At the time – about twelve years after the Metropolitan Police had been formed – there were no official detectives because the new police service had been set up firmly to prevent crime rather than to investigate it. It was before the age of telephones or telegraph equipment and messages were distributed to police stations around London by officers, sometimes on horseback, meeting on their station boundaries to exchange handwritten 'route papers' giving details of crimes that had been committed. The V Division superintendent, Thomas Bicknell, arranged for 1,000 'wanted' posters to be printed and distributed overnight. The next morning, Sergeant Golding questioned Good's son and then visited No. 18 South Street, near Manchester Square, Marylebone, where his mother, Good's common-law wife, Jane Jones (or Sparks) took in washing. It turned out that Jane Jones was the victim. Immediately after the murder Good had fled to South Street by cab, the identification number of which had been noted by a patrolling officer, but the wanted man had moved on. At that time cab drivers invariably returned to the same rank, so it was relatively easy for the police to find the driver. He had taken Good to the Spotted Dog public house in the Strand, and from there Good had temporarily visited Flower and Dean Street, a notorious location for criminals in Spitalfields, where he had changed his clothes.

One of the joint commissioners at Scotland Yard, Richard Mayne, appointed Inspector Nicholas Pearce to co-ordinate inquiries. Pearce had formerly been employed as a Bow Street patrol officer, and had recently returned from conducting an investigation into the murder of Jane Robinson, a farmer's wife in Eskdaleside, Yorkshire. He was one of several officers in whom Mayne took an interest because of their flair for conducting investigations, but he was not formally a detective.

Good had left London on Saturday, 9 April without being caught by the police.

The case was widely reported in the press, and on 11 April 1842, *The Times* published an article severely criticising the new police system and the lack of co-ordinated inquiries it was making into catching Daniel Good. A number of murders had taken place in London, including that of Lord Frederick Russell by his butler, and although most of these cases had been solved quite quickly, *The Times*, influenced perhaps by some magistrates who resented their loss of control over policing arrangements, argued that what was needed was a body of specialist detectives, such as those who had been employed by the Bow Street magistrates.

The level of concern was raised further six weeks later, on 29 May 1842, after an assassination attempt against Queen Victoria by John Francis. Richard Mayne sent a long report to the Home Secretary, pointing out the relative success of the new police system but, using an argument that would be repeated in later years, wrote that he needed more resources if a new detective branch was to be formed. This resulted in the employment of eight officers, on 15 August 1842, with Inspector Nicholas Pearce in charge of the new branch. These eight officers were, in fact, the first formal detectives to be employed at Scotland Yard.

By this time the case against Daniel Good had been solved: he had been recognised whilst working as a labourer on the new railway line being built in Tonbridge, Kent, and had been arrested, tried and then executed at Newgate on 23 May 1842, unaware that his bolting of the stable door had contributed to the establishment of detectives at Scotland Yard.

Death Mask of Franz Müller

FRANZ MÜLLER BECAME the famous subject of a chase across the Atlantic and an early extradition case from America, as well as having committed Britain's first railway murder. For many years, detectives recorded their inquiries and arrests in diaries, such as Inspector Richard Tanner who had been an assistant to the famous detective Jonathan Whicher and had taken over from him as officer in charge of the Detective Branch. Tanner's diary, which recorded his involvement with the Müller case, has survived as the earliest example of such diaries.

Two bank clerks boarded a Highbury-bound North London train on the evening of Saturday, 9 July 1864 and found their first-class compartment was soaked in blood. They found a walking stick that had apparently been used as a weapon, a leather bag allegedly belonging to a Mr Briggs and a hat.

Soon afterwards, the victim, Thomas Briggs, the chief clerk of Messrs Robarts, Curtis & Co. in the City of London, was found unconscious beside the railway line with a serious head wound. His watch and chain were missing, and he died a few hours later. Richard Tanner arranged for the circulation of a description of Briggs' stolen gold watch and chain, and this resulted in a silversmith, John Death, describing a man who had come to his shop to exchange the chain, but not the watch, for a cheaper version and some cash. The suspect had a sallow complexion, was dressed in a black frock coat

DATE:
1864

FACT:
Franz Müller's last words were *'Ja. Ich habe es getan'* (Yes. I did it)

43

and hat, and was probably German. The second clue was that the hat found in the railway carriage had not belonged to Briggs, whose silk top hat was missing. It appeared that the murderer had, perhaps inadvertently, left wearing the wrong hat. The hat from the scene of the crime was unusual because it had been cut down in size; the alterations had not been made by a hatter, but the sewing was very neat, as if done by a tailor. A £300 reward for information resulted in a cab driver called Jonathan Matthews coming forward, who at one stage had bought a hat for a young German tailor called Franz Müller who had given Matthews' young daughter a box bearing John Death's name two days after the murder. Matthews supplied the police with Müller's address in Bethnal Green, but when Richard Tanner called there, the suspect had already left the country on the sailing ship *Victoria*, bound for America.

Tanner went to Bow Street, obtained an extradition warrant and then set sail for New York from Liverpool on the faster steamship SS *City of Manchester*, accompanied by Sergeant George Clarke, John Death and Jonathan Matthews. Tanner arrived in New York no less than three weeks before Müller, who was identified by the two witnesses and was arrested with Briggs' hat and watch still in his possession. Extradition proceedings were in their infancy in those days, but Tanner could bring his witnesses to the New York court to be heard by the commissioner, a Mr Newton. There was some public hostility expressed against Britain in New York at the time because of Britain's perceived naval interference in the Civil War and a certain corresponding sympathy for Germany, so the result was not a foregone conclusion. Nevertheless, Newton decided that Müller should be returned to Britain to face trial.

Large crowds had assembled at Euston station to express their indignation at Müller who was then driven off to Bow Street court, which, until its closure in 2006, was the traditional court for dealing with extradition cases. In due course Müller stood trial at the Old Bailey and was convicted of the first murder on the railway. He was executed on 14 November 1864, about four months after the crime had occurred, a very rapid process by today's standards, especially when much of that period had involved the long sea voyages to and from America and the three-week wait for the sailing ship to arrive. John Death had been away from his business for a considerable period whilst helping the police with this inquiry.

A letter offering £55 as a reward to the detective 'as a small token of our appreciation of the courteousness and delicacy with which he conducted the case in all communications with the family' was one of the final outcomes from the case. Rewards for success in individual cases were often paid to detectives during this period. The system had originated with payments made direct to Bow Street officers before the Metropolitan Police was established in 1829, and continued for much of the nineteenth century – provided that the Metropolitan Police commissioner approved of the individual circumstances. Rewards were also paid to officers direct from police funds, balanced, no doubt, by deductions in pay in the form of fines for disciplinary misdemeanours.

One of the William Hartley courtroom sketches was of a witness in the case of Elizabeth Camp, who was found murdered in a London and South-Western Railway carriage at Waterloo, on 11 February 1897. The body was removed from the railway station to St Thomas' Hospital and from there, after a medical inspection, to the mortuary, but the police had not been informed of any crime having been committed. The subsequent investigation revealed that the probable murderer had been drinking in a certain public house, but 'the opportunity of taking him red-handed was lost, and evidence was afterwards lacking to justify an arrest', according to the Commissioner's Annual Report for 1897.

London These are to certify that at the General Session of the Delivery of the Gaol of our Lord the King of Newgate holden for the City of London at Justice Hall in the Old Bailey within the parish of Saint Sepulchre in the Ward of Farringdon Without in London aforesaid on Thursday the twenty eighth day of October in the Fifth year of the Reign of His late Majesty King George the Fourth before certain Justices of our said late Lord the King assigned to deliver the said Gaol of Newgate of the prisoners therein being **Henry Fauntleroy** late of London Gentleman was in due form of Law tried on a certain Indictment against him for that he on the first day of June in the Fifty fifth year of the Reign of His late Majesty King George the Third with force and arms at London that is to say at the parish of Saint Mary le Bow in the Ward of Cheap in London aforesaid feloniously did falsely make forge and counterfeit and also feloniously did utter and publish as true a certain deed with intention to defraud the Governor and Company of the Bank of England Against the Statute &c and against the Peace &c And the said Henry Fauntleroy was thereupon found Guilty of feloniously uttering and publishing as true the said deed and acquitted of forging the same And was thereupon Ordered and adjudged to be hanged by the Neck until he should be dead. Dated the eighteenth day of June 1832.

John Clark

Clk of the Session
of Gaol Delivery.

9

Execution Order

THE HANDWRITTEN LEGAL document pictured is the formal notification from the clerk of the session at the Old Bailey of Henry Fauntleroy's conviction and death sentence. He was the last person to be hanged in Britain for a forgery-related crime, having committed the offence in 1815. The clerks responsible for writing out such legal documents were often paid by the total number of words they wrote, perhaps an incentive for the convoluted legal style employed in such documentation. The gist of the case is that Henry Fauntleroy was convicted at the Old Bailey of using or 'uttering' a forged document, acquitted of the forgery itself, but sentenced to death:

> These are to certify that at the General Session of the delivery of the Gaol of our Lord the King of Newgate holden for the City of London at Justice Hall in the Old Bailey within the parish of Saint Sepulchre in the ward of Farringdon Without in London aforesaid, on Thursday the twenty eight[h] day of October in the fifty fifth year of the reign of his late Majesty King George the Fourth [*sic*] before certain Justices of Oier said late Lord the King assigned to deliver the said Gaol of Newgate of the prisoners therein being Henry Fauntleroy, late of London, gentleman, was in due form of law tried on a certain indictment against him for that he on the first day of June in the fifty fifth year of the reign of his late Majesty King George

DATE:
1824

EXHIBIT:
Henry Fauntleroy's execution order from the Old Bailey, for forgery

the Third [1815] with force and arms at London, that is to say at the parish of Saint Mary le Bow in the ward of Cheap in London aforesaid, did falsely make, forge and counterfeit and also feloniously did utter and publish as true a certain deed, with intention to defraud the Governor and Company of the Bank of England. Against the statute etc and against the peace etc. And the said Henry Fauntleroy was therefore found guilty of feloniously uttering and publishing as true the said deed, and acquitted for forging the same. And was thereupon ordered and adjudged to be hanged by the neck until he should be dead. Dated the eighteenth day of June 1832 [*sic*].
John Clark
Clerk of the session of Gaol delivery

Henry Fauntleroy was a clerk in the banking firm of Marsh, Sibbald and Co., which his father had founded, and then, after being made a partner and left to run the business largely on his own, found that the company was accumulating debts that it could not pay. He therefore forged a power of attorney document to sell three per cent stock investments without the client's knowledge, but continued to pay the dividends to the clients, so that his ruse would not be immediately detected. Fauntleroy's arrest, on 10 September 1824, was on a warrant from Marlborough Street court for an investment worth £10,000. Businessmen would invariably place their records in a locked box in those days and Fauntleroy's box was found to contain a list of other similar transactions that had not been passed through the bank's books. The total sums acquired by this method were in the region of £170,000, a vast amount for pre-Victorian England. The false signatures were a straightforward issue of proof once the matter had come to light. Fauntleroy was given the benefit of the doubt about whether he had personally forged the document, but was convicted of 'uttering' it, the legal term for knowingly passing on a forged or counterfeit item. Despite the pleas of many character witnesses and legal appeals, he was sentenced to death. His execution took place on 30 November 1824 and was apparently witnessed by a large crowd, 100,000 strong.

Forgeries can encompass a wide range of situations – at one end of the scale simply writing another person's signature on a document, or the more complicated end of the spectrum can involve complex, false documents. The financial loss involved in forgery can be extremely high.

One of Fauntleroy's counterparts, James Townshend Saward, born in 1799, was an English barrister from the Inner Temple who used a network of accomplices to acquire blank or stolen cheques, which thieves would otherwise throw away as being of no value to them. He became known as 'Jim the Penman'. It was a common practice at the time to present a cheque at a bank for payment in cash, but it was also a time when bank cashiers would readily recognise their customers. Saward took pains to research and copy the signatures of those who owned the accounts to which the stolen cheques related, and used an accomplice named James Anderson to present the cheques on bank premises. Anderson himself would often sub-contract the transaction to others in return for a commission from the proceeds. When the London banks became progressively more suspicious, Saward used another accomplice, William Hardwicke, to present forged cheques further afield.

Whilst visiting a bank in Great Yarmouth, Hardwicke got confused over false names and had to write to Saward for instructions. When Saward's reply came back, the police had already arrested Hardwicke, and this led to the prosecution of Saward and Anderson at the Old Bailey on 2 March 1857, where his accomplices Hardwicke and Henry Atwell gave evidence for the prosecution. Saward and Anderson were transported to Australia for fourteen years.

'Jim the Penman' was a nickname also given to Emanuel Ninger (1845–1924), who drew American banknotes by hand in New Jersey in the 1880s and forged a number of Bank of England notes later in his career. *Jim the Penman* is also the title of numerous films made in Britain and America.

10 Arthur Orton's Handkerchief

A HANDKERCHIEF WITH the word 'Tichborne' written on it was one of a number of personal items in the possession of Arthur Orton, also known as Thomas Castro, who became the centre of controversy and extremely lengthy court cases that tried to determine whether he was the long-lost heir to a fortune, or a fraudster. If the word 'Tichborne' was on the handkerchief at the time, it indicated either that Orton could be the missing heir, or that he had appropriated or created it as part of a blatant fraud. The handkerchief, perhaps more than any other exhibit held at Scotland Yard's Crime Museum, was something that could not have been the subject of a mistake or misunderstanding; it indicated either that Orton was indeed the missing heir, or that he had committed a blatant fraud.

One of the most complicated and celebrated cases in Victorian England centred around the missing eldest son of the baronet Sir James Tichborne, who possessed

DATE:
c. 1854–74

EXHIBIT:
Arthur Orton's handkerchief with the name 'Tichborne'

great wealth. Roger Tichborne, the immediate heir and an officer in the 6th Dragoon Guards, had hoped to marry Katharine Doughty, but she was a first cousin and the family disapproved of the match. Roger, therefore, resigned his commission and, on 1 March 1853, left for a private tour of South America. He was last seen in Rio de Janeiro in April 1854, awaiting passage to Jamaica on board the ship *Bella*. A few days later, a capsized boat from *Bella* was found off the coast of Brazil, and Roger was presumed to have died in the shipwreck; no survivors were found.

Roger's father, Sir James, the 10th baronet, died in 1862 and at that point the title passed to Roger's younger brother Alfred. Lady Tichborne, Sir James' widow, steadfastly refused to believe that her son Roger had died and, following rumours that he had made his way to Australia, advertised a reward for information about his whereabouts. She commissioned Alfred Cubitt, who ran an agency to trace missing people, to make inquiries. In 1866, Cubitt informed Lady Tichborne that he had identified a butcher, Thomas Castro, from Wagga Wagga, Australia, as the missing heir. Castro smoked a pipe with the initials RCT engraved on it and claimed to have been picked up from the wreck of *Bella* and taken to Australia where he had become a butcher and a postman. Castro then came to England with his wife and child, and Lady Tichborne accepted him as her son; she had meanwhile suffered the loss of Alfred. Some servants and acquaintances also accepted Castro, but others did not or changed their minds after a time. Castro was a man of unrefined habits unlike Roger, and other members of the Tichborne family disputed Castro's claim. The case divided the country: those who believed that he was the inheritor of the vast Hampshire estate, and those who thought he was a fraud.

The legal case took five years to prepare and during this time inquiries suggested that Thomas Castro was in fact Arthur Orton, a butcher's son from Wapping who had gone to sea as a boy and had last been heard of in Australia. Lady Tichborne also died before the case came to court, thereby depriving Castro of his main supporter. The civil court case was opened in May 1871 to clarify the claim of Thomas Castro or Arthur Orton to be heir to the Tichborne estate and title. It lasted 103 days and culminated in March 1872 with a decision against him. Orton was then charged with perjury, the trial starting in April 1873 and ending in February 1874 with him being convicted and sentenced to fourteen years' penal servitude for impersonating Roger Tichborne. It created a record for the longest criminal trial in the records of English courts. Orton was released in 1884 and briefly confessed his true identity in 1895, only to recant shortly afterwards. He died in poverty in 1898.

The case had many threads of inquiry, one of which was a list of personal items that Lady Tichborne had listed as being in Roger's possession when he had set out to sea. A set of possessions belonging to Arthur Orton that might have matched Lady Tichborne's list is held at the Crime Museum. The objects are keys, a snuff box, a pair of scissors, a knife and a comb, but there is also a sample of Orton's hair, cut in Millbank prison.

The case provoked great public attention, not least because of campaigning undertaken by Orton and his lawyer. The retired detective inspector Jonathan Whicher worked on the case, demonstrating his painstaking attention to detail.

11 Cybercrime Equipment

THIS EQUIPMENT WAS used by 53-year-old Tony Colston-Hayter in his flat in Colindale to perpetrate frauds and 'smishing' offences. This occurs when people are sent bogus text messages inviting them to ring a certain telephone number if they had not spent money at a specified shop. When the calls were answered, Colston-Hayter's system would elicit personal and bank details so that he could defraud the victims' bank accounts. The equipment is a computerised system that plays a preprogrammed series of messages according

DATE:
2018

EXHIBIT:
Telephone
banking
simulation tool

to the responses made on people's telephone keypads. His mobile telephone had apps for changing a voice from male to female, a facility for impersonating police, utility companies and banks, and the means to make it appear that his messages came from a different telephone number.

One bank calculated the proceeds of his frauds to be over £22 million. A credit card company found over $53,000 charged to credit cards registered at his address. In total, his frauds amounted to more than £500,000 and potentially over £23 million. Despite committing the offences while released from prison under licence for similar offences and having a confiscation order for £800,000 against his assets, he was sentenced to twenty months' imprisonment with a nominal confiscation order of £1.

In 1995, at the lower end of the scale of sophistication, but nevertheless effective for at least one sufficiently gullible victim, modern-day fraudsters made up a suitcase that appeared to contain vast quantities of banknotes. Some genuine banknotes were included within the suitcase, but the bulk of the contents were pieces of paper cut to the exact size of US dollar banknotes and coloured black. The fraudsters told their victim that the money was part of a large fortune that had been smuggled out of Nigeria and that the cash had been dyed black to evade the authorities. The victim needed to buy the fraudsters' special chemicals to treat the money and reveal the true nature of the banknotes. The process of removing the dye was shown with genuine banknotes, and appeared plausible when a real US dollar bill would emerge once the black dye was removed in a staged demonstration.

The victim paid £20,000 to buy the chemicals and pay a chemist to treat all the money in the suitcase, an 'investment' that would result in his receiving money ten times what had been paid. Having handed over his cash, the victim held the security of the suitcase and its contents whilst the fraudsters undertook to return with the chemist and other necessary equipment. When the fraudsters did not return, the victim realised the scam and, to his credit, reported the matter to the police.

As always, a proposition that sounds too good to be true normally *is* too good to be true.

A notable fraud took place in 1877 and involved a number of senior detectives at Scotland Yard. Sometimes known as the Turf Fraud trial or the Trial of the Detectives, this scandal had its origins in a scam conducted by Harry Benson and William Kurr who created an elaborate, fraudulent system of passing on racing tips to unwary victims. They printed a fictitious newspaper containing reports about an English tipster who was so successful that no bookmakers would take his bets, and who therefore needed people in France to lend their names to bets he would place on horses in return for a commission. They invited others to add their own money to the investment.

A rich Parisian lady, Madame de Goncourt, was approached, fell for the ruse and asked her attorney for £30,000 for the purpose of betting on horses in England. The attorney was less gullible than his client and he duly reported the matter to Scotland Yard. Superintendent Adolphus 'Dolly' Williamson, the head of the Detective Branch, allocated Chief Inspector Nathaniel Druscovich to bring back Benson from Amsterdam where he had been arrested, but progress in the case seemed unduly slow. Sergeant John Littlechild and two colleagues pursued Kurr, but he seemed to evade arrest by moving on just as he was about to be caught. They finally detained the two offenders in Edinburgh, however, and, as the prisoners talked, the real reason for the lack of success in catching them earlier became apparent – Inspector John Meiklejohn had been taking bribes to forewarn bookmakers of impending arrests. Sergeant Littlechild reported his concerns, and his integrity led to convictions being obtained against Kurr, Benson and three senior detectives. The scandal resulted in a reorganisation of the detectives as the Criminal Investigation Department.

12 Courtroom Sketch of Horatio Bottomley MP

WILLIAM HARTLEY (1862–1937) was a journalist who composed courtroom sketches of the characters involved in many trials from 1893 to 1919, and whose original drawings are part of the Crime Museum's collection. One of his subjects was Horatio Bottomley who had entered Parliament in 1906 as Liberal member for Hackney South. A year later, Bottomley launched *John Bull*, a patriotic journal. He also started the John Bull Victory Bond Club, a forerunner of premium bonds, and had a notable talent for persuading people to spend money on the bonds. A mixture of fraud and mismanagement resulted in the collapse of the scheme, his conviction for fraud, a sentence of seven years' imprisonment and expulsion from Parliament. Bottomley is one of a number of politicians who have appeared in the courts.

DATE:
c. 1912

EXHIBIT:
Horatio Bottomley, possibly in court here for bankruptcy proceedings

Jabez Balfour (1843–1916) was the Liberal MP for Tamworth from 1880 to 1885 and for Burnley from 1889 to 1893. He had been mayor of Croydon, and, in 1887, was involved in setting up an investment underwriting firm with two City of London financiers. He was involved in a series of companies that largely traded with each other, but he did in fact construct some substantial buildings in London. In 1892 he was engulfed

in scandal involving the Liberator Building Society, then the largest in the country, whose members were often Nonconformist church members, perhaps influenced by Balfour's ostensible position as a pillar of the Congregational church. Instead of advancing money to large numbers of prospective house purchasers using their homes as security, the Liberator Building Society bought property already owned by Balfour at inflated prices. When Balfour's companies failed, they owed about £7 million. Balfour fled the country to Argentina and was arrested there in 1895 by Detective Inspector Frank Froest. Froest was a strong and determined man, who could tear up a pack of playing cards with his hands. He became impatient with what seemed interminable extradition wrangling and bundled Balfour on to a train, then a ship bound for London. Balfour was convicted at the Old Bailey and sentenced to fourteen years' penal servitude, notwithstanding the breach of extradition procedures.

Maundy Gregory (1877–1941) was a British theatre producer and political fixer who acted as a broker to sell political honours, with prices ranging from £10,000 for a knighthood to £40,000 for a baronetcy, on behalf of Lloyd George. In 1933, Gregory was the first person to be convicted under the Honours (Prevention of Abuses) Act 1925, which made it illegal to agree to give or accept any gift, money or valuable consideration in any connection with the grant of any honour. He was fined £50 and jailed for two months. There were claims that Gregory continued to offer various honours for sale when he no longer had influence to implement his promises, but he was protected from legal action by the fact that his victims could not complain for fear of also being prosecuted under the 1925 Act.

Tony Blair was Labour prime minister from 1997 to 2007 and at one stage became embroiled in an investigation conducted by Assistant Commissioner John Yates. The police inquiry had been initiated by a complaint from members of the Scottish National Party and others that £14 million in loans given by wealthy individuals to the Labour Party during the 2005 general election campaign were made in breach of the 1925 Act after some donors were subsequently recommended for life peerages. The prime minister was interviewed three times but was not cautioned, a procedure that would have been necessary for his answers to be made admissible in any prosecution against him. Lord Levy, a fund raiser for the Labour Party, was arrested and twice interviewed under caution, along with other staff who worked for No. 10 Downing Street, but the Director of Public Prosecutions decided against legal action in July 2007. The case was relevant both for the way in which political parties were funded and also for the process by which prominent people in public life who also contributed to political parties could justifiably be recognised through the honours system.

Reginald Maudling (1917–79) resigned as Home Secretary for the Conservative Party in 1972 when the Metropolitan Police commenced fraud investigations against John Poulson, a bankrupted property developer and architect whom Maudling had assisted to win con-tracts. As Home Secretary, he acted as police authority for the Metropolitan Police under arrangements in force at that time and resigned to ensure that there were no conflicts of interest. He was not prosecuted.

An opposition Labour MP, John Stonehouse (1925–88) set up a number of business interests, but, concerned about an investigation by the Department of Trade and Industry, faked his own death by leaving his clothes on a Miami beach on 20 November 1974. He then went to Australia where he adopted the false identity of Joseph Markham, the dead husband of a constituent, and lived there with his parliamentary secretary, Sheila Buckley. 'Markham' was arrested in Melbourne, on Christmas Eve 1974, by Australian officers who first supposed he was Lord Lucan. Eventually, he was extradited, convicted and sentenced to seven years' imprisonment for fraud. He continued to act as an MP whilst in prison, but finally gave up the Labour whip in April 1976, resigning as an MP on 28 August 1976.

In 2009, *The Daily Telegraph* published details of expenses claimed by MPs that had previously been confidential. Many of the problems arose from MPs needing to live both in London and in their constituencies, and from how the inevitable expenses relating to these second homes were dealt with. There was widespread connivance in an expenses system that had been interpreted as compensating for salaries seen as insufficient. A panel headed by former civil servant Sir Thomas Legg reviewed the expenses and referred a small minority of cases to the police where the claims for expenses amounted to criminal conduct rather than breaches of parliamentary rules about allowances. Members of Parliament were held not to be protected from prosecution in relation to these financial, rather than political, issues.

Elliot Morley MP pleaded guilty to two cases of false accounting to the value of £30,000 relating to payments for a mortgage that had been repaid, and was sentenced to sixteen months' imprisonment. David Chaytor MP pleaded guilty and was sentenced to eighteen months on three counts of false accounting amounting to about £18,000 for instalments on a mortgage that had already been redeemed, and claiming rent for a flat he owned. Jim Devine MP was convicted of false accounting relating to an invoice for work on his home from a non-existent company and was sentenced to sixteen months. Lord Hanningfield was jailed for expenses relating to overnight stays in London when he had, in fact, returned to his home in Essex, and was jailed for nine months. Lord Taylor was convicted of wrongful claims relating to travel costs and overnight London accommodation by wrongly using an address in Oxford as his base, and was sentenced to twelve months. In December 2012, Margaret Moran, by then no longer the MP for Luton South, was sentenced for claims relating to her partner's house in Southampton, and received a two-year supervision and treatment order because of illness. Denis MacShane received six months' imprisonment for claims based on false invoices worth £12,900.

These cases provide examples of how police officers are sometimes called to investigate and deal with offenders regardless of their position in life, and how the system in Britain can enable the law to apply to all, regardless of status.

Counterfeit Currency

IN 1935, SCOTLAND Yard was notified by the Berlin police that Bank of England £5 notes were being sold there at half their face value. Detective Inspector George Hatherill, who was fluent in foreign languages and had been a liaison officer in Antwerp, posed as an illegal arms trader and smuggler and met up with members of a gang who agreed to sell him 1,000 notes, to be delivered the following week. The German police conducted a surveillance operation and arrested the gang, but the forger himself was not arrested.

In 1937, £5 and £10 notes started to circulate in Paris and Hatherill went to France to assist the French police. They did not know the source of the forgeries, so he spent his time notifying many foreign currency outlets about the forged notes. He was no nearer to tracking their source after two weeks than he had been at the start of his inquiries and so returned to London.

Two weeks afterwards, a man was arrested in Paris in possession of counterfeit Bank of England banknotes, no doubt detained because of the heightened awareness of the forgeries that had been circulating. The man refused all details of his background. Hatherill then went to Paris and recognised the similarity with the high-quality forgeries he had seen previously in the Berlin inquiry. Hatherill questioned the prisoner in a number of languages. He knew that the suspect was German, with a Württemberg accent, but with some knowledge of English idiomatic phrases that he could only have

DATE:
1937

EXHIBIT:
Frederick Beckert's identity documents and forgery items

known if he had lived in London, but the prisoner admitted nothing. Turning to other lines of inquiry, Hatherill investigated a laundry mark 'K157' on his clothing and eventually traced the identity of the man as Frederick Beckert of No. 2A Shoot-Up Hill, Cricklewood.

When this address, which included a photographic studio, was investigated, it was found to be empty. The young lady who occupied the premises had moved out a fortnight earlier, but had been burning material that spoilt her neighbour's washing on the line. Hatherill undertook a thorough search of the empty house, removed floorboards and found negatives and partly burned plates that had been used to produce counterfeit German, British and Belgian banknotes, some of them corresponding to his Berlin inquiries two years earlier. Beckert had lived at the address for the previous six years with his 26-year-old niece Beatrice. Hatherill traced Beatrice's boyfriend and found two of her suitcases, one of which contained ties that had apparently been purchased to generate genuine money as change, and the other held a large number of wallets that had apparently been used to carry the banknotes. Hatherill quickly went to an address in Brussels and helped the Belgian police arrest Beatrice, who had been on the verge of moving to Germany because of a telegram from her boyfriend warning of the police interest in her. When confronted with Beatrice's arrest, Frederick admitted his identity and eventually pleaded guilty to counterfeit currency offences at his trial at the Old Bailey. He had used his knowledge of colour photography to produce banknotes that often escaped detection until they reached the national banks of the countries concerned. He was sentenced to four years' penal servitude, and was then interned until he was deported after the Second World War.

In the Second World War, Heinrich Himmler and Reinhardt Heydrich had printing plates made for Bank of England £1 and £10 notes with a view to undermining the British economy. The plan was delayed by the lack of availability of the right quality paper, but, by 1942, up to 140 concentration camp inmates of different nationalities were brought to the Sachsenhausen camp, 22 miles north of Berlin, to produce forged Bank of England notes in £1, £5, £10 and £20 denominations. It is believed that notes to the face value of around £200 million were produced, and placed into five categories: those without faults that could be used for purchasing war materials from neutral countries; those with a minor fault that could be used by German agents abroad; notes with more than one fault, but presentable, were to be used for payments made in occupied countries; banknotes of lower quality were to be dropped over England from aeroplanes; and the lowest quality were reserved as worthless junk notes.

Having been forced into taking part in the largest counterfeiting operation in history, the prisoners involved were liberated in May 1945 when much of the equipment and banknotes had been destroyed. Nevertheless, 425,000 'Bank of England' notes were recovered, packed in wooden cases, from Lake Toplitzsee, Austria. A further 100,000 notes were found and destroyed in 1959 and 1963.

In December 1976, the Counterfeit Currency Squad started to receive very convincing forged American $20 and $50 banknotes. They had been produced using an offset lithographic printing process that involved taking a photograph of a genuine banknote and then transferring the image to a printing plate. The serial numbers all differed and were hard for banks to detect. In fact, these forgeries were circulating on a worldwide basis.

Eventually, inquiries led to a house in Bromley, Kent, where Charles Black was arrested after police had found no fewer than 85,000 forged banknotes on the premises concealed in his kitchen door, as well as the negatives crucial for producing the printing plates.

At the home of his accomplice, Brian Katin, in Pagham, Sussex, the police found a complete set of printing equipment in the garage, and 3.5 million forged notes. The intention was to produce and distribute $2 million per month through an international network. In January 1979, at the Old Bailey, Black was sentenced to ten years, and Katin received three years' imprisonment.

14 Counterfeit Coins

THE PROSPECT OF literally making your own money has been a temptation for criminals for hundreds of years, and posed a problem for Isaac Newton when he was Master of the Royal Mint from 1699 to 1727. Adding milled edges to coins and including other features into the design gradually made counterfeiting more difficult. Notwithstanding that printing false banknotes can create currency with a higher return for their efforts, criminals have nevertheless not completely stopped their efforts to make their own coins.

James Steel was in his 80s when, in 1964, he created the die to make the florins now exhibited in the Crime Museum. Florins were 2s coins, equivalent to 10p today. The only easily discernible difference from those of the Bank of England was the milling around the edges, where Steel's coins had two fewer milling marks than the genuine article.

Steel claimed to have limited his activities so that he simply made 'beer money', but he manufactured 15,144 coins (with a face value of £1,514). Sentenced to two years' imprisonment, he was released early because of failing health.

DATE:
Various

EXHIBIT:
Selection of nineteenth- and twentieth-century counterfeit coins

15 Collapsible Ladder

THE LADDER PICTURED was the means by which burglar Charlie Peace would climb down from the roofs of houses.

In the early hours of Thursday, 10 October 1878 the police were on special alert in Blackheath, south-east London, because of a spate of night-time household burglaries. PC Edward Robinson noticed a flickering light to the rear of a house in St John's Park and sought assistance from his colleagues. When Sergeant Brown rang the doorbell of the house, Robinson saw a figure escape from the dining-room window and run across the back lawn. The officer gave chase and was shot at five times and wounded in the arm before the burglar was finally overpowered with assistance from PC William Girling. The man gave his name as John Ward and refused to state his address, but was duly charged with burglary and with wounding Robinson. At the Old Bailey the burglar was convicted and sentenced to penal servitude for life. It was before the introduction of a gallantry medal for these circumstances, so the grateful residents of Blackheath presented Robinson with a pocket watch. It was also before the introduction of the fingerprint system to identify criminals with records under a different name.

Two weeks before the Old Bailey trial was due to begin, Ward, who was held in Newgate prison, had requested a visit from a Mr Brion. So, still uncertain about Ward's identity, Detective Inspector Henry Phillips arranged for Brion to be followed from the prison to his address in Peckham Rye. Brion, a respectable cartographer, knew Ward as Mr Thompson, who

DATE:
1878

EXHIBIT:
Folding ladder for hooking on to windowsills, etc.

claimed to be working on an unsinkable boat that required him to go out late at night to test his invention. With Brion's assistance, Phillips then interviewed Susan Thompson who refused to disclose any details of John Ward, with whom she was living, notwithstanding that an apparently stolen watch had been found in her bedroom. She would not speak about Ward's true identity, but eventually wrote down in Phillips' pocketbook that Ward's real name was Charles Peace of Sheffield.

Peace (46) had been living a seemingly respectable life in Peckham. He dressed well to avoid suspicion, entertained friends with his violin playing (apparently being referred to as 'the modern Paganini') and took part in amateur dramatics. By night, he would carry his collapsible wooden ladder to burgle houses. Other housebreaking equipment used by Peace is in the museum, along with his violin, letters and a wanted poster of the time. Peace had two fingers missing on his left hand, which would have been an easy identification feature, so he fitted himself with a tube and a hook to give the appearance that he had lost his whole hand and part of his arm.

Henry Phillips, whose unpublished recollections of the case are in the museum, travelled to Sheffield and recovered a large amount of stolen property that he traced to no fewer than thirty-six burglaries across the country. Peace was also wanted by the police in Sheffield for murdering Arthur Dyson in 1876, who had objected to Peace seeing so much of his wife, Katherine Dyson. Locally, Peace was wrongly believed to have died in a coal pit accident in Derbyshire.

Peace was escorted to Sheffield (throwing himself from a train in an escape attempt on the way), stood trial for murder and was sentenced to death in 1879. After the sentence had been passed, he also admitted to the murder of Manchester's PC William Cock for which 18-year-old William Habron had been sentenced to death but later reprieved. Peace had even attended Habron's trial, apparently watching him being sentenced to death for a crime that he, Peace, had committed. His confession did at least spare William Habron further imprisonment.

Susan Thompson received the £100 reward that had been advertised for Peace's apprehension.

16 Henry Miller's Lantern

THE BULL'S EYE lantern, fuelled with paraffin and owned by 15-year-old Henry Miller, was found at a murder scene. It is a typical Victorian lantern, not unlike those used by police officers on patrol, but Miller knew that it was his own lamp because of a broken red and green glass panel, some sandpaper marks and an improvised wick he had devised from material his mother had used for a child's dress.

The small lamp had been found at the house of Henry Smith, a wealthy 79-year-old man who lived alone at Muswell Lodge, Muswell Hill. Henry Smith had been a gas engineer, but had saved significant sums of money. He owned a number of houses and received rents, and he kept a safe in his bedroom that might typically contain about £250 in gold. Although independent by temperament and in wealth, Henry Smith was concerned about burglars. Before the days of modern burglar alarms, Smith had set up a trip-wire running between a fence and some iron supports upon which a loaded gun was set up. An intruder would be liable to set off the gun. On the morning of 14 February 1896, the gardener, Charles Webber, arrived for work and was surprised that the garden gate had not been unlocked, as was usual, by Smith. The wire of the gun alarm had also been dismantled. Webber went to the house and found signs that a window had been jemmied open. Henry Smith was lying dead on his kitchen floor with head wounds, dressed in his nightshirt and tied up with strips of tablecloth.

11cm

7cm

DATE:
1896

EXHIBIT:
The Bull's Eye lantern that proved to be a vital clue

Upstairs, the safe was open and had been emptied. The mattress of the bed had been disturbed as if a search had been made under it for money. When Detective Chief Inspector Henry Marshall and Inspector Charles Nutkins were called in to investigate, they found two penknives, some tools and the small lantern in a basket that had apparently been left behind by the burglars. There were tracks seemingly indicating that the intruders had left by the rear of the premises, climbing over the fence and going into Coldfall Woods.

The police consulted the records of convicts recently released from prison on licence and under police supervision (known as 'ticket-of-leave' men) and found that two criminals, Albert Milsom (33) and Henry Fowler (31), had been seen in the neighbourhood. A local resident, Miss Kate Good, had seen two men answering their description asking questions about access to Coldfall Wood from the rear of the houses, and had also seen the men catching a train to London some days earlier. Following up on the suspicions about Albert Milsom, Marshall went to No. 133 Southam Street off Harrow Road where Milsom had been living with his wife and two children. Marshall brought the lamp with him and it was immediately recognised by Henry Miller as his own missing lantern. Miller gave an account of how he had bought the lamp just after Christmas and had tried to remove some varnish from the glass with sandpaper. He had originally bought the lamp without a wick or paraffin, but he had got it to work and had played with it after dark. It had then gone missing.

Albert Milsom had married Henry Miller's older sister Emily, had recently been in possession of money to buy new clothes but had then moved away. Henry Fowler had often visited Milsom but had been an unwelcome visitor. Miller also recognised a tobacco box found in Henry Smith's garden as belonging to Albert Milsom.

Marshall went to the same shop where young Miller had bought the lamp, and made a test purchase of a similar item that also had varnish that clouded the glass. He took a pawn ticket from Miller's mother and redeemed a child's dress, the material of which matched the improvised wick that Miller had put in his lantern, and confirmed the boy's explanation of how using a penholder had helped the light burn better. Miller's lamp had apparently been stolen by Milsom and then used in the course of his burglary exploits.

A letter arrived at the house – postmarked Bath – that eventually led to the arrest of Milsom and Fowler who had, using the names of Taylor and Scott, joined a travelling show organised by a man called Sinclair. Their show went from town to town in the south-west of England in an unsuccessful attempt to entertain the public, and had eventually arrived in Bath, where the police raided the house where the men were lodging. Milsom was very strong and put up a violent struggle before being subdued and arrested. A £10 note from Smith's safe was traced to Fowler through its serial number. It transpired that Fowler had identified Henry Smith's house as a burglary target and had persuaded Milsom to join in on the enterprise. Needing a candle at the last minute before setting off, Milsom admitted that he had taken Henry Miller's lamp instead, without realising that it would act as evidence linking him to the crime scene. Both men admitted the burglary, but blamed each other for the murder of Henry Smith. In May 1896, both were convicted of murder and sentenced to death.

Other exhibits in the case were entered into the museum's catalogue as a spring gun, a portion of windowsill, a brace and bits, two iron chisels, a gimlet and a revolver. The ropes used to execute Albert Milsom and Henry Fowler are also in the museum and were used in the last triple execution at Newgate prison, on 9 June 1896. The authorities had to keep the two men separated from each other and hanged William Seaman in the centre position because of antagonism and violence displayed by Milsom, who had tried to kill Fowler in the dock at the Old Bailey. William Seaman apparently commented that it was the first time in his life that he had ever acted as a peacemaker! When the executioner, James Billington, pulled the lever to withdraw the bolt of the trapdoor to carry out the execution, he did not realise that his assistant, William Warbrick, was still standing on it, securing one of the prisoner's feet. As the bolt was drawn, Warbrick started to fall into the pit below, but managed to save himself by holding on to the dying prisoner's legs.

17 Hatton Garden Vault Hole

OVER THE EASTER weekend of 2–5 April 2015, a group of criminals abseiled down the lift shaft of a building in Hatton Garden and drilled three holes through a 50cm-thick wall to gain access to a vault containing safety deposit boxes. Three concrete cylinders were drilled out from the wall and the resulting hole measured only 46 x 25cm. The replica was made to demonstrate to the jury how access to the vault had been achieved. The security alarm was activated but, because the premises appeared secure from the outside, it was concluded that the alarm was faulty. The gang stole £20 million worth of valuables.

DATE:
2015

EXHIBIT:
Replica hole drilled in the wall of a vault, and a gold smelter

The gang disguised themselves as a precaution, and whilst CCTV footage showed a white van with registration number DU53 VNG, this vehicle transpired to have been sold on a roadside and was never found. A white Mercedes car was then traced, and was found to be driven by Kenneth Collins, a career criminal. Further inquiries linked him to Daniel Jones, Terry Perkins and Brian Reader. A month later, the gang met up to divide the proceeds, which included large quantities of jewellery hidden behind skirting boards in their houses and in a cemetery in Edmonton. Seven men were convicted, mostly career armed robbers in their 60s and 70s, but one further member of the gang, known as Basil,

46cm

25cm

escaped arrest. After three years of inquiries, 53-year-old Michael Seed was arrested in his one-bedroom council flat where proceeds from Hatton Garden were found with the smelting machine with which he was disposing of the stolen gold. He was sentenced to ten years' imprisonment.

From 1918 until 1937, a series of burglaries in various parts of London became known as the work of 'Flannelfoot', a nickname given to the criminal by newspapers because he wore socks or other material over his shoes to reduce any noise when he was entering houses. Flannelfoot was very careful not to leave finger marks. He worked entirely alone, did not associate with known receivers or other thieves and took care to vary his travel arrangements to outer suburbs and housing estates by using a bicycle, trams or trains. He often committed his crimes on Friday nights when pay packets would be more likely to be available and tended to enter houses by forcing rear windows or by picking locks. He rarely seemed troubled by dogs. Eventually, police received information about 48-year-old Henry Edward Vicars who lived in Holland Park. A surveillance team arrested him in 1937 after he had broken into a house in Eastcote and found him in possession of keys, pliers, gloves and other housebreaking equipment that became part of the Crime Museum's collection. Vicars was said to have committed over a thousand burglaries.

In 2019, Kosovo Serb Astrit Kapaj (43), known as the Wimbledon Prowler, was arrested for a series of burglaries in Wimbledon that had started in 2008. He was identified partly because of a distinctive snood that he wore. He had taken steps to avoid detection by CCTV cameras and often stole only some of the available valuables so that the theft might not immediately be noticed. His DNA was detected from glove marks, but there was no corresponding entry on the database. It transpired that he travelled from Manchester to commit over 224 burglaries and was sentenced to fourteen years' imprisonment.

18 Chignon

THE CHIGNON ONCE worn by murder victim Harriet Lane – equivalent, no doubt, to those then worn by many women on the back of their heads – was a coil of hair, amongst which was not only an immense number of hairpins, some of which can still be seen attached to the ringlets, but also a lead bullet found by a surgeon. At one stage Harriet Lane's wig was encased in a glass dome, and it featured in an 1890 newspaper sketch of the interior of the Crime Museum.

In 1874, Henry Wainwright was a brush manufacturer who had a shop in Whitechapel Road in London's East End. The premises were long and narrow. Most of the floor of the building was stone, but at the extreme end of the building, which was 40yds deep, there was a raised portion known as the paint room. Despite being married with four children, Wainwright set up a separate home in Mile End with his 22-year-old mistress Harriet Lane, who bore him two children and was also known as Mrs Percy King. Under financial strain, Wainwright cut Harriet's allowance whilst he himself

DATE:
1875

EXHIBIT:
Harriet Lane's hairpiece in its display box

moved to Sidney Square, Stepney, but he soon became bankrupt. Harriet disappeared on 11 September 1874.

About a year after her disappearance, Wainwright, by now manager of the premises under a new proprietor, asked a former workman named Alfred Stokes to help him move some oilcloth-wrapped parcels from the shop premises to London Bridge. They were so smelly and heavy that Stokes complained, and Wainwright agreed to search for a cab. Whilst Wainwright was absent, looking for a cab, Stokes saw that one of the parcels contained a severed hand and a decomposing head. After helping Wainwright load the parcels into the cab, Stokes followed it on foot and called police to the address where Wainwright was unloading the parcels into premises occupied by his brother Thomas.

There were two bullets in the head and the throat had been cut. The body was identified as Harriet Lane, partly because she had been scalded on the leg as a child and a corresponding scar was found on the victim's body. Wainwright had shot her, slit her throat and buried her under the paint shop floor, but made the mistake of using lime chloride that actually preserved, rather than destroyed, her remains. A year afterwards, the unpleasant smell was arousing too much attention: a dog had started to become inquisitive, for instance. Wainwright had decided to move the remains elsewhere, and, with the assistance of his brother, Thomas, had cut the body into ten parts to make its transfer and disposal easier. The museum catalogue records the acquisition of a chopper, a spade, a piece of rope, a piece of cigar, three lead bullets and an old umbrella that were also seized by the police as exhibits.

Henry Wainwright was executed for murder on 21 December 1875, Thomas Wainwright was imprisoned for seven years and Alfred Stokes received a reward of £30 for his part in informing the police about the body.

The position of Harriet Lane was a difficult one, shared by many unmarried Victorian women who were unable to maintain financial independence in their own right. Henry Wainwright disposed of her by violence, a fate that Lane also shared with a number of other women in similar situations.

19 Pin Cushion

ANNIE PARKER SPENT most of her life in prison and had appeared over 400 times at Greenwich magistrates' court charged with drunkenness. The lace bordering the pin cushion was made by her, supposedly to mark her 200th conviction. It was embroidered entirely with her own hair and is an example of the skilful handiwork that can be achieved by prisoners. She gave it to Revd J.W. Horsley, the chaplain of the Clerkenwell House of Detention for many years, who in turn donated it to the Crime Museum in 1884. Annie Parker died of consumption in 1885 at the age of 35.

The work of a prison chaplain is not any easy one, but Revd Horsley must have appreciated the gift, not least for the sentiments expressed. The four virtues of

DATE:
1879

EXHIBIT:
Sampler, or pin cushion, embroidered with a prisoner's hair

justice, fortitude, prudence and temperance appear on the corners, with 'Let Thy Priests be clothed with righteousness – 1879' and 'I will instruct thee and teach thee in the way which thou shalt go. I will guide thee with Mine Eye. Thy home is in heaven.'

Charging prisoners with simple drunkenness is now a rare occurrence and the criminal justice system probably deals with fewer cases of vagrancy and drunkenness than in the past, when the police were sometimes the only agency that took responsibility for them on the streets. The police would keep them in the cells overnight, feed them and take them to court where they could be diverted to a probation officer or to a charity if appropriate.

Annie Parker was no doubt one of the characters well known within the prison system. With time on their hands, prisoners would often construct detailed handiwork using great initiative in utilising what little resources they had at their disposal. The results have sometimes been exemplary work of this type, or elaborately sculpted tobacco tins. These artefacts are a product of a prison's regime; the other side of the coin is that sometimes prisoners can spend inordinate amounts of time generating elaborate grievances, concocting plans for escape, or becoming obsessively concerned with the details of the enclosed communities in which they live.

20 Courtroom Sketch of John Williams

WHEN JOHN WILLIAMS was arrested and first taken to court in 1912, the detective in charge of the case, Scotland Yard's Detective Chief Inspector Eli Bower, put a spotted apron over Williams' head to avoid his face being publicised by press photographers waiting outside the court. This was the start of the tradition of giving an element of privacy to prisoners as they entered the courthouse, and may also have been motivated by a wish not to compromise any issues of formal identification of the defendant.

DATE:
1912

EXHIBIT:
John Williams at Lewes Assizes

The arrival at the courthouse was the culmination of an investigation that contained many interesting aspects. The story started on Wednesday, 9 October 1912 when Countess Flora Sztaray of Southcliffe Avenue in Eastbourne was due to go out to dinner with friends. A one-horse brougham carriage arrived at the house at 7.20 p.m. to take the countess and her companion the short distance to their friend's house, but the driver noticed a man lying on top of a flat canopy above the front door of the house. He reported this to the countess after they had left, and she, worried about her servant who was still at the house, returned home and

telephoned the police. The message was passed to Inspector Arthur Walls who then went the ½ mile from the police station and challenged the man, but was shot dead. The culprit escaped. The chief constable of Eastbourne, Major Teale, telephoned Scotland Yard at 8.25 p.m. and Detective Chief Inspector Eli Bower was deputed to take up the inquiry, taking the first train to Eastbourne the following morning.

There was no accurate description of the suspect from witnesses and no sign of fingerprints, but that evening, Dr Edgar Power from Finsbury Park went to the Eastbourne police and gave information that he believed the man responsible to be John Williams, who also used other names, including Frank Seymour. Williams had lived in Finsbury Park and had been treated by Dr Power for an injury caused whilst escaping from a burglary in Bournemouth. Power was due to take the train back to London with Florence Seymour, with whom Williams had been living. Power was adamant that his name was not to be used in the inquiry and would not make a written statement. This was very valuable information, but Eli Bower believed that Power was not being completely honest and concluded that Power wanted Williams out of the way because he had designs on the attractive Florence Seymour.

Back in London, Power told the police of an arrangement that he had to meet Williams in Moorgate at lunchtime on 11 October. This enabled Bower, Sergeant Hayman and other officers to arrest Williams, who was taken to Cannon Row police station but denied any involvement with the murder. Bower then intercepted Florence in Victoria Street and invited her to his office at Scotland Yard. She admitted being in Eastbourne with her 'husband' at the time, but said that he had been absent for a period whilst they had been walking near Southcliffe Avenue and that he had lost his hat there. Power was present during part of the interview and when Florence managed to throw a left-luggage ticket into a fire burning in the grate of the detectives' office, Power gave the police sufficient details of the ticket to enable them to recover a gun holster. There was little doubt about the identity of the murderer, but there was still insufficient evidence to support the murder charge.

After discussing the case with Bower, Power then managed to persuade Florence to try to recover the murder weapon from its burial place on Eastbourne beach and travelled down to Eastbourne with her for this purpose on 15 October. The police kept discreetly in the background. Officers on surveillance duty saw Florence linger at a certain point on the promenade, but she did not go on to the beach itself. Without modern equipment such as metal detectors, the investigators then undertook a search of the beach in the dark and eventually recovered parts of a gun.

It was before the advent of forensic science laboratories, so Eli Bower took the gun components and the bullet from the crime scene to Robert Churchill, a firearms expert who had previously assisted his uncle Edwin Churchill with ballistics evidence for the 1903 Moat Farm murder case, which had also been investigated by Bower. Robert Churchill reassembled the gun using a new hammer and springs, and then test-fired the weapon. Churchill had assembled a comprehensive index of guns and their characteristics, including the rifling patterns inside their barrels that made bullets spin and therefore fly straighter. Using this knowledge, Churchill concluded that the bullet that had killed Inspector Walls was a .25 automatic pistol of the same make and type as that found on Eastbourne beach. There had been no substantive evidence against Williams, but the discovery of this gun and the link with Florence did complete a chain of evidence linking Williams to the murder. Florence and Williams also had a number of items in their possession that were traced back to burglaries on the south coast.

The differences in the number, direction and degree of twists in rifling grooves of various makes of gun barrel were demonstrated to the jury by creating impressions from dental wax and withdrawing them from the gun barrels. William McBride, a pioneer police photographer, then took close-up photographs. It was the first time in Britain that evidence of this type had been introduced to show that a bullet from a crime scene had been fired from a particular make of gun, and is an excellent example of early close-up photography.

William McBride had spent a long time rotating the cast of the gun barrel grooves to demonstrate that it matched the bullet, and he was able to bring a fresh approach to demonstrating technical evidence to a jury.

John Williams had enlisted into the Royal Scots Regiment under the name of George McKay on 9 October 1899 and had deserted in October 1901. He was convicted of the murder and executed in January 1913. As for Dr Edgar Power, whose information and collaboration with the police was crucial for solving the case, he did not make romantic progress with Florence Seymour, possibly because she realised that he had betrayed her as well as John Williams. The police paid him a generous reward, but, worried that he would spend the money too quickly, he asked for the payment to be delayed until immediately before he left the country for America.

There had been notable ballistics cases before this date. In 1794, John Toms was traced as the killer of Edward Culshaw, in Lancashire, after wadding made from broadsheet newspaper used for his muzzle-loading gun was matched to the remainder of the document found in his possession. This method of examining improvised wadding also solved an 1860 case, when newspaper used in the undischarged barrel of a double-barrelled shotgun fired by Thomas Richardson was found to fit another piece, torn from the same page of a newspaper, that had been used as wadding for the shot that killed PC Alexander McBrian in Lincolnshire.

In 1835, Henry Goddard, a Bow Street officer, was called down to Southampton to investigate armed burglars who had raided a house, where the butler, Joseph Randall, had supposedly fired his gun to defend the property. Goddard found an identical pimple in the bullets apparently fired by the intruders and the same feature in the butler's own home-made ammunition, upon which Randall confessed that the story was concocted so that he would find favour with his mistress for his bravery.

The first recorded ballistics case investigated by the Metropolitan Police was the murder of PC George Cole, who, on a foggy night on 1 December 1882, caught a young thief trying to break in to a Baptist chapel in Ashwin Street, Dalston, but his prisoner escaped and shot the officer dead. Inquiries were made by N Division police, but these grounded to a halt, the only clue being a chisel that had been left behind at the scene. Scratched into the chisel were the letters 'R. O. C. K.', the meaning of which was unclear. Eventually, Inspector Thomas Glass received information that Thomas Orrock may have been the murderer. This suddenly made sense of the letters, and pioneering photographic techniques did indeed then reveal Orrock's full name scratched on to the chisel. Using the ruse of a self-compiled anonymous letter to extract information from Orrock's wife, Inspector Glass identified Orrock's burglary accomplices from the fateful night, one of whom showed Sergeant Cobb a tree on Tottenham marshes where Orrock had been involved in target practice. Cobb then recovered a bullet from the tree that was of the same type and weight as those recovered from Cole's body and from his truncheon case (a long leather pouch used in Victorian times before truncheons were concealed in a trouser pocket). The truncheon case, a black felt wide-awake hat discarded by the gunman, and a wedge used for burglary also found their way into the museum.

James Squire, a gunmaker from Whitechapel, confirmed the similarity of the bullets and that they were all of a type fired from the pin-fire cartridges used by the gun that had been bought from his shop (and later thrown away) by Orrock who was in due course convicted of George Cole's murder and executed in October 1884.

The Moat Farm case concerned the murder of Camille Holland, who had bought a farm in Essex on behalf of Samuel Dougal, in April 1899. Camille Holland then disappeared, but cheques drawn from her London bank account *after* her disappearance gave rise to suspicion against Dougal, who in turn also disappeared. A search of the farm in 1903 revealed Holland's dead body with a bullet in her head. The distance from which the gun had been fired was a crucial factor in Dougal's trial, but, four years after her death, there was no evidence of powder burns to indicate a close-range shot. Edwin Churchill, the uncle of Robert and original owner of a gun shop in Agar Street, Strand, in central London, experimented with shooting bullets into a sheep's skull, and, with Robert's assistance, concluded that the shot must have been fired from a range of 6–12in. This contradicted the defence's assertion that the shot was accidental.

Dougal was executed at Chelmsford prison on 14 July 1903. A stone with his initials was let into the wall of the prison to mark his grave. The gravestones were transferred elsewhere in 1923 when Chelmsford prison was emptied. Gilbert Harris, the governor of Wandsworth prison, donated Dougal's tombstone to the museum in May 1939.

A more modern ballistics exhibit of international interest in the museum is the test bullet used to make a comparison for the murder of John Lennon by Mark Chapman in New York in 1980.

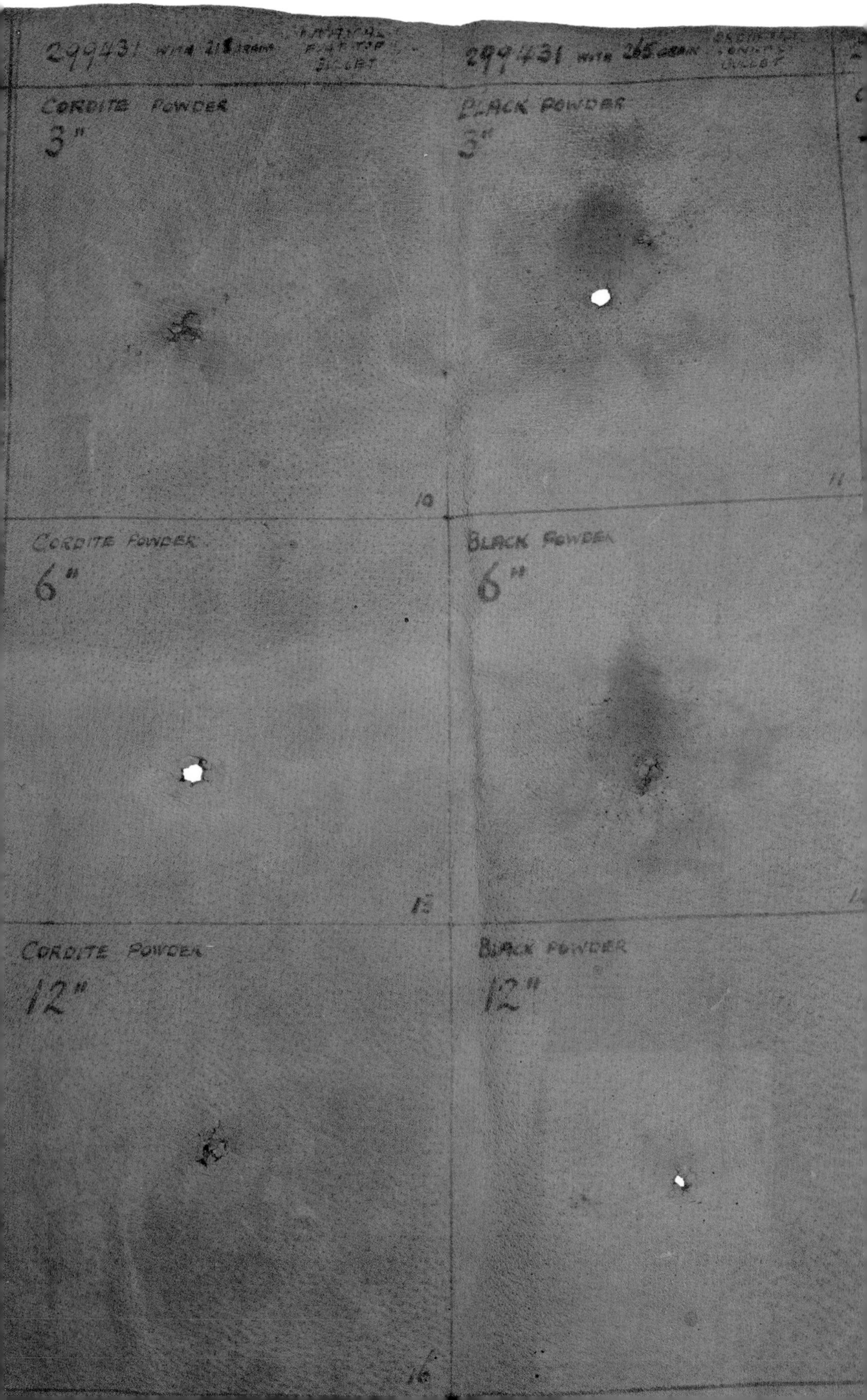

299431 with 218 grain FLAT TOP BULLET | 299431 with 265 grain BULLET

CORDITE POWDER
3"

BLACK POWDER
3"

10

11

CORDITE POWDER
6"

BLACK POWDER
6"

13

CORDITE POWDER
12"

BLACK POWDER
12"

16

Pigskin with Bullet Holes

BY 1927, ROBERT Churchill was an established firearms expert and conducted further experiments about the penetration of bullets in another milestone ballistics case. He used a pig's skin to test how far bullets fired from a particular weapon penetrated, and used this method of calculating the distance from which the gun would have been fired to murder a police officer. The case was also important because of a distinctive mark on a cartridge case, which then became the centre of ballistics evidence that, for the first time in British legal history, proved one particular firearm had been used in a murder.

On 27 September 1927, PC Gutteridge, an Essex officer, was found dead in a lonely lane at Howe Green. He had been shot four times in the face, including through both eyes. This may have been because of a belief that the last image of a dying person is retained on their retina. The officer's pencil was clenched in his hand and his pocketbook was nearby, as if he had been questioning a suspect, but there were few other immediate clues.

Detective Chief Inspector James Berrett from Scotland Yard was appointed to investigate. A Morris Cowley motorcar, stolen 10 miles from the murder scene, was recovered in Brixton, south London, with bloodstains on one of the running boards. There was tree bark stuck to the springs, which was consistent with a mark in the bank of the road at the scene, and

DATE:
1927

EXHIBIT:
Pigskin marked into 6in squares to test bullet impacts

tests showed that the 42 extra miles recorded on the car's milometer was consistent with a route that would have taken in PC Gutteridge's beat, so the car seemed to be linked to the murder. Also found in the car was an unusual cartridge case.

The cartridge case found was marked 'RLIV', indicating a type of soft ammunition produced at Royal Arsenal, Woolwich, for soldiers in the First World War. But the most significant feature was a small raised pimple that appeared to have been created by a corresponding small scar in the smooth face of the breech shield of the gun that had fired the bullet; officers speculated at the time that the gun had been damaged by a cleaning rod. Robert Churchill examined the bullets from the crime scene and concluded, because of their rifling marks, that the murder weapon had been a Webley revolver. Months of intensive inquiries followed, during which a number of Webley revolvers were found, but these were all systematically excluded because they did not create that exact mark on the cartridge cases of the bullets they fired.

Eventually, an appeal in January 1928 in the *News of the World*, and a doubling of the reward to £2,000 for information, created a breakthrough. The Sheffield police reported that one of Berrett's suspects, an elusive car thief named Frederick Browne, had resumed his old habits. Mrs Hutton from Tooting had recently travelled to Sheffield to identify her car that had been stolen from her garage in Tooting two months earlier, for which Browne was a prime suspect. Berrett then heard that Browne had been visiting a prisoner at Dartmoor and arranged for the police to be waiting for his likely return to his garage at Clapham Junction. When Browne did return, he was promptly arrested. The police found four guns, two of which were Webleys and one of which made precisely the same mark on a cartridge case when it was fired. Items from the stolen car's owner were found in Browne's garage, thus completing a chain of evidence. The murder weapon is on loan from Essex Police Museum.

Later, a Sheffield informant identified Patrick Kennedy as Browne's accomplice. Kennedy was arrested in dramatic fashion in Liverpool. In a poorly lit street,

Sergeant William Mattinson of Liverpool City police approached Kennedy, whom he knew, and was arresting him when Kennedy took a pistol from his pocket, held it to the officer's ribs and said, 'Stand back or I'll kill you.' As Kennedy pulled the trigger, the officer heard a click, but grappled with the prisoner until assistance arrived. The bullet in the gun had jammed part way up the gun's barrel because the safety catch was on. The sergeant was later awarded the King's Police Medal for his bravery. At the police station, Kennedy made a long statement about how PC Gutteridge had stopped them in the stolen car in the early hours of the morning and how Browne had shot the officer. The two men were convicted of murder and executed on 31 May 1928. The *Sunday Dispatch* newspaper summarised the case with the headline 'Hanged by a Microscope', reflecting the nature of the ballistics evidence that proved Browne and Kennedy's involvement in the murder.

Ballistics is the science of comparing firearms with ammunition that might have been fired from them, determining the trajectory and distance from which ammunition has been fired, and judging whether firearms could have been fired accidentally. The rifling grooves, machined into the barrels of handguns and rifles to make the bullets spin, create a pattern on the lead bullet as it is pushed through the barrel by the explosive force of the gun being fired. As well as the marks of these easily visible grooves and lands (the spaces between the grooves) there are also much smaller striation marks that transfer themselves on to the bullet. Viewed through a microscope, no gun barrel is completely smooth; they all have a unique pattern of minute marks created by the manufacturing process. These create their own much less visible pattern on the bullet, resembling a barcode. Robert Churchill commissioned Messrs Watson of High Holborn to make a comparison microscope to a specification he had devised with Hugh Pollard (who had experimented with two microscopes linked together) to enable a bullet from a crime scene to be compared with a second bullet test-fired from a suspect firearm. One bullet would be rotated to clarify whether the rifling marks matched each other.

METROPOLITAN POLICE.

MURDER

£100 REWARD.

WHEREAS at 1.15 p.m., on Sunday, the 9th March, 1884, ANNIE YATES was found dead at No. 12, Burton Crescent, St. Pancras, supposed having been suffocated by a man unknown; and whereas a verdict of Wilful Murder against some person or persons unknown has been returned by a Coroner's Jury :—

A Reward of £100 will be paid by Her Majesty's Government to any person (other than a ~~n~~ belonging to a Police Force in the United ~~K~~ ~~ing~~dom) who shall give such information ~~as shall lead to the discove~~ ~~ry a~~nd co~~nvicti~~on of the Murderer or Murderers; and ~~S~~ecretary of State for the Home Department will advise the grant of Her Majesty's gracious

PARDON

to any accomplice not being the person who actually committed the murder, who shall give such evidence as shall lead to a like result:

Information to be given to the Director of Criminal Investigations, Great Scotland Yard, S.W., or at any Police Station.

Metropolitan Police Office,
4, Whitehall Place,
3rd April, 1884.

E. Y. W. HENDERSON,
The Commissioner of Police of the Metropolis.

Printed by M'Corquodale and Company Limited, "The Armoury," Southwark—21355

22

Reward Poster

PUBLIC POSTERS WERE a significant part of police methods to appeal for information, with considerable rewards regularly being offered from government funds. The earliest such reward poster, issued by the Metropolitan Police in 1829, related to a man known as John Berrigg who was wanted for horse theft, whilst that issued for Charlie Peace in 1876 was an early example of a poster containing an illustration of the wanted man.

What became known as the Burton Crescent Murder was discovered on Sunday, 9 March 1884 when a young woman, Mary Anne (or Annie) Yates, was found dead in her lodgings at No. 12 Burton Crescent, near Euston, by her friend Annie Ellis, who also lodged in the house. Annie Yates had a wound to her head caused by a blunt instrument, bruising on her chest, and injuries consistent with being strangled to death. In the general untidiness of her room, a half sovereign was found amongst her bedclothes. Annie was an 'unfortunate' (or prostitute), who had a paralysed right arm. She had originally come from Reading and her real name was Mary Anne Marshall. On the previous evening Annie Ellis had walked out with Annie Yates, but had parted company from her at about 1.15 a.m. when Yates had gone to speak to a man on the corner of Euston Road and Tottenham Court Road before heading off with him towards Burton Crescent. The street door of the house had been banged shut with some violence at about 4 a.m. after some 'hysterics' or 'screaming' had been heard.

DATE:
1884

EXHIBIT:
Poster seeking information about the Annie Yates murder

The landlady, Mrs Eliza Evans of Lewisham, told the inquest that she had rented the room to Yates on the basis that she was a married woman accompanied by her husband, and that a Mrs Sarah Apex acted as a caretaker for the premises. Evans owned two other houses and the coroner was distinctly unimpressed when she claimed not to know whether her tenants in those houses were also prostitutes. Yates' background was a sad one: she had been found abandoned as a 5 year old in Regent Street by a police officer from Great Marlborough Street. Detective Sergeant James Scandett told the inquest that she had been sent to Westminster Workhouse, then to St James's Industrial School in Tooting and was put into domestic service but then 'fell into evil ways and lived an immoral life'. The inquiries to trace the man who had been with Yates that night were unsuccessful, and the case remained unsolved.

It was a reflection of the tragic circumstances of young women who fell into prostitution, but the posters did result in a number of people coming forward in unsuccessful attempts to identify her as a missing relative. The inquest ended with the coroner taking note of a deputation of local residents who pointed out that their neighbourhood was largely a respectable one, that houses of prostitution such as No. 12 Burton Crescent should be prosecuted, and that they wished the name of their street to be changed. Burton Crescent had been built around 1810 by James Burton and named after its builder; it became Cartwright Gardens, after the political reformer Major John Cartwright who had lived at No. 37.

The murders of prostitutes have often caused problems for the police because of the difficulty in identifying their clients. Twelve years earlier, another notable case had occurred where the police caused controversy by pursuing inquiries into the clients of Harriet Buswell, another 'unfortunate'. The comments in newspapers of the time blamed the police for arresting the wrong person, but also expressed outrage at the prospect of a gentleman ever being accused of such a crime.

The idea of the police investigating into a prostitute's clients was seen as abhorrent.

On Christmas morning 1872, Harriet Buswell, like Annie Yates, was found murdered in her lodgings. For many years a plaster cast of a half-eaten apple was stored in the museum in the hope that it might provide the means of confirming or disproving the identity of a future suspect by comparing details of his bite marks.

Late on the morning of 25 December 1872, the occupants of No. 12 Great Coram Street became concerned that they had not yet seen 27-year-old Harriet Buswell, who lodged at the address. They opened her room and found that she had been brutally murdered. There was a bloodstained thumbprint on her forehead and other bloodstains in the room, but the modern techniques of crime scene investigation – blood grouping and fingerprint analysis – had not yet been developed. The body was taken to St Giles Workhouse where the recent development of photography was utilised in order to assist in the issue of identification. Harriet Buswell was also known as Clara Burton, and had a daughter who had been fostered out to a neighbour for 5s per week. Buswell lived in poverty, relying on her activities as a prostitute to get by. Her situation was in one sense summarised by the discovery of a pawn ticket for five pairs of ladies' drawers. She had borrowed 1s from a fellow lodger the previous evening and had returned at about midnight with nuts, oranges, apples and enough money to be able to pay her landlady half a sovereign. She had brought a man home with her who had been heard leaving the house at about 6.30 a.m. on Christmas morning.

Superintendent James Thomson from E Division took charge of the investigation rather than an officer from Scotland Yard, but whether this was significant is difficult to judge. The Detective Branch was in the last five years of its existence before the introduction of the Criminal Investigation Department (CID), and had been under great pressure, not least from investigations into the Irish Republican Brotherhood and their 1867 Clerkenwell explosion. Harriet Buswell's movements from the Alhambra Theatre were traced. Various witnesses had seen her with a foreign man, possibly German, who had a swarthy complexion and blotches or pimples on his face. A reward, this time for £200, was offered for information.

The reward posters appeared to pay dividends when a development came from Ramsgate, where the local police suspected a man, Carl Wohlebbe, the assistant surgeon of German brig *Wangerland* that had been put into the port at Christmas for repairs. Superintendent Thomson sent Inspector Harnett down to Ramsgate with George Fleck, the greengrocer who had served Harriet Buswell her nuts and oranges, and a Mr Stalker, a waiter from the Alhambra who had served Harriet and her companion with drinks on Christmas Eve. Carl Wohlebbe was placed on an identification parade of about twenty members of the ship's crew, but both witnesses stated that Wohlebbe was not the man that they had seen. Amongst the other members of the crew making up the parade was Dr Gottfried Hessel, the ship's chaplain. Both witnesses positively identified him, rather than Carl Wohlebbe, as the man that they had seen with Harriet Buswell. Both Wohlebbe and Hessel had in fact been in London that night. Hessel was duly arrested and charged with murder.

On 20 January 1873, Hessel appeared at Bow Street magistrates' court and was remanded. Sir Richard Mayne had died three years earlier and murder cases no longer had the supervision of a barrister-trained commissioner. Mayne's successor, Colonel Henderson, was a military man. The police sought legal assistance from a firm of solicitors to conduct the case, an early form of the role later played by the Solicitor's Department at Scotland Yard, the Director of Public Prosecutions and the Crown Prosecution Service. A week later, two further witnesses identified Hessel in the Bow Street dock as having accompanied Harriet Buswell that night, but others expressed doubts. A housemaid from the Royal Hotel in Ramsgate testified that Hessel had asked for turpentine and a clothes brush when he had returned from London, and one of his handkerchiefs had been saturated with blood. Hessel gave alibi evidence that he had never left his London hotel that night because of illness, and this was supported by Carl Wohlebbe, but there is no record of this alibi being investigated by the police. It is possible that the prosecution simply decided not to call evidence that they knew would not support the case against Hessel, or that the advocate summarised such evidence to the court.

The magistrate, Mr Vaughan, discharged Hessel and declared that he was being released without suspicion attached to him. Hessel was cheered by crowds and a public subscription was raised for him by the *Daily Telegraph* before he continued his voyage to Brazil. The money may have been more welcome than antici-pated: an anonymous letter received after his acquittal outlined a catalogue of spendthrift conduct, drunken-ness and debts left behind by Hessel in Germany. The case reflected the speed with which suspects were charged in those days; nowadays there would be a much more thorough investigation before commitment to a prosecution. It was also an example of how identi-fication parades could have unintended consequences. A modern investigator would have checked whether any of Hessel's fingerprints matched the mark on the victim's forehead and would have checked his teeth. Analysis of the bloodstains, not least on Hessel's hand-kerchief and, perhaps, on his clothing and at his hotel rooms, would be likely to have confirmed or disproved his involvement.

The Commissioner's Annual Report for the year referred to the case and stated: 'It was held at the time that the Metropolitan Police, to whose custody the person charged was committed, were to blame in the matter; but, in fact, they had no alternative what-ever, and acted throughout strictly in accordance with their duty.'

METROPOLITAN POLICE.

Fac-simile of Letter and Post Card received by Central News Agency.

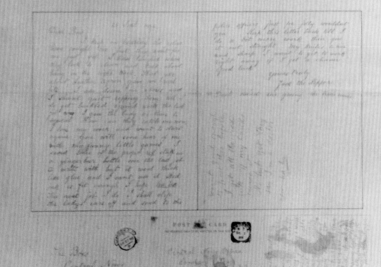

Any person recognising the handwriting is requested to communicate with the nearest Police Station.

Metropolitan Police Office,
3rd October, 1888.

Printed by M'Corquodale & Co. Limited, "The Armoury," Southwark.

Appeal Poster

THIS POSTER WAS a high-profile appeal issued by the police in an attempt to identify the author(s) of a letter and postcard sent to the Central News Agency about the Whitechapel murders. The letter was the most famous one in a whole series of taunting or hoax letters, and was dated 25 September 1888. Addressed 'Dear Boss', and sent to the Central News Agency in the City of London rather than to the police, it was the first to use the name Jack the Ripper. It read:

> 25 Sept 1888
>
> Dear Boss
>
> I keep on hearing the police have caught me but they won't fix me just yet. I have laughed when they look so clever and talk about being on the right track. The joke about Leather Apron gave me real fits. I am down on whores and I shan't quit ripping them till I do get buckled. Grand work the last job was. I gave the lady no time to squeal. How can they catch me [now]. I love my work and want to st[art] again. You will soon hear of me with my funny little games. I saved some of the proper <u>red</u> stuff in a ginger beer bottle over the last job to write with but it went thick like glue and I can't use it. Red ink is fit enough I hope <u>ha ha</u>. The next job I do I shall clip the lady's ears off and send to the police officers just for jolly wouldn't you. Keep this letter back till I do a bit more work, then give it out straight. My knife's

DATE:
1888

EXHIBIT:
Appeal poster publicising the handwriting of Jack the Ripper

so sharp I want to get to work right away if I get a chance. Good Luck.
Yours truly
Jack the Ripper
Don't mind me giving the trade name.
[At right angles] Wasn't good enough to post this before I got all the red ink off my hands curse it. No luck yet. They say I'm a doctor now **ha ha**.

The letter below (known as the 'saucy Jacky' postcard), postmarked 1 October 1888, was also sent to the Central News Agency. It was apparently bloodstained and had a smudged finger and thumbprint:

I wasn't codding dear old Boss when I gave you the tip. You'll hear about saucy Jacky's work tomorrow. Double event this time. Number one squealed a bit. Couldn't finish straight off. Had not time to get ears for police. Thanks for keeping back last letter till I got to work again – Jack the Ripper.

The significance is partly the linked references to the victim's ears, but also the reference to the 'double event' and whether the card could have been written before one or both of the two murders that occurred on Sunday, 30 September 1888 – those of Elizabeth Stride (between 12.45 a.m. and 1 a.m.) and Catherine Eddowes (between 1.35 a.m. and 1.45 a.m.).

The Whitechapel murders are perhaps the most famous unsolved series of murders in the world. Certainly they have generated an unprecedented amount of attention and speculation, driven, in recent years, by a series of books and television programmes that have drawn both on documents released by The National Archives and on other techniques that try to bring fresh light to bear on investigations that are more than 120 years old. The Whitechapel murders illustrate the difficulty of being certain, particularly in Victorian times, about how many crimes are committed by one person when dealing with serial murders.

Most commentators focus on five murders as being committed by one man, starting with that of Mary Ann Nichols on 31 August 1888, but the killings, at least as far as public anxiety was concerned, started earlier, with two beforehand and four afterwards for a total of eleven, and, when victims were identified, all involved prostitutes.

On Tuesday, 3 April 1888 at 1.30 a.m., Emma Elizabeth Smith was badly assaulted by a group of three men in Osborn Street and died of peritonitis the following day. She had suffered internal injuries from a blunt weapon, her head was bruised and her ear was torn. One of Emma Smith's friends had suffered a similar attack. The police were only informed of the attack on 6 April.

On Tuesday, 7 August 1888 between 2 a.m. and 3.30 a.m. Martha Tabram (or Turner) was stabbed thirty-nine times, probably with a dagger. Martha's colleague Mary Connelly (or 'Pearly Poll') said that she and Martha had been with two soldiers from 10 p.m. until 11.45 p.m. when they had paired off. Identification parades were held at the local barracks. Although Mary picked out two soldiers, they had alibis. A police officer, PC Thomas Barrett (226H), had spoken to a soldier outside George Yard that night but two that he picked out from the line-ups were also eliminated from suspicion.

The first of the core group of five murders occurred on Friday, 31 August 1888 between 2.30 a.m. and 3.45 a.m. at Buck's Row when Mary Ann Nichols was found disembowelled and with her throat deeply cut from left to right, as if by a left-handed person. She had told another woman that she was trying to obtain 4d to pay for her bed for the night. At this point, some police officers started to think that all three murders could be linked. A newspaper report referred to gangs who would blackmail prostitutes in the early hours of the morning and abuse them if their demands were not met. Inspector Helson reported that inquiries were being made to trace a man named John or Jack Pizer (nicknamed 'Leather Apron'), who had been in the habit of 'ill-using' prostitutes.

When the next murder occurred just over a week later, on Saturday, 8 September, Annie Chapman (alias Ann Siffey) was found, also with her throat cut, in the rear yard of No. 29 Hanbury Street in Spitalfields. Some of her intestines were found on her right shoulder. Her uterus and part of her bladder had been removed with a fair degree of skill. The injuries were similar to those suffered by Mary Ann Nichols, and the murders were only eight days apart. Two brass rings were missing from the victim's fingers and were never recovered. A witness, Mrs Long, saw the back of a man talking to Annie Chapman at 5.30 a.m. and described him as being shabby but genteel. Dr George Phillips, the police divisional surgeon, believed the weapon was a small amputating knife, or a well-ground butcher's knife, narrow and thin, with a blade about 6–8in long, used by somebody with some anatomical knowledge. John Pizer was arrested two days after Annie Chapman's murder, but had an alibi for the night of Mary Nichols' murder, corroborated by a lodging house proprietor from Holloway Road. Pizer also accounted for where he had been on the night of Annie Chapman's murder, despite being picked out on an identification parade by somebody who identified him as bullying a woman in Hanbury Street.

An unemployed butcher, Joseph Isenschmid had been seen with blood on his hands at 7 a.m. on the morning of Annie Chapman's murder. He was suffering from mental health problems, his wife had reported him missing and he carried large butcher's knives around with him, but no blood was found on his clothing so he was confined to an asylum.

Three weeks later, two murders occurred on one night. On Sunday, 30 September 1888, Elizabeth Stride (also known as 'Long Liz') was killed between 12.45 a.m. and 1 a.m. at Dutfield's Yard, by No. 40 Berner Street, Commercial Road East. Her throat was cut and it is possible that the murderer was disturbed by the arrival of members of a nearby Socialist club. There was no trace of the weapon. PC William Smith (452H) had seen the victim talking to a man aged about 28 years, 5ft 7in in height, with a dark complexion, a small black moustache, and dressed in a black coat with a white collar and tie.

The second murder on the night of 30 September occurred in Mitre Square, Aldgate, on City of London police territory within about an hour of the first. Catherine Eddowes (or Kate Kelly) was killed between 1.35 a.m. and 1.45 a.m.. Her throat was cut, she had been disembowelled, her right ear was cut through and her uterus and left kidney had been removed. Part of her bloodstained apron was found a few streets away in Goulston Street in the Metropolitan Police District. A message was found on the wall above it, written in chalk: 'The Jewes are the men that will not be blamed for nothing.' The Metropolitan Police Commissioner, Sir Charles Warren, ordered this to be erased, something that was done before the arrival of the photographer called up to record it.

After a respite of five weeks, Mary Jane Kelly was murdered on Friday, 9 November 1888, not in the street, but in her lodgings at No. 13 Miller's Court, No. 26 Dorset Street, Spitalfields. She suffered a cut throat, numerous gashes and mutilations and her heart had been removed. Her body was found at 10.45 a.m. the next day when Thomas Bowyer called to collect the rent. Mary Cox, another prostitute, had seen Mary Jane Kelly return to her room, drunk and with a man, at about 11.45 p.m. This was the last of the five main murders in the series.

Six weeks later, Rose Mylett was found dead in Clarke's Yard, High Street, Poplar, in the early hours of 20 December 1888. There were no signs of violence or a struggle, but she had been strangled with a moderately thick cord and one of her earrings was missing.

The next year, Alice McKenzie was found dead on 17 July 1889 in Castle Alley, Whitechapel, with her throat cut and knife wounds to her abdomen. She had died between 12.20 a.m. and 12.50 a.m. Dr Bond, who had started to analyse the patterns of the deaths from a medical perspective, performed a second post-mortem and concluded that it had been a 'sudden onslaught on the prostrate woman, the throat skilfully and resolutely cut, with subsequent mutilation, each mutilation indicating sexual thoughts and a desire to mutilate the abdomen and sexual organs'. Dr Phillips, who had examined earlier Whitechapel murder victims, disagreed with his colleague, however, because of the difference in abdominal wounds.

On 10 September 1889, the remains of a female torso were found at Pinchin Street, Whitechapel, under a railway arch. Donald Swanson concluded that this was not one of the main Whitechapel murders. There was no blood at the scene, which was a lonely spot away from habitation, and it looked as if the torso had been dumped there at a distance from the murder scene itself.

Finally, at 2.15 a.m. on Friday, 13 February 1891 in Swallow Gardens, Whitechapel, PC Ernest Thompson (240H) found the body of Frances Coles with her throat cut. She had not been mutilated in any other way. Dr Phillips thought that the nature of the wound and posture of the body suggested that this murder was not linked to other Whitechapel murders. Police inquiries did, however, result in the arrest of a sailor, James Sadler, who had consorted with Frances Coles, and there was a belief at the time that Jack the Ripper had at last been caught. Sadler was charged with Frances Coles' murder and he was investigated in relation to the earlier crimes. Sadler was not identified by the witness in Mitre Square for the Catherine Eddowes murder, and the dates of his employment on various ships were examined to verify whether he could have been involved in the other murders. He was released on 3 March 1891 at Thames magistrates' court when the prosecuting advocate offered no evidence against him. Later, on 16 May 1892, he was bound over to keep the peace at Lambeth court after his wife complained that he had threatened to cut her throat.

The Whitechapel murders caused a sensation in the newspapers, which reported crime and court proceedings in far greater detail than today. The press articles were fuelled by reported opinions of police officers, by private detectives and journalists conducting investigations, by correspondence from well-meaning members of the public, and by letters received by the police and the press purporting to come from the killer himself. The first such letter was dated 24 September 1888, after the Annie Chapman murder: 'I do wish to give myself up ... I have found the woman I wanted that is Chapman and I done what I called slautered [sic] her ... Keep the Boro' Road clear or I might take a trip up there ...'

Hoax letters about murders are not unusual in high-profile murder cases. The motives of the writers would include ridiculing the police, creating mischief, seeking attention for their writing, or simply a perverted obsession with the murders. The flood of such letters about the Whitechapel murders continued for about two years, with a wide variety of handwriting.

A handbill dated 30 September 1888 appealing for information about the murders, copies of which were distributed to local residents, is also in the museum, but most surviving material about the Whitechapel murders is available in The National Archives.

Modern investigations are able to keep much tighter control over what details are released as public knowledge, and which facts could be known only to a perpetrator. There was a suspicion, even soon afterwards, that the two communications in the police's appeal were part of a hoax from a member of the press. Detective Chief Inspector John Littlechild wrote, in retirement, that officers at Scotland Yard had suspected Tom Bulling of the Central News Agency, or his chief, John Moore, of writing the 'Dear Boss' letter and the 'saucy Jacky' postcard. Bulling and Moore signed the museum's visitors' book as having visited the collection on 26 July 1892, giving their address as 'No. 5 New Bridge Street, EC' (Central News).

It would have been wonderful for the Victorian police to have had access to modern crime scene technology and forensic science, not least the opportunity to have analysed the now lost, apparently bloodstained, 'saucy Jacky' postcard. Even today, murders of prostitutes can be notoriously difficult to solve, not least because of the transitory and anonymous nature of the transactions involved. Senior officers and medical experts disagreed with each other at the time; and disagreement by those who have studied the murders continues to this day.

24 The Swanson Marginalia

THE LIGHTER SIDE of My Official Life, published in 1910, was the title of the autobiography of Sir Robert Anderson who was assistant commissioner at Scotland Yard from 1888 to 1901, the period in which the Whitechapel murders took place. Detective Chief Inspector Donald Swanson, who played a key role in many of the inquiries, was given a copy of Anderson's book. The identity of the donor is not known. After Swanson died in 1924, the book was passed to other family members and was on loan to the Crime Museum from 2006 to 2012. The printed text of the book mentioned the disapproval of retired officers 'telling tales out of school' but then stated 'the only person who had

DATE:
c. 1910

EXHIBIT:
Handwritten notes in a book owned by Donald Swanson

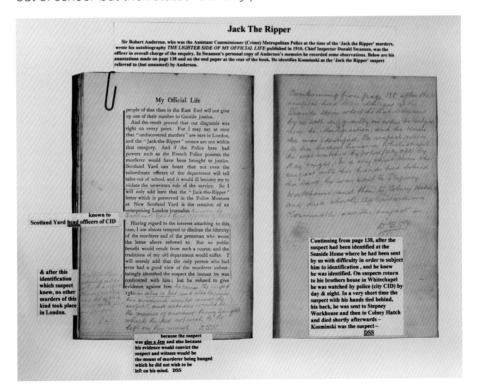

Jack The Ripper

Sir Robert Anderson, who was the Assistant Commissioner (Crime) Metropolitan Police at the time of the 'Jack the Ripper' murders, wrote his autobiography *THE LIGHTER SIDE OF MY OFFICIAL LIFE* published in 1910. Chief Inspector Donald Swanson, was the officer in overall charge of the enquiry. In Swanson's personal copy of Anderson's memoirs he recorded some observations. Below are his annotations made on page 138 and on the end paper at the rear of the book. He identifies Kosminski as the 'Jack the Ripper' suspect referred to (but unnamed) by Anderson.

known to Scotland Yard head officers of CID

& after this identification which suspect knew, no other murders of this kind took place in London.

because the suspect was also a Jew and also because his evidence would convict the suspect and witness would be the means of murderer being hanged which he did not wish to be left on his mind. DSS

Continuing from page 138, after the suspect had been identified at the Seaside Home where he had been sent by us with difficulty in order to subject him to identification , and he knew he was identified. On suspects return to his brothers house in Whitechapel he was watched by police (city CID) by day & night. In a very short time the suspect with his hands tied behind, his back, he was sent to Stepney Workhouse and then to Colney Hatch and died shortly afterwards – Kosminski was the suspect – DSS

ever had a good view of the murderer unhesitatingly identified the suspect the instant he was confronted with him; but he refused to give evidence against him'. Donald Swanson then apparently added his own comments in the margin of the book, and these are regarded as significant in the speculation about the identity of Jack the Ripper.

Researchers of the Whitechapel murders have studied many files and documents, but the earliest surviving official analysis of the suspects is an 1894 report by Sir Melville MacNaghten, then chief constable in the CID who, apparently from memory, set out the case against three suspects. The immediate reason for writing this memorandum was a series of reports in the *Sun* newspaper about Thomas Cutbush, who had been detained for stabbing women in Kennington with a speculative reference to Jack the Ripper. There are in fact three versions of MacNaghten's document, two of which survive. The three suspects listed are described as:

Montague John Druitt, born 1857, was found dead in the river Thames on 31 December 1888 and an inquest returned a verdict of suicide. A rail ticket in his pocket was dated 1 December 1888, and he probably died about that date. MacNaghten described him as sexually insane and recorded that Druitt's family believed him to have been the murderer.

Kosminski, born 1865, was a Polish Jew whom MacNaghten described as having become 'insane owing to many years indulgence in solitary vices. He had a great hatred of women, specially of the prostitute class, and had strong homicidal tendencies; he was removed to a lunatic asylum about March 1889.'

Michael Ostrog was described by MacNaghten as 'a Russian doctor, and a convict, who was subsequently detained in a lunatic asylum as a homicidal maniac. The man's antecedents were of the worst possible type, and his whereabouts at the time of the murders could never be ascertained.' One version of the memorandum records that Ostrog was 'known to have carried about with him surgical knives and other instruments'. He had a record of passing himself off as a Russian nobleman and was known to have acted as a confidence trickster.

There is no single suspect that is consistently quoted as the person whom Scotland Yard believed to have been responsible for the murders. It is, perhaps, a human characteristic for any senior officer of the time to want to be regarded as knowing the truth of the matter, but their versions are not consistent. Against that background, the handwritten comments in the margins of Donald Swanson's book have created understandable excitement. In the margin of p. 138, Swanson had apparently written, in pencil, enlarging on the comment in the printed text about the witness who refused to give evidence:

> because the suspect was **also a Jew** and also because his evidence would convict the suspect and witness would be the means of murderer being hanged which he did not wish to be left on his mind. DSS

> & after this identification which suspect knew, no other murders of this kind took place in London

And on the book's endpaper:

> Continuing from page 138, after the suspect had been identified at the Seaside Home where he had been sent by us with difficulty in order to subject him to identification, and he knew he was identified. On suspects [*sic*] return to his brothers [*sic*] house in Whitechapel he was watched by police (city CID) by day & night. In a very short time the suspect with his hands tied behind, his back, he was sent to Stepney Workhouse and then to Colney Hatch and died shortly afterwards – Kosminski was the suspect – DSS

25 Witness Album Photograph

DATE:
c. 1890-95

EXHIBIT:
Police photograph of Michael Ostrog

THE DEVELOPMENT OF photography transformed the way that criminals were circulated and identified. Although the photography of prisoners largely developed in prisons, the pictures of prisoners were also used to help witnesses identify suspects involved in crime and were displayed in albums in a format that would enable witnesses to glance through many pictures at once in an attempt to recognise their suspect. The process was primarily a screening process before a formal identification parade. This early example of a witness album shows a picture of Michael Ostrog, a suspect for the Whitechapel murders. In modern times this process has been transferred to a computer-based system, and the identification parade process now takes place with a witness observing a sequence of good quality video clips of suspects.

The photographs of prisoners were also used for the distribution of an *Illustrated Circular of Expert Criminals* that was published, in 1924 for instance, so that all of the police forces could have access to a list of travelling criminals, who might then be recognised when they were perpetrating particular methods of crime, such as fraud, in different parts of the country.

According to *The Development of Criminal Records* by Dennis Luke, it was as early as 1842 when the Swiss police circulated daguerreotypes (a photographic process dating from around 1839) of a man who was caught breaking into a church. The governor of Bristol prison, Captain Gardiner, began to take daguerreotype pictures of every prisoner he thought was a habitual criminal. Birmingham City Police undertook photographs of prisoners from 1857 by employing a local private photographer who used collection plates, one of the earliest being that of criminal Dennis Desmond. With the introduction of photographic paper from about 1860, this task then began to be undertaken by the police themselves.

One of the first references to photography at Scotland Yard was a police order dated 3 April 1868, drawing attention to the availability of equipment for photographing prisoners, especially Fenians. By 1870, the record pages of the Habitual Criminals Register, kept by Scotland Yard, had a space for a photograph, and by 1872 the Paris police had 60,000 photographs. In 1878, the commissioner wrote to the Home Office saying that he proposed to set up a collection of photographs of criminals, and Sir Howard Vincent wrote to the Home Office on 2 March 1882 for approval to consult all chief constables about improving *Police Gazette*. This publication had started in the eighteenth century under the auspices of the Bow Street magistrates to circulate details of crimes and wanted criminals, and it was part of Howard Vincent's reforms to transfer responsibility for *Police Gazette* to Scotland Yard.

By January 1884 photographs of wanted criminals were being circulated in special editions of a supplement to *Police Gazette*. A special illustrated circular of

'Race Course Thieves, Welshers, Three Card Trick and Confidence Men' from July 1894, for instance, showed photographs of thirty-seven criminals who might be expected to travel to various horse racing venues. Later, photographs of all prisoners sentenced to penal servitude were taken at the prison prior to their release and sent to Scotland Yard's Convict Supervision Office who would then circulate them. The possibility of crime being committed by recently released prisoners was seen as a real problem. Some police forces exercised a supervision role with some of these men, directing them towards lawful employment but also keeping an eye on whether they were reoffending.

The modern technology for easily making copies of pictures was not available. Detective Inspector William McBride, who joined as a constable in 1900 and became a notable police photographer, described how John Ashley, then a sergeant in the Criminal Records Office and later to become a chief constable in the CID, had wished to circulate a picture of a wanted criminal to police stations in London. Ashley borrowed a quarter-plate camera and then distributed copies of his photograph, this method then being quicker than the alternatives. This led Detective Superintendent Frank Froest to set up a photographic section. The first officer to perform the job retired within a year, but William McBride then applied for the vacancy and succeeded in impressing Assistant Commissioner Melville MacNaghten with a picture he had taken of an Italian woman playing a street piano. From those beginnings, the Photographic Branch of Scotland Yard developed, but the members of staff were far more involved with photographing scenes of crime and fingerprints than taking pictures of prisoners.

The advances of photographic technology enabled increasing use of new techniques in the years that followed. One notable exponent of new technology was Ken Creer MBE, whose work with the Serious Crime Unit at the Metropolitan Police Forensic Science Laboratory in the 1980s developed the use of lasers, light sources and chemical, physical and biological methods to reveal fingerprints and other features that would otherwise be invisible to the human eye.

OLD
BAIL

Courtroom Sketch of Adolf Beck

WILLIAM HARTLEY'S COURTROOM sketch of Adolf Beck is a record of a controversial miscarriage of justice that was very nearly repeated in relation to the same man.

The story commenced with a man named Weiss who had been convicted, under the false name of John Smith, in 1877 and had been imprisoned for five years for frauds of a very distinctive method that overshadowed other details of the case. The man befriended and entertained women, passed himself off as an aristocrat, invited them to go cruising with him and offered to finance a set of new clothes by giving them a cheque. He would borrow a ring or other item of jewellery from them so that he could obtain a superior version of the right size. The man would then disappear, his cheque would be found to be worthless and the woman's jewellery would have been pawned or sold. Some of the victims, invariably unmarried women, may well have been too embarrassed by their agreement to the proposition to report the incidents, thus some cases may have gone unrecorded.

In 1895 the frauds started again, with their victims describing exactly the same method, and one of the victims recognised Adolf Beck in the street, found a police officer, and had him arrested. Beck denied any involvement, but he was put on a series of identification parades and picked out by no less than ten women. On the basis that Beck was the same man renewing this

DATE:
1904

EXHIBIT:
Adolf Beck at the Old Bailey in 1904

distinctive fraud against women, and had been repeatedly identified, Beck was prosecuted and convicted, regardless of his repeated denials.

There was no doubt that the 1895 frauds had been committed by the man who had carried out the 1877 offences, and, indeed, the arresting officer from 1877 gave evidence that Beck was the same man that he had arrested eighteen years earlier. In fact, the trial judge, Sir Forrest Fulton, had been the prosecuting counsel in the 1877 trial. Beck's evidence that he had been in South America at the time of the 1877 trial was held to be inadmissible. As well as being identified by the ten women (of a total of twenty-two), handwriting evidence was heard. At the time, Thomas H. Gurrin of Holborn Viaduct was commissioned by the Home Office, Admiralty and Scotland Yard to act as an expert witness in handwriting. He had been earning his living in this way for about nine years when he took part in Beck's trial. Gurrin testified that the handwriting used in the 1877 case was all written by one person, in a Scandinavian style, and that the 1895 case documents were also written by the same person, who had been disguising his handwriting, regardless of the very significant difference in style. So, on the basis of identification and handwriting evidence, Beck was convicted and sentenced to seven years' penal servitude.

Whilst in prison, Beck maintained his innocence, using various arguments including the fact that the convict 'Smith' had been circumcised, whilst he had not. This succeeded in removing the 1877 offences from his criminal record, but Sir Forrest Fulton maintained that Beck had been convicted of the 1895 offences on the trial's own merits, so Beck remained in prison until 1901.

In 1904, the same frauds recommenced, and one of the victims, accompanied by a police officer, recognised Beck in Tottenham Court Road as Beck went from his lodgings to the City of London. This time all five female victims identified him and he was again taken to the Old Bailey where he was convicted of a set of frauds for a second time, yet again on the basis of identification evidence and that of Thomas Gurrin, who repeated his professional belief that Beck had disguised his hand-writing from the style that had been used in 1877.

Fortunately, the 1904 trial judge, Mr Justice Grantham, had a lingering doubt about the case and delayed Beck's sentencing. On 7 July 1904, a few days into Beck's remand in prison, another of the frauds took place. Not only could Beck not have committed this offence from his prison cell, but there was also an immediate arrest of 'William Thomas' at a pawn-broker's after two sisters had asked their landlord to follow him from their lodgings, after he had borrowed their rings as part of exactly the same fraud. Detective Inspector John Kane made a thorough investigation into 'William Thomas', established his real identity as a German man named William Weiss who had indeed been convicted in 1877, and demonstrated the strik-ing similarity of Weiss' handwriting to the documents produced in all three trials. The handwriting similarity proved the miscarriage of justice in Beck's 1895 and 1904 convictions. Beck was Norwegian and was not dissimilar to Weiss in appearance.

Adolf Beck was pardoned and awarded £5,000 in compensation, his case being instrumental in the introduction of the Court of Criminal Appeal in 1907. A repetition would be avoided by the introduction of fingerprints to prove previous convictions.

Comparison of handwriting is often accompanied by the close examination of questioned documents at a forensic science laboratory, where modern scientific techniques can reveal many details about the paper, inks and other details to detect forgeries and incon-sistencies. Thomas Gurrin had become a handwriting expert by developing a long-term interest in the sub-ject and had then started to earn his living from his considerable skill. He gave expert evidence in a number of cases at the Old Bailey from 1888 onwards. In some cases he would use a microscope and different col-oured light to reveal traces of writing that had been erased, for instance, but expressing an expert opinion about whether a second set of writing was by the same person *disguising* his handwriting style was an entirely different proposition.

27 Identikit and Photofit

THE IDENTIKIT SYSTEM was developed in 1959 by Hugh C. MacDonald, a detective in the Los Angeles Identification Bureau who had seen the need for a system for recording facial descriptions. MacDonald would sketch descriptions himself but then decided to save time by drawing different eyes, noses, hairstyles and face shapes on transparent plastic sheets that could be selected by witnesses and overlaid on each other so that they built up a composite picture. In due course he approached the Townsend Co. in Santa Ana California, who then collaborated with him to develop a kit of 525 coded and numbered transparencies, with 102 pairs of eyes, thirty-two noses, thirty-three sets of lips, fifty-two chins and twenty-five moustaches and beards. The coding system could be used to circulate

DATE:
1961

EXHIBIT:
The Metropolitan Police's first Identikit pictures

descriptions and, by 1960, a number of police forces had started to use the system.

Britain first used the system on 3 March 1961, when 59-year-old Elsie Batten was found stabbed to death in an antique shop owned by Louis Meier and Maria Gray in Cecil Court off Charing Cross Road. Detective Superintendent Pollard led the investigation and called in Keith Simpson, the pathologist, and Superintendent Ray from the Fingerprint Branch. Meier recalled an

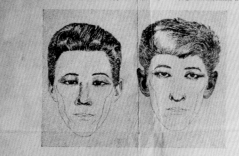

Special Notice

MURDER

M.P. (ED).—At 12.16 p.m. 3rd inst., Elsie May Batten, aged 59 years, was found stabbed to death in an antique shop at 23, Cecil Court (L.), W.C.2.

It is desired to trace the after-described MAN, b. about 1941, 5ft. 7 or 8in., slim build, c. lt. coffee colour (Indian appearance), long face (high cheekbones), h. black (crew cut, grown long and bushy, brushed back at sides), long thin nose, speaks perfect English with trace of London accent; wearing tight dk. blue faded jeans (no turn-ups), mid-brown shoes with rounded toe caps and rubber heels. Spoke of having an Indian Father. May attempt to leave the country.

Is believed to be a collector of antique or oriental daggers and may have made purchases at antique shops or second-hand dealers, or do so in the future.

Has recently been in the company of a girl aged 17-20 yrs., 5ft. 3in., round face (pleasant looking, red cheeks), h. blonde (wavy).

The photograph produced is based on witnesses impressions and suggestions as to identity are requested.

Indian youth who had been in the shop the previous day with a young female companion. The youth had shown a great interest in daggers, one of which had clearly been the murder weapon as it had been found protruding from the victim's chest. A dress sword, in which the youth had been interested, was missing. The sword was recovered at the premises of a nearby gun dealer at No. 53 St Martin's Lane, where a youth had offered it for sale for £10, but had not returned after the son of the shop owner had asked the youth to return later to see his father, Joseph Roberts. Detective Sergeant Raymond Dagg from the local police station, Bow Street, had just been trained in the new Identikit method, and became the first British police officer to use the system when he compiled two independent facial pictures of the youth from the descriptions supplied by Meier and Roberts. The two resulting pictures were notably similar to each other, and were published in newspapers and circulated to police stations.

Soon afterwards PC Arthur Hilton Cole was patrolling Old Compton Street in Soho when he saw somebody whose appearance corresponded to the Identikit images; he arrested the youth, whose name was Edwin Bush, and took him, with his female companion, to Bow Street police station. He was placed in an identification parade, identified by Roberts but not by Meier, and then confessed to the murder. The soles of his shoes had a pattern similar to marks left at the scene. The paper that had been used to wrap the sword had afterwards been reused to parcel up some goods bought from Roberts' gun shop; when this paper was recovered by police and examined with the chemical ninhydrin, an imprint of Bush's palm print was revealed. The use of the Identikit system and PC Cole's sharp observation had led to a rapid conclusion to the inquiry. Bush had been released from borstal training just over six months earlier and was convicted of the murder. He was executed at Pentonville prison on 6 July 1961.

In 1938, before Identikit had been developed, a facial topographer, Jacques Penry, had been researching facial characteristics and found it possible to build complete faces from photographed eyes, ears and so on. Because the images had more of a photographic appearance, they seemed more lifelike than those from Identikit. Penry approached the Home Office in 1968 and by April 1970 had devised a kit that the police service could use. The new system was called 'photofit' and was first used in October 1970 after James Cameron was murdered at his home in Burgh Street, Islington. Detective Chief Superintendent Bill Wright's investigation team needed to trace a man who had been seen loitering outside James Cameron's home and used photofit to compile a picture of the suspect's face.

The murder victim's bank account showed that some cheques had been used after his death, and this led to the belief that the suspect had purchased an airline ticket and flown to Scotland. Detective Sergeant Thompson and Detective Constable Stuart Douglas, who had both originated from Fife, then started to make inquiries north of the border. The murder investigation team realised that widespread publicity would be needed to identify the man. Shaw Taylor, the presenter of the television programme *Police 5*, gave advance notice that the broadcast on 22 November 1970 would be featuring the new photofit system, and this publicity attracted a wide audience. The programme was widely watched, including being screened in Scotland, and resulted in a success that enhanced the reputation of the programme, and of Shaw Taylor, at a time when both their futures were in some doubt.

One of the many people who responded to the programme was a central London shop assistant in Victoria who recognised a man to whom he had sold an umbrella. The man had paid by cheque and, to verify his identity, had produced a firearms certificate, the number of which had been written on the back of the cheque. This information led the police to John Ernest Bennett's home in Nottingham, where the murder weapon and items stolen from the murder scene were found. Bennett was found guilty and sentenced to life imprisonment.

28 E-FIT

DATE:
1997–2003

EXHIBIT:
The E-FIT image of Kunowski and his photograph

AS COMPUTER TECHNOLOGY developed, the techniques for assisting witnesses in reproducing images of suspects has changed. On 4 October 1988, the Home Office announced the introduction of new computer software called Electronic Facial Identification Technique (E-FIT). The program uses computer graphics based on a number of databases of facial features. The features can be stretched and manipulated to create a distinctly individual result. Scotland Yard's first case involved a burglary near St Ann's Road police station where the offender had been seen jumping out of a front-room window. E-FIT operator Peter Bennett used the freestyle drawing facility of the system to illustrate the suspect's dreadlocks as there was no equivalent hairstyle on the system's database at the time. The process of establishing a good image is not just a matter of technology; operators are trained to ensure that a witness' recollection is not skewed by external suggestions or premature viewing of the images the computer generates.

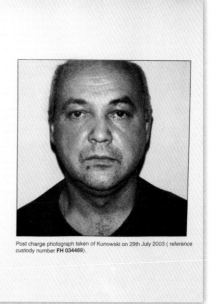

Post charge photograph taken of Kunowski on 29th July 2003 (reference custody number **FH 034469**).

In 1993 a series of murders of gay men took place in London, the victim in each case apparently taking the perpetrator back to his home and being attacked when he was rendered helpless to resist because of being tied up. The case was notable for the efforts made by Scotland Yard and the investigating officer, Detective Superintendent John, to gain the trust of the gay community by providing a telephone contact number staffed by members of the Gay and Lesbian Police Officers' Association (GALOP). The fifth and final victim of the murders was Emmanuel Spiteri, who had been seen on CCTV images at Charing Cross police station on his way home, accompanied by a large, dark-haired man with discoloured teeth. The image illustrating the suspect for Emmanuel Spiteri's murder was publicised and resulted in Colin Ireland going to a solicitor's office to admit that he was the man in the picture. After giving himself up to the police and claiming that he had parted from Spiteri soon after the CCTV images had been taken, he confessed to the murders when confronted with the fact that his fingerprints matched marks left at the scene of another murder in the series.

In due course, Detective David Parker found that witnesses could often describe the build and clothing of a suspect and arrive at a helpful image: this then became the Clothe-IT system. A murder inquiry in May 1997 used E-FIT and Clothe-IT to circulate descriptions of the suspect prior to the arrest of Andrezej Kunowski, an illegal immigrant who had committed many sexual attacks in Poland before his arrival in Britain.

In May 1997, a 12-year-old girl was attacked by a man as she returned to her flat in Hammersmith. She was dragged into her home and was slowly throttled to death. The attack was disturbed by the girl's father who chased off the assailant, but was threatened with a knife. The man escaped by hijacking a passing car at knifepoint. The father returned to the flat, forced open his daughter's room and found that she had been murdered.

The suspect's finger mark and palm print were found on a window frame. His DNA was found on a pen used for the ligature and from hair found on his victim's cardigan, but this evidence did not lead to the identification of the suspect from police records. An E-FIT image of his face was then produced, but unfortunately this did not result in anybody recognising the culprit and so the case went cold.

In 2003, Andrezej Kunowski was arrested, charged and convicted of the rape of a foreign student in London. A sample of his DNA was then found to match that from the murder scene and he was then tried and convicted of the murder of the 1997 case. At the time of the murder, Kunowski had been wanted for the rape of an 11-year-old girl in Poland after having been granted bail when he claimed that he need a heart operation. His DNA matched a sample taken from his Polish victim's underwear. At the time of sentencing, the trial judge recommended that Kunowski would never be safe to be released.

W.H.C.

Mrs Williams
(Dairy Farmer)
hanged for Murder

Courtroom Sketch of Ada Chard Williams

ADA CHARD WILLIAMS was sketched by William Hartley as she stood trial for the murder of a 21-month-old infant, Selina Jones. Ada Williams had been baby farming, a Victorian crime where women were paid to look after young babies but in fact killed them through deliberate acts or by gross neglect. Some mothers may have turned a blind eye to what would happen to their unwanted babies, but others were grievously exploited in their vulnerable situations. There was no equivalent of the modern social services departments.

Florence Jones had lived with her mother and father in Woolwich, but she became an unmarried mother when she gave birth to Selina in December 1897, in a home for unwed mothers in Clapham. In Victorian England it was not realistic for a single woman to try to bring up her own children. The lady who ran the Clapham establishment recommended a Mrs Muller, who looked after the baby for the first six months, and then for a further four months the infant was cared for by a Mrs Wetherall of Gee Street in St Lukes. At that point, Selina's father stopped contributing towards the 5s per week cost of maintaining the child, but Florence continued to pay half a crown. Then, in August 1899, she saw an advertisement in the *Woolwich Herald* about a young married couple who wished to adopt a healthy baby and wrote a letter to 'Mrs Hewetson' of No. 4 Bradmore Lane, Hammersmith. Mrs Hewetson replied, said that she

DATE:
1900

EXHIBIT:
Baby farmer Ada Williams (24) and husband William (41)

117

would be asking for a down payment of £5 and met Florence in Woolwich. Florence and her mother made it clear that the arrangement would be temporary, and that they would provide clothing for the child. In due course Florence withdrew Selina from Mrs Wetherall's care, met Mrs Hewetson at Charing Cross station and they then travelled to Hammersmith together.

Hewetson took Florence not to her own home, but to a friend's house, where Florence handed over Selina, a bundle of clothing and £3. Hewetson stated that she would write and give details of where they should meet so that Florence could pay the remaining balance on the following Sunday. No letter arrived, but Florence travelled to Hammersmith on the date arranged, 3 September, but could find no trace of 'Mrs Hewetson'. No. 4 Bradmore Lane was in fact a post office that acted as an accommodation address. Florence returned the following day and reported the matter to the police.

On 27 September 1899, a waterman found a parcel in the River Thames and called V Division's PC David Voice to deal with it. The parcel contained the body of a small dead infant, which was taken to Battersea mortuary. The child had been dead for a number of days, had suffered severe bruising and had been strangled. Florence came to the mortuary and identified her daughter's body. The police made a number of inquiries to trace Hewetson, and eventually, on 8 December, Detective Inspector James Scott went to Hackney and arrested the woman, whose real name was Ada Chard Williams. He also arrested her husband, William Chard Williams, who had been involved in collecting letters from the post office for his wife's dealings with children. They were remanded in custody and charged with Selina's murder. Whilst in prison, Ada Williams wrote a letter to Scotland Yard, using the name of Hewetson, claiming that she had undertaken a form of baby farming where she had taken over the adoption of a number of infants and then had them readopted for about half the price she had paid. She had received five children in this way, but two of them had died, regardless of the care and expense she had taken with them. She claimed she had likewise transferred Selina Jones to another woman before the child died, but had destroyed her letters.

The court heard evidence from a neighbour of Ada Williams about her cruel treatment of a child in her care. Thomas Gurrin, the handwriting expert, gave his opinion that the letters sent to the *Woolwich Herald*, other applications for advertisements, the letters sent to Florence, and her letter of defence of her conduct that she sent to Scotland Yard were all written by the same person. Ada Williams was convicted and executed on 6 March 1900, aged 24, at Newgate prison, the last woman to be hanged there. Her husband was acquitted.

A letter from Amelia Dyer was part of a small hoard of correspondence and telegrams that related to the adoption and fostering of small children at an address used by a 'Mrs Thomas'. The address was found on wrapping paper inside a package found in the River Thames near Reading. The package, wrapped in string, contained the dead body of a baby girl that had dressmaker's white edging tape round her neck, and had been found by a bargeman on 30 March 1896. The same edging tape, matching that used by Amelia Dyer, was found at her daughter's house in Willesden, and had also been used in the deaths of other children whose bodies were found in the river. Police inquiries at the address of Mrs Thomas soon revealed the woman's real identity as Amelia Dyer, who had been convicted and sentenced to six months' hard labour in 1879, after a doctor had become suspicious of the number of deaths amongst the children she was looking after. The police then started an inquiry to trace other children that Dyer had taken into her care and discovered it was a case of baby farming. Women would advertise to take children to nurse, usually in return for a payment of between £3 and £10. Victorian Britain reflected a different world from today's environment. There was great shame attached to being an unmarried mother, no reliable means of birth control or social security, and severe financial pressure for many when an extra child was born. Infant mortality was high by today's standards. Some women looked after their charges with care, but others simply took their fee, neglected the babies or killed them. In some cases, baby farmers were also a route of access to illegal abortions.

Also found in the river was a carpet bag that contained the little bodies of 13-month-old Harry Simmons and Doris Marmon. Doris' unmarried mother, 25-year-old barmaid Evelina Marmon, had given birth to her and then advertised for a 'respectable woman to take care of child', apparently hoping one day to be able to reclaim her daughter. The advertisement was answered by 'Mrs Harding' to whom Evelina handed over her child, a cardboard box of clothes and £10 as an upfront fee, which Harding had insisted upon rather than a regular payment. Harding then travelled to Willesden, murdered the child and dumped the body in the River Thames near Caversham Lock with the body of Harry Simmons. Amelia Dyer admitted her involvement in these murders during the investigation. By some estimates she had murdered up to 400 infants, classifying her as a prolific serial killer.

Amelia Dyer stood trial at the Old Bailey on 22 May 1896 for murdering Doris Marmon and unsuccessfully attempted a defence of insanity. She was convicted of murder and executed three weeks later. In 1902 the governor of Holloway prison presented the rope with which James Billington hanged her to the Crime Museum, where a knife, stolen by Dyer from Barton Regis workhouse, is also on display. Dyer's letters were donated to the museum in 1970 by the son of an Inspector Bennett from the National Society for the Prevention of Cruelty to Children, who received them from Granny Smith who had a peripheral involvement in the case.

Amelia Sach, 28 years old, and Annie Walters, 54, were known as the Finchley Baby Farmers and were sketched on 12 January 1903 by William Hartley at their Old Bailey trial for murdering the newly born baby of Ada Galley.

Ada Galley was in domestic service and found herself pregnant. In 1902, she saw an advertisement in *Dalton's Newspaper* for a nursing home that stated, 'Accouchement, before and during. Skilled nursing. Home comforts. Baby can remain', and went to an establishment run by Amelia Sach at Claymore House. She agreed to pay 1 guinea per week, then 3 guineas per week during her confinement, and in due course gave birth to a baby son after a difficult delivery that required forceps. Prior to the birth, Amelia Sach asked Ada whether she would like the baby to be adopted, and this was agreed, for a payment of £25. The baby's father came to the establishment and paid this sum in cash to Sach after seeing the baby alive and well. He gave evidence to this effect at the trial, with his name being kept confidential by the court. The baby was then transferred to Annie Walters who lodged at No. 11 Danbury Street in Islington, telling the landlord, police officer Henry Seal, that she worked as a nurse for Sach.

Whilst Ada Galley was staying at Claymore House, she got to know Rosina Pardoe, in a similar condition to herself. Rosina Pardoe gave evidence that she came to a similar arrangement with Amelia Sach, had seen Annie Walters at the house and had been told by Sach that Ada's baby had been taken away. The father of her child also paid £25 to have the baby adopted.

Detective Constable George Wright kept observation in Danbury Street and followed Walters, who was carrying a bundle, to South Kensington where he stopped her and demanded that he inspect what she was carrying. It was Ada Galley's dead baby boy who had not yet been named. Walters admitted giving the baby chlorodyne, a powerful sedative with chloroform and morphine that, according to Augustus Pepper of St Mary's Hospital, would be fatal for a baby of that age. The post-mortem revealed that the baby had died from asphyxia and suffocation caused by a narcotic drug. The stories that Sach had given to three women about placing their babies for adoption were proved to be untrue, and both defendants were convicted of murder and sentenced to death. The jury recommended mercy on the basis that they were women, but Sach and Walters were the last double execution of women when they were hanged at Holloway prison on 3 February 1903.

A generation before these cases, and shortly after his promotion, Sergeant Richard Relf investigated the deaths of eighteen infants in the Brixton area. In 1870, 276 babies were found dead on the streets of London. Relf undertook an observation at a 'lying in establishment' where he discovered that a newly born baby had been taken to Margaret Waters' house. Relf demanded entry and found seven sickly infants living in filthy conditions. He arrested Waters for child neglect and had the babies taken to the workhouse, where six of them, including one named John Cowen, later died. John Cowen's grandfather was the only relative to come forward as a witness, stating that he had paid Waters £4 to look after the child in an attempt to avoid his daughter being stigmatised by having become an unmarried mother.

It was one of the first cases of baby farming to be prosecuted successfully, and led to the conviction and execution of Margaret Waters. Waters herself was a widow whose attempt to establish a clothes business had failed, leaving her in debt. She had then taken an unwanted baby in and managed to have it adopted, on both occasions for a fee, and then gradually expanded her activities. She admitted adopting about forty infants for cash, produced receipts for doctors' fees and for milk and admitted that sometimes she had been unable to afford proper burial for those who had died. She claimed to have looked after the babies as best she could in difficult circumstances and when infant mortality was high in any event. Waters was convicted and executed. Her sister, Sarah Ellis, pleaded guilty to conspiring to obtain money by false pretences and was sentenced to eighteen months' imprisonment.

Relf's experience from the case led to his becoming perhaps the first semi-officially recognised specialist officer who then gave his advice in other similar cases. He was presented with a testimonial by the vicar of Christ Church, Camberwell, in recognition of his efforts.

30 Box of Dr Patterson's Female Pills

DATE:
Early to
mid-1900s

EXHIBIT:
Box of pills
sold to induce
abortions

THE 'FAMOUS FEMALE pills' were sold through the Hygienic Stores, No. 95 Charing Cross Road, WC2, where the store's literature described their use as to restore 'females to their usual health, when Penny Royal and Steel, Pil Cochiae, Bitter Apple &c. fail'. The ordinary price was 2s 9d, with 'Special' available at 4s 6d per box and 'Special Strong for Obstinate Cases' 11s and 21d. Customer testimonials included comments such as 'I am pleased to be able to tell you that your pills were successful in relieving my wife of her trouble'. The Crime Museum's collection also includes a black stethoscope, a rubber tube with a pump, aridone analgesic tablets, a uterine repository, curette spoon, a tin of pennyroyal, amenorone and various other items used for procuring illegal abortions.

Several items are in the museum from 'The Great Harley Street Mystery' of 1880. Pieces of embroidery, underwear, some hair and plaster casts of teeth survive from an investigation of a body of a woman found in a barrel of lime, in a cellar of a house in Harley Street. Medical examination revealed a stab wound in her left breast and concluded that death had occurred at least two years before the body was discovered. The victim was never identified and the case remains unsolved. The case was debated many years later by the Medico-Legal Society, with Sir Bernard Spilsbury proposing that the woman might have died as the result of an abortion, and that the abortionist had inflicted the stab wound after death as a method of diverting any post-mortem examination away from internal organs that would have revealed the true cause of her death.

Backstreet abortions were carried out in a completely unregulated manner prior to the Abortion Act of 1967 (when abortion was legalised), and there was a significant risk to the health and life of women who found themselves needing to terminate their pregnancy, often putting themselves at the mercy of untrained and inexperienced abortionists. The provisions of the 1967 Act almost eliminated this dangerous practice. Abortions are controversial and the Department of Health reported that the number conducted in England and Wales in 2011 reached 189,000.

One abortionist prosecuted in 1969 had a set of equipment so comprehensive that pathologist Professor Keith Simpson, a witness at the trial, thought that it should be displayed in the Crime Museum for police training purposes. The case had originated in September 1969 in a three-storey terraced house in Southampton Way, Peckham, where Matthew Okenarhe had advertised himself as an osteopath. Information had been given to the police that drugs were being kept under the bath at the house and that abortions were being performed there. When the police raided the house, they found phials of the drug ergot, a substance used for inducing abortions, a large number of gynaecological instruments and medical textbooks. Okenarhe, from Nigeria, had no medical training, and had been previously imprisoned for theft of mail and fraud in his former occupation with the Post Office. He had been collaborating with his brother-in-law Matthew Esegine, a local hospital porter, in attempting to perform abortions on a number of West Indian women who had been staying at a local boarding house for nurses run by Mrs Retornella Wright. He was convicted on fourteen counts of conspiracy to procure illegal abortions and of indecent assault on women by posing as a doctor. Okenarhe was sentenced to eight years' imprisonment, Esegine was given four years, and Wright two years.

31 Doctor's Pill Box

DATE:
1891–92

EXHIBIT:
Cream's medicine case with seven tubes containing strychnine

THE MEDICAL CASE containing various pills also contained strychnine, and it belonged to the infamous Dr Thomas Neill Cream.

At about 7.30 p.m. on 13 October 1891, a 19-year-old prostitute, Ellen Donsworth, collapsed in the street in Lambeth and died. With her last words she was able to describe a tall, dark, cross-eyed man with a silk hat who had given her some white stuff to drink just before her death. It was a tonic prepared to clear the complexion and brighten the skin. Six days later, on 19 October, the coroner received a letter apparently written from a 'Detective A. O'Brien' offering to solve the case for the spectacularly high fee of £300,000, but payable only if he was successful. The offer was not taken up. Later it was discovered that this letter had been written by Cream.

125

A week later, on 20 October, a 27-year-old prostitute, Matilda Clover, suffered a slow death and was reported to be convulsing and sweating. As she lay dying she was able to say she had taken some white pills from a man she only knew as 'Fred'. She described him as tall, wearing a silk hat and speaking with a transatlantic accent. But Matilda's death was recorded as alcohol poisoning on account of her being a very heavy drinker. Using a pseudonym, Cream then wrote to a doctor threatening to expose him as the murderer unless he paid Cream £2,500.

There was then a gap in the series of deaths, but, on 12 April 1892, two more prostitutes, Emma Shrivell and Alice Marsh, died slow, painful deaths. Both lived at a house in Stamford Street, Southwark, and had been given pills by a tall, bald doctor called Fred, who spoke with a transatlantic accent. The deaths were investigated by Inspector George Harvey, from Lambeth.

On Easter Sunday, 17 April, Cream was reading about the case with his landlady's daughter and told her that he would bring the culprit to justice. He went on to allege that a fellow lodger in the house, Dr Walter Harper, a medical student, was the murderer. Cream then wrote to Walter's father claiming to hold evidence that proved his son was the killer, and that he would sell his silence for £1,500. Cream's downfall came when he started to repeat the same allegation in a pub to a private inquiry agent named John Haynes, a former New York detective who had been in America gathering intelligence about Irish terrorism. Haynes then introduced Cream to Detective Sergeant Patrick McIntyre from the CID at Scotland Yard. Cream showed the officer a letter apparently received by the Stamford Street victims warning them about Harper and mentioned the murders of Matilda Clover and Louise Harvey. Louise Harvey had indeed been given pills in October 1891, but she had only pretended to take them before throwing them away. She remained very much alive and was able to give evidence about the incident.

When police did visit Cream he willingly showed the officers the leather case, including the strychnine pills, explaining the quantity involved by stating that they could only be sold to chemists and doctors. Cream had been in England in October 1891, but had then gone to America and Canada for a few months, returning to England on 9 April 1892, a few days before the deaths of Emma Shrivell and Alice Marsh. Cream had been born in Glasgow on 27 May 1850, but his parents immigrated to Canada around 1856 and he had become a doctor in Canada. Three women (Kate Gardener, Mary Faulkner and Flora Brooks) had died under his care in his early years as a doctor and so had his first wife. He had then moved to Chicago, where, in the first six months of 1881, he had had an affair with Julia Stott, the wife of his 65-year-old patient Daniel Stott, who would go to Cream to collect her husband's medication. Cream poisoned the husband and falsely informed the coroner that the man had died from strychnine given by the local chemist. Cream was sentenced to life imprisonment, but was released in July 1891. Cream worked as an obstetric clerk at St Thomas' Hospital whilst studying there but otherwise did not appear to have formally practised as a doctor in Britain, but he did claim to deal in patent medicines, and certainly developed a habit of accusing other people of crimes in order to blackmail them.

Cream was put under surveillance. When Detective Inspector John Tunbridge and Detective Sergeant Patrick McIntyre became aware that Cream was planning to leave the country, they were forced to act, despite the lack of proof at that stage that any murders in Britain had been committed by Cream. Patrick McIntyre could only arrest him in relation to the threatening letters in which he attempted to extort money. Matilda Clover's body was exhumed and it was established that she had been poisoned with strychnine. Cream was then charged with murder.

On 17 October 1892, Cream stood trial at the Old Bailey. Thomas Stevenson gave evidence of finding strychnine in the victim's organs after her body had been exhumed, and that Cream's pill case contained a number of bottles of strychnine. Cream had been sold the poison by a chemist who had also sold him empty capsules, which could have been filled with a fatal dose of strychnine transferred from those pills. Evidence of the other victims also found to have been poisoned with strychnine was allowed at the trial. To Cream's surprise he was convicted of Clover's murder and was hanged on 15 November 1892 at Newgate prison. It is alleged that, as the trapdoor was opening and he fell to his death, he said, 'I am Jack the ...', perhaps seeking a last-minute reprieve to allow an investigation into public speculation that he might have been responsible for the Whitechapel murders. These had, in fact, occurred whilst he was in prison in Illinois.

Poisons can come from many different sources (strychnine is extracted from the seeds of the nux-vomica tree that is native to India and South-East Asia). Sometimes poisons have been readily available for household purposes, such as the destruction of vermin or insects, and sometimes they are overdoses of medication that are legitimately available for treatment of an illness. There is often an element of disguise by which the perpetrators trick their victims into consuming the poison. The stronger the taste of the poison, the more difficult it is to swallow it undetected. If the poison has not been detected at the time of consumption, it is sometimes a matter of good fortune that an accurate diagnosis is reached by a discerning doctor, or that suspicion is formed, reported and investigated. Because of the nature of the subject, the involvement of medical training is a notable trend amongst the perpetrators. Political assassination by means of poison has been a crime known for centuries and this threat has certainly not disappeared.

32 Bottle of Valentine's Meat Juice

DATE:
1889

EXHIBIT:
Florence Maybrick's meat juice bottle

THE BOTTLE OF meat juice that contained 38mg of arsenic came from a Liverpool case when cotton broker James Maybrick died from poisoning. Arsenic is a metallic substance that occurs naturally in many minerals and became a common by-product associated with the mining of lead and iron.

Maybrick met the 19-year-old American Florence Chandler whilst they were fellow passengers on a voyage from America. They married in 1881 and lived in Battlecrease House, in Aigburth, a Liverpool suburb. James Maybrick was much older than Florence and was a hypochondriac who regularly took arsenic as an ingredient of various patent medicines. He had a number of affairs and Florence began to follow his example. James was taken ill on 27 April 1889 after giving himself a dose of strychnine, and his condition started to deteriorate despite medical treatment. A letter that Florence wrote to her lover, Alfred Brierley, was intercepted and James' brothers became very suspicious of her. She had soaked flypapers in water, apparently to retrieve the arsenic ingredients for cosmetic purposes, but this may have been the source of arsenic intended to kill her husband. On 9 May, a nurse reported that Florence had tampered with the bottle of Valentine's Meat Juice, which was later found to contain half a grain of arsenic. James Maybrick died two days later.

129

James' brothers requested a post-mortem examination, which found some arsenic in his body but not enough to have caused his death. A local pharmacist had sold arsenic to James Maybrick and it is feasible that he took it as an aphrodisiac. There were copious amounts of arsenic in the house, not least because the substance was legitimately used as rat poison. An inquest charged Florence with murder, and her subsequent trial in Liverpool was a complicated story involving intrigue, adultery and drug abuse. She was convicted and sentenced to death in an atmosphere of great public controversy about the case. Because of the doubts about the precise cause of death rather than any challenge to her intention to kill her husband, Florence Maybrick's sentence was commuted to life imprisonment and she was released in 1904. She died in America in 1941.

Although there was no Scotland Yard involvement in this famous murder, which was investigated by Superintendent Isaac Bryning and Inspector Baxendale from Liverpool, the bottle of Valentine's Meat Juice was later presented to the museum by the son of Dr McAllister, who gave medical evidence at the trial. The case contributed to two important changes in the law. The first was the Criminal Evidence Act of 1898, which for the first time allowed people accused of murder to give evidence on their own behalf. It also contributed, together with the Adolf Beck case, to the creation of the Court of Criminal Appeal in 1907.

Arsenic acquired the nickname of 'inheritance powder' on the basis that it might be used by those who had an interest in benefitting from legacies. It was a favourite method of poisoning for centuries, partly because the effects of taking arsenic, which has little taste, include vomiting and diarrhoea, signs common to a number of illnesses like cholera and dysentery. The effects are cumulative, giving the poisoner the chance to administer small doses that would create an illness over a period of time. Its legitimate uses included rat poison, fly killer, wallpaper dye, weedkiller, medicinal tonics, sheep dips, dyeing and cosmetic preparations. In 1836, James Marsh published details of a sensitive mirror test that could detect small amounts of arsenic in human tissue. The Arsenic Act 1851 prohibited the sale of arsenic to a customer not known to a pharmacist and required colouring agents to be added to all arsenic compounds to reduce the risks of accidental poisoning.

Mary Ann Cotton (1832–73) was a nurse who had moved around the County of Durham and elsewhere quite frequently. Cotton was a widow and spent periods in destitution. In 1872, Thomas Riley, a parish official in West Auckland, asked her to nurse a woman suffering from smallpox, so she asked for her stepson Charles to be taken to the workhouse to enable her to carry out the task unimpeded. When Mr Riley refused, Cotton commented that the boy would not last long and, five days later, on 12 July 1872, reported the lad's death to Riley, who was also the assistant coroner. She became distressed when Riley persuaded the doctor to delay issuing a death certificate. This in turn prevented payment of an insurance policy she had taken out on the boy's life.

Rumour and suspicion then started to circulate and it transpired that in various locations she had lost three husbands, a lover, her mother and twelve children, all apparently from stomach fever. A post-mortem examination showed that the contents of the dead boy's stomach contained arsenic, and two other exhumations from the Cotton home were also found to have traces of the poison. She was charged with murdering her stepson and appeared at Durham Assizes where her defence was that the boy must have died from arsenic contained in the wallpaper of her home. However, evidence that Cotton had purchased significant quantities of arsenic, ostensibly for dealing with bed bugs, counted against her. She was convicted of the murder and hanged at Durham prison on 24 March 1873. She had apparently made a habit of poisoning her husbands and children with a view to collecting insurance money and leaving herself free to move on to a new relationship. When Mary Cotton was hanged, it apparently took three minutes for the rope to strangle her to death because the length of the drop had been miscalculated. A longer drop would have broken her neck and caused instant death.

Courtroom Sketch of Louise Masset

WILLIAM HARTLEY'S COURTROOM sketch is of Louise 'Louisa' Masset.

On 27 October 1899, the naked body of a 3-year-old child was found in a toilet at Dalston railway station; at about 6 p.m. Miss Mart Teahan, a governess, discovered the body when she visited the ladies' waiting room after a journey from Richmond with her friend, Margaret Briggs. The stationmaster, David Bundy, called the police, and noticed that the body was still warm. A clinker brick was nearby and had apparently been used to batter the child to death. The infant was identified as Manfred Louis Masset, the illegitimate son of Louise Josephine Jemima Masset, aged 36 years, a French governess. The cause of death was strangulation.

Louise Masset had given her child to Helen Gentle to be looked after, for which she was paid £1 17s each month. Masset visited her son once a fortnight and then once a week, but then decided to make other care arrangements, asking Gentle to meet her at London Bridge so that she could take her son to live in France. The boy was duly handed over, but with some distress on the part of the child. Masset went to Brighton to spend the weekend with her lover, 19-year-old Frenchman Endor Lucas, who had lived next door to her in Bethune Road, Stoke Newington, for a period. The attendant in the waiting room at London Bridge station, Ellen Rees, saw Masset with her son around 3 p.m. and then again at about 7 p.m.,

DATE:
1899

EXHIBIT:
Louise Masset in court

this time without the child, when Masset asked about the next train to Brighton.

Inspector Frederick Forth was in charge of the case and gave evidence that the brick found in the toilet, which later became an exhibit in the museum, was consistent with other bricks found in Masset's garden at Bethune Road. A shopkeeper gave evidence that he thought he recognised Masset as the customer who had bought the shawl in which her son's body had been wrapped. Masset herself claimed that she had given her son into the care of two women at London Bridge, who had agreed to look after the child for a payment of £12, an arrangement sometimes undertaken by baby farmers. The prosecution alleged that Louise Masset had disposed of her child by killing him, so that she could make a new start with the younger Endor Lucas. She was found guilty and sentenced to death, and was executed on 9 January 1900 at Newgate prison.

One of the most famous cases involving the murder of a child by a female was the Road Hill House murder investigated by Scotland Yard in 1860. Inspector Jonathan Whicher was sent down to the village of Road, Wiltshire, to investigate the death of 3-year-old Francis Savill Kent (known as Savill). The victim's father was 59-year-old Samuel Kent, a factory inspector who lived with his second wife who had formerly been his children's governess. Constance, one of his children from his first marriage, was 16 years old and lived at the family home whilst not away at boarding school. The second Mrs Kent was eight months pregnant with her third child at the time when, early in the morning of Saturday, 30 June 1860, her second child, the ill-fated Savill, was found to be missing from his cot.

The children's nurse, Elizabeth Gough, had woken, found the child's cot empty, and had wrongly presumed that he had been taken into his mother's bedroom. The house was searched, but there was no sign of Savill. One of the windows was partly open, but there was no sign of forced entry into the house. The family had a dog, which had not been heard to bark.

Mr Kent drove personally to see Superintendent Foley of the Wiltshire Police. He did not wish to rely on a messenger or to spend time speaking to two constables he passed on his way. It was not long before Savill's body was found in an outside privy with his throat cut and a stab wound to his chest. The murder appeared to have been committed by somebody in the house, and there began an inquiry that coincidentally formed the basis of many a future detective story by Agatha Christie and other authors. The servants were questioned thoroughly and the children of the family to some extent, but the notion of members of a respectable middle-class family committing a crime and being questioned by the police was a novel idea that some would not have countenanced. At one stage the local police held Elizabeth Gough in custody, but the Trowbridge magistrates then decided to write to the Home Secretary, Sir George Cornwall Lewis, asking for the assistance of a detective officer from Scotland Yard. Sir Richard Mayne, the Metropolitan Police Commissioner, first turned down the request on the basis that the county police had been established for the area and should deal with the case. He might have been influenced by the fact that the local police were decidedly not in favour of calling in 'The Yard'. But, when the request was repeated and backed up by a request from Mr Kent's solicitor, Mayne sent Jonathan Whicher, the head of the Detective Branch.

Called to the scene two weeks after the murder, Whicher concentrated on the fact that the child's injury must have created bloodstains, but no such clothing could be found in the house. One of Constance's night-dresses was missing, however, and she was known to have expressed jealous thoughts about the children of her father's second marriage. Samuel Kent was not a popular man locally. His reputation suffered from gossip about whether his second marriage had been preceded by an affair with the governess before his first wife had died, and the local villagers were prone to suggest that history was repeating itself with Elizabeth Gough. Whicher needed more time, but the magistrates issued a warrant for Constance Kent, who was duly arrested, given the services of a legal team by her father, and remanded for a week.

Whicher was given the assistance of Sergeant Adolphus Williamson from Scotland Yard and was under pressure, especially as the local police's opinion was to suspect Elizabeth Gough and Mr Kent, but Whicher could find no additional evidence in the following seven days and Constance was released. This process polarised opinions and Jonathan Whicher was roundly criticised by newspapers, particularly those that reflected resentment about the local police being bypassed. It would have been a difficult investigation by any standards without an admission by the perpetrator or some other direct evidence. The case lingered on, unsolved by the local police.

Constance Kent was sent to a finishing school in France, and then went to a religious institution in Brighton. Five years later, in 1865, she unexpectedly arrived at Bow Street court, admitted the murder to the chief magistrate and was sent for trial to Wiltshire Assizes where she pleaded guilty and was sentenced to death before being reprieved by Queen Victoria. The sentence was commuted to life imprisonment but she was eventually released in 1885, and died in Australia in 1944. She never answered any detailed questions about the crime, but this sensational development vindicated Jonathan Whicher's suspicion about her. By this time Whicher had retired from the police, suffering from 'congestion of the brain'. The case blighted his career, and remained a vivid example of the difficulties of investigating local men of substance, the inexperience of some police forces and the importance of effective collaboration when a member of another police force was brought in to head a major crime investigation.

34 Bywaters' Knife

DATE:
1922

EXHIBIT:
The 26cm
knife used
by Frederick
Bywaters
to kill Percy
Thompson

THE KNIFE USED by Frederick Bywaters was recovered from a drain after the murder of Percy Thompson, whose wife Edith had been having an affair with Bywaters. It was a case notable for the interpretation of love letters.

Edith Thompson, 28, and her husband Percy, 32, lived in Ilford and went on holiday to the Isle of Wight in 1921 with Edith's sister Avis and her boyfriend Frederick Bywaters, 20. Frederick and Edith were attracted to one another and no doubt this affection increased when Frederick, who soon lost interest in Avis, went to live with the Thompsons for a period, during which Percy was aggressive towards his wife. Frederick intervened in the quarrel between man and wife, and tried to persuade Percy to agree to a separation from Edith, but Percy declined. Unsurprisingly, Percy withdrew his hospitality and Bywaters moved out of the house to stay with his mother in Upper Norwood. Edith worked in the City of London for a millinery company whilst Frederick was a ship's clerk with the P&O shipping line. They met at lunchtimes when he was not at sea and Bywaters continued to meet up with Edith until he sailed on a voyage to the Far East. Edith wrote a series of sixty love letters to him in the course of a year during which he had been at sea five times. The letters referred to at least one occasion when she had visited his room at night and left no doubt about the extent of their affair.

On Tuesday, 3 October 1922, Edith and Percy Thompson went to the theatre in London and, around midnight, were walking back home from Ilford station when Bywaters overtook them in a dark street, pushed Edith out of the way, began a furious argument with Percy about giving Edith a divorce, stabbed him several times and then ran off, dropping the knife into a drain and eventually arriving at his mother's house at 3 a.m. Meanwhile, Edith went to her dying husband and implored a passing couple for help. The police arrived and a doctor attended to Percy Thompson, who soon died as the result of the attack. Edith remarked to Sergeant Mew, 'They'll blame me for this,' which was, at best, a curious thing to say. Bywaters was arrested the following evening and initially denied any involvement in the attack but later admitted that he had stabbed Percy in self-defence as their argument was escalating and Percy had apparently threatened to shoot him (regardless of the fact that no gun was in Percy's possession). Edith Thompson was arrested later. During the investigation, the police searched Bywaters' cabin on his ship, the *Morea*, which was docked at Tilbury, and found Edith's love letters. They also found some letters sent from Bywaters at Edith's place of work. Both Frederick Bywaters and Edith Thompson were charged with the murder, and the details of their affair became central to the motivation for the murder.

The jury did not hear about all the letters. Some of them referred to abortions and would have been even more prejudicial as to how the jury would have regarded Edith's reputation in a period when adultery and divorce were regarded far more seriously than today. Her letter of 10 February 1922 contained comments about poison, such as 'It would be so easy ... if I had things ... I do hope I shall ... have enclosed cuttings of Dr Wallis's case ...', and she sent newspaper cuttings about the case of a curate poisoned by his wife, and poisoned chocolates sent to a university chancellor. Twelve days later she wrote, 'Will you do all the thinking and planning for me ... be ready for every little detail when I see you ... I am relying on you for all plans and instructions ... What about Wallis's case?' On 1 May, Edith referred to making up pills and avoiding leaving finger marks on the box. A theme could be seen running through the letters that expressed her wish to be rid of her husband and to discuss poisoning him. The jury apparently decided that it was not merely a fantasy on her part.

Bywaters told the court that he did not take any of Edith's comments seriously, that he thought her comments referred to a future elopement or possibly suicide, and that he had supplied her only with relatively harmless quinine in order to humour her. Edith Thompson disregarded her barrister's advice by choosing to give evidence in court and faced cross-examination. She said that she had wanted Bywaters to believe that she would do anything for him. The jury convicted both of them of the murder and, despite an appeal and protests, Edith Thompson was hanged at Holloway prison on 9 January 1923 at the same time that Frederick Bywaters suffered the same fate at Pentonville.

The *Nottingham Evening Post*, dated 25 November 1937, saw the exhibits in the Crime Museum and wrote about the 'Love Letters Clue':

> The passionate and extraordinarily-worded love letters written by Edith Thompson to her lover, Frederick Bywaters, played a big, indeed the principal, part in sending them both to the gallows for the murder of the former's husband. Actually, it has been a matter of speculation whether the crime would have ever been brought home to the guilty pair had not Bywaters kept these strange and incriminating letters.

Weedkiller Tin

THE TIN, BELONGING to 33-year-old Charlotte Bryant, contained arsenic weedkiller and was found with boiler ashes at the back of her cottage.

Charlotte Bryant lived with her husband Frederick in Coombe, near Sherborne, Dorset. They had five children, but they may not all have had the same father. Charlotte started to have an affair with a horse dealer, Leonard Parsons, who lodged with them. Charlotte became the subject of gossip but Frederick seemed to tolerate his wife's behaviour because of the extra income it provided. In May 1935, Frederick was taken ill. The doctor diagnosed gastroenteritis and within a few days Frederick returned to work. On 11 December, Frederick was again taken ill with violent stomach pains: again he recovered. On 22 December 1935 he suffered further violent stomach disorder after drinking Oxo prepared by Charlotte, and died. Doctors found four grains of arsenic in his body. On 10 February 1936, Charlotte was arrested and charged with the murder of her husband. At her trial, Dr Roche Lynch, a prominent scientist specialising in poisons, found that ashes in the garden, where the battered and burnt arsenic tin had been found, contained 149 parts per million of arsenic, which he considered high compared to normal. Traces of arsenic were also found in the pocket of a coat apparently owned by Charlotte. Her general character would not have endeared her to a jury, and she was convicted of murder and hanged at Exeter prison on 15 July 1936.

DATE:
1935

EXHIBIT:
Charlotte Bryant's burnt weedkiller tin and an undamaged version

Frederick Seddon, 40, was an insurance agent who had become obsessed with money and lived with his wife Margaret in a large house in Tollington Park, London, N4. In July 1910, Miss Eliza Barrow, 49, started to rent the top-floor flat of the property, which she shared with Robert Hook and his wife. The house was becoming crowded, so Seddon gave Barrow and the Hooks notice to quit. The Hooks moved out, but Barrow remained, and started to worry about her financial affairs. Seddon arranged for her to buy an annuity. Barrow started to mistrust her bank and she withdrew large amounts of money in cash. Seddon and his wife became more involved in Eliza Barrow's finances and when Barrow became ill, she made a will naming Frederick Seddon as executor. She died in September 1911, and Seddon arranged a cheap funeral.

When Eliza Barrow's long-standing friends, Frank Vonderahe and his wife, called to see her, they were shocked to learn that she had died and even more surprised to learn that she had been buried in a public grave when she owned a private vault. They had further anxieties about the will and her investments, which seemed to have disappeared, and reported their concerns to the police. Eliza Barrow's body was exhumed and found to contain enough traces of arsenic to have been the cause of death rather than the diarrhoea and heart failure written on the death certificate. Because the Seddons had been entirely responsible for Barrow, and Frederick Seddon had profited from the financial transactions, they were charged with murdering her, the suggestion being that arsenic could have been extracted from flypapers, now exhibited in the museum. At their trial, Margaret was acquitted, but Frederick was found guilty and hanged on 19 April 1911.

Before his sentence, Frederick Seddon made a speech declaring his innocence, ending it with a salute and an oath to the 'Great Architect of the Universe', a reference to being a freemason, to which movement the judge, Mr Justice Bucknill, also belonged. In sentencing, Bucknill, visibly moved, acknowledged their shared membership of the movement, but reminded him that freemasonry condemned crime and asked Seddon to make his peace with the Great Architect of the Universe before condemning him to death. The judge then wrote a letter reflecting on the situation, that is now on display in the museum, with the result of the Marsh mirror poison test, bottles of Valentine's Meat Juice, brandy, and Mather's flypaper. A newspaper published a confession by Margaret Seddon, later retracted by her, that she had seen her husband administer poison to Eliza Barrow. Frederick Seddon had visited the Crime Museum on 1 December 1905, possibly with his father, and his signature appears in the visitors' book.

Herbert Rowse Armstrong practised as a solicitor in Hay-on-Wye and held a respectable place in the local community, becoming the sole practitioner in his office at Broad Street when his partner died in 1914. In November that year, he enlisted in the Royal Engineers, was promoted to major in 1916 and demobilised in 1920. Armstrong did not go abroad on military service and whilst away from home had been seeing Mrs Marion Gale, whom he had met in 1915. In 1919, Armstrong's wife, Katherine, whose health was weak, became ill, and, in 1920, she went to live in a private asylum near Gloucester. She was also suffering some physical symptoms, including vomiting. She was discharged and sent home in January 1921, but died a month later. The cause of death was given as 'gastritis'.

In 1921, Armstrong was dealing with a case that involved Oswald Martin, the only other solicitor in Hay-on-Wye, who was acting for the other side in a property transaction, but it appeared that Armstrong no longer had the money entrusted to him as a deposit by his client. On 26 October 1921, Armstrong invited Martin to tea and handed him a buttered scone, which Martin ate; he was violently sick afterwards. Martin's father-in-law, John Davies, was the local pharmacist who had made several sales of arsenic to Armstrong, supposedly to kill dandelions in his garden. Davies, Martin and Dr Hincks, who had remained puzzled by Katherine Armstrong's death, discussed their suspicions, which may have been raised by a case of a solicitor in Wales who had poisoned his wife a year or two earlier. They sent a sample of Martin's urine and the remains of some chocolates (that had been sent anonymously to the Martin family and made a relative violently ill) to the Clinical Research Association in London. It transpired that the chocolates contained arsenic.

Martin began to refuse Armstrong's increasingly urgent invitations to have tea with him, and eventually Armstrong was visited by Detective Chief Inspector Charles Crutchett of Scotland Yard with Superintendent Weaver from Herefordshire. Packets of arsenic were found in Armstrong's desk and in one of his pockets. His wife's body was exhumed and found to contain arsenic. He appeared at Hereford Assizes charged with murdering his wife and was found guilty, despite the defence argument that Katherine Armstrong had committed suicide. Armstrong was hanged on 31 May 1922, perhaps the only solicitor to have suffered this punishment. His diaries for the years 1919–21 are in the Crime Museum with a nine-page statement, two packets of arsenic, books, maps and correspondence.

36 Ruth Ellis' Gun

DATE:
1955

EXHIBIT:
.38 Smith &
Wesson revolver

THE .38 SMITH & Wesson revolver was the weapon used by Ruth Ellis – the last woman hanged in Britain – to murder David Blakely.

Ruth Ellis was born in 1926 in North Wales but moved to London during the Second World War, where she worked in a munitions factory, later becoming a photographic model and drifting into work as a nightclub hostess. She gave birth to a son after having an affair with a French-Canadian soldier, and in 1950 married George Ellis, an alcoholic dentist and client at one of the clubs where she worked. The marriage did not last and she began an affair with Blakely, a 24-year-old racing driver. They became besotted with each other, and Ellis neglected her job as a nightclub manager, which led to her being dismissed.

Both Blakely and Ellis had affairs with other partners, and their relationship deteriorated into violence, drunken arguments and mutual recriminations. Ellis became obsessed with establishing whether Blakely was having another affair, tracked him down to the Magdala public house in Hampstead on Easter Sunday 1955 and waited until he emerged before firing at him six times. Four bullets struck and killed him, a fifth missed, and the sixth hit and injured a passer-by after a ricochet. A police officer, Alan Thompson, had been in plain clothes having a drink in the pub and removed the gun from her grasp. Ellis said that she had been given the gun by one of her nightclub contacts in the past, but gave no further details.

At her trial at the Old Bailey, she pleaded not guilty but admitted that she had shot David Blakely intending to kill him. A Dr Whittaker gave evidence that he considered that she was sane, and on that basis she was sentenced to death. A petition with 50,000 signatures called on the Home Secretary to reprieve her, but the arguments were rejected. A last-minute claim that Ellis had been given the gun by Desmond Cussen, who had been jealous of David Blakely, did not delay the execution and she was hanged on 13 July 1955.

Whether a more modern argument about the nature of provocation, particularly as experienced by women, would have made a difference to Ellis' conviction for murder remains a matter of debate. She had lived a complicated life with many relationships and clearly planned the crime rather than acting on impulse. A prison sentence can be adjusted for mitigating circumstances, but capital punishment cannot, so the case is probably one of the examples where the existence of the death penalty can distort the legal and sentencing processes. Ruth Ellis, her name remembered far more than that of David Blakely, formed one of the milestones in the process of abolishing the death penalty.

The Homicide Act 1957 reduced the circumstances for capital punishment to the categories of homicide caused in the course or furtherance of theft, by shooting or explosion, by resisting or preventing a lawful arrest, for the murder of police officers or somebody assisting them, for killing of a prison officer by a prisoner, or for a second conviction for murder. Capital punishment for murder was suspended in 1965 and this was converted into a permanent abolition in 1969 (and 1973 for Northern Ireland). Two offences, treason and piracy with violence, retained the death penalty until 1998.

William Hartley sketched the court appearance of another woman who had resorted to murder on 10 November 1902, the day of the Lord Mayor's show. Kitty Byron, 23 years old, was not married, but lived with Arthur Baker, who was often drunk. They often quarrelled and when Byron left their room dressed only in her nightgown, as if taking refuge from Baker's violence, their landlady gave them notice to leave. Baker, who worked in the City of London, tried to persuade the landlady to let him stay if Byron left, and when Byron heard of this from the maid, she became extremely angry. A woman in her position was unlikely to find any kind of respectable occupation and might well have to resort to prostitution. She bought a knife and sent a message for Reg, as her 'husband' was known, to meet her urgently. When he turned up they had another furious argument that ended with Byron producing the knife and stabbing him to death in the street. Byron collapsed over his body, sobbing violently, and was arrested and prosecuted for murder. The defence argued that she should be convicted only of manslaughter because she had only been trying to frighten Baker by the prospect of her committing suicide, but the judge, Mr Justice Darling, directed the jury that it was a clear case of murder. She was convicted of the charge and sentenced to death in December 1902, but with a strong recommendation for mercy. A petition of 15,000 signatures asked the Home Secretary to reprieve her, and the Home Secretary commuted the sentence to life imprisonment. In 1907 the sentence was reduced to ten years' imprisonment.

A female murderer of a different kind was Te Rangimaria Ngarimu, a 27-year-old Maori woman working in England. She was propositioned by one of her New Zealand compatriots to murder his business partner, Graeme Woodhatch, for £7,000. The proposed victim was 38 years old and a patient in Hampstead's Royal Free Hospital, recovering from an operation for haemorrhoids. Deith Bridges instructed her to shoot Woodhatch twice in the head and once in the body. That is exactly what she did when she visited the hospital, on 24 May 1992. Woodhatch was in a ward corridor using a telephone when Ngarimu shot him with the .22 Colt Trooper revolver that is now a museum exhibit. Ngarimu caught the next flight to New Zealand and was out of Britain before her murder was discovered. This was because he was first thought to have died from a brain haemorrhage, and it was not until five hours later that the bullets were discovered in his body.

The background to Woodhatch's business dealings revealed the bad blood between him and his two partners, Bridges and Paul Tubbs, and they became suspects. Woodhatch was already on bail for threatening to kill not only his secretary, but also Bridges and Tubbs whom he had defrauded of £50,000 as well as owing £400,000 in unpaid tax. The investigation also discovered the connection to Ngarimu, who firstly denied involvement, telling New Zealand officers, 'I could not kill a chicken. I'm a vegetarian,' but she then converted to Christianity and agreed to return to Britain to face trial and give evidence in court. Her evidence helped to convict Tubbs and Bridges, who were jailed for life in 1994 for their part in the murder. The judge recommended that they serve a minimum of sixteen and fifteen years respectively. Being in prison might have been a protection for Bridges; he himself was shot and wounded in Ruislip one evening, apparently as the result of another grudge against him. The case was investigated by Detective Superintendent Duncan MacRae and Detective Inspector John Dixon.

Te Rangimaria Ngarimu is believed to be the first female contract killer to have committed murder in Britain. She was sentenced to life imprisonment, but the judge accepted that she had expressed deep remorse and was satisfied that she was not in fact a professional killer.

37 Umbrella Pellet

DATE:
1978

EXHIBIT:
The 1.53mm platinum-iridium bead containing ricin that killed Gorgi Markov

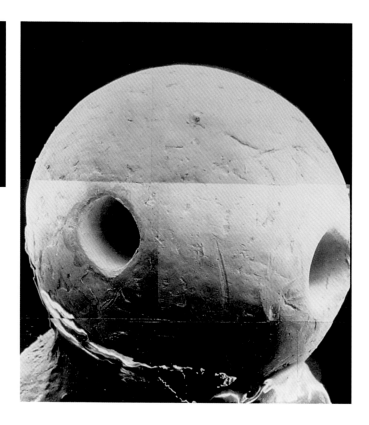

THE TINY METAL pellet was the means of delivering poison and killing a man on the streets of London in broad daylight.

Georgi Markov was a successful playwright and writer in Bulgaria, but defected in 1969, first to Italy and then to London, where he became a radio presenter working for the BBC World Service in Bush House in Aldwych. He became highly critical of the Bulgarian regime under President Zhivkov. In August 1977, Georgi Markov's brother, Nikolai, passed on a warning that Georgi was being blamed for the defection in Paris of Vladimir Kostov, a television commentator with a far higher profile. The Bulgarian government were apparently seeking revenge. On 24 August 1978, Kostov was on an escalator on the Paris metro when he felt a stinging sensation low down on his back. He had the 'sting' treated, the wound having small metallic fragments cleaned from it, and went home, none the worse for the experience. The incident was only seen as relevant in hindsight, after what happened to Georgi Markov a fortnight later, on Thursday, 7 September 1978.

As Markov was waiting for a bus at around 6.30 p.m. on Waterloo Bridge, he felt a jab in the back of his right thigh, kicked back, and saw a man drop an umbrella. The man apologised and then hailed a taxi. Shortly afterwards, Markov complained that his leg was stiff, and he began to feel ill. He went to hospital and stated that he thought he had been the victim of a 'hit', but the doctor believed that he was suffering from a virus. Three days later he died. The post-mortem examination showed an inflamed area at the back of his thigh, which the pathologist cut out and sent to Porton Down, the UK's research centre for chemical, biological, radiological and nuclear defence. Their detailed examination revealed the tiny metal capsule with holes made in it that contained ricin. (Ricin is a highly poisonous substance that originates from castor oil plant seeds.) A dose of pure ricin powder equivalent to a few grains of salt can kill an adult.

The pellet on a pinhead in a tube as displayed in the Crime Museum

The investigation clearly regarded agents of the then Bulgarian government as prime suspects. The killers of Georgi Markov have never been prosecuted in Britain, but media reports have pointed towards General Stoyan Savov, the head of their secret service, sending an assassin named Francesco Gullino to commit the crime. According to historian Hristo Hristov, General Savov committed suicide two days before he had been due to attend an inquiry ordered by a new government in Bulgaria, and General Oleg Kalugin admitted in his memoirs the involvement of Soviet Union KGB officers in giving assistance to their Bulgarian counterparts for their plans to kill Georgi Markov. Francesco Gullino, said to have been given the codename 'Piccadilly', has denied involvement.

Ricin has also been used by terrorists. On 14 January 2003, Greater Manchester police officers raided a flat in Crumpsall, north Manchester in relation to immigration offences. During this operation one of the occupants of the flat, an Algerian illegal immigrant named Kamel Bourgass (b. 1974) became violent and murdered Detective Constable Stephen Oake, who was subsequently awarded the Queen's Gallantry Medal for his bravery. In fact, Bourgass was wanted in connection with a plot to attack the London Underground system with ricin. The police had found evidence of this plot during a raid on a flat above a pharmacy in Wood Green, on 5 January. Although his co-defendants were acquitted, Bourgass was convicted of conspiracy to commit a public nuisance by the use of poisons and/or explosives to cause disruption, fear or injury. The evidence against him was based on five pages of written notes on how to make ricin, cyanide and botulinum. Already serving a life sentence for the murder of Stephen Oake, Bourgass was sentenced to seventeen years' imprisonment.

In November 2006, Alexander Litvinenko (b. 1962), a British-naturalised Russian defector who had accused the Russian President Vladimir Putin of various crimes, died after being poisoned with a radioactive substance, polonium-210, after meeting two Russians, Andrey Lugovoy and Dmitry Kovtun, in London. The two suspects could not be extradited from Russia, and the European Court of Human Rights held Russia responsible for the crime in 2021.

In March 2018, another Russian defector, Sergei Skripal, 66, and his daughter Yulia, 33, were poisoned in Salisbury with a Novichok nerve agent. Although they and a police officer survived, a member of the public, Dawn Sturgess, died after handling a perfume container that held the poison after it had apparently been carelessly disposed of by the two suspects, Alexander Mishkin and Anatoly Chopiga.

38 Courtroom Sketch of Laura Horos

THEO AND LAURA Horos were members of an occult sect named Theocratic Unity or Theocratic and Purity League, supposedly connected with the 'Hermetic Order of the Golden Dawn'. Laura Horos styled herself 'Swami' Laura Horos with supposed Indian connections, but she had convictions for fraud in Illinois under the name of Vera Ava, and in New Orleans, also being known as Editha Jackson. Theo Horos was the name used by Frank Dutton Jackson. They indulged

MADAME HOROS.
(A "Star" Artist's Sketch in Court.)
Madame Horos (cross-examining Olga Rowson): Did I ever make any hypnotic passes over you?

DATE:
1901

EXHIBIT:
Madame Horos at Marylebone court sketched by William Hartley

in fortune telling and acted as spiritual mediums. They placed advertisements for young women interested in matrimony and persuaded those who responded to take part in an admission ritual, which would lead to a 'revelation of truth as would ensure salvation'. The 'Order' involved vows of poverty, chastity and obedience. The admission ritual was Editha luring the victim into agreeing to sexual intercourse with Frank; the victim assuming that she would be married into a wealthy family if she complied. At the Old Bailey on 20 December 1901, Frank and Editha Jackson were convicted of raping two young women. Editha Jackson was sentenced to seven years and Frank Jackson to fifteen.

In November 2003, a schoolgirl, BM, an Angolan national, was found in a stairwell by Hackney street wardens. She had injuries to her eye and head. BM explained that her 'aunt', Sita Kisanga, had punched her in the face and accused her of being a witch. Further investigations revealed that BM had suffered a history of physical abuse: scars were found on her face, there was a tender area on the base of her skull, and there were vertical and linear scars on her abdomen. She had sustained injuries from being hit by a belt, a shoe and blows from fists and feet. BM alleged that her 'uncle', Pinto, had been trying to poison her school lunch and that she had suffered chilli powder being rubbed into her eyes. She was forced into a laundry bag (an exhibit in the Crime Museum) with the intention of being thrown from the third-floor balcony of the flats where she lived and then thrown into a nearby river. A diary entry in this case was translated as 'it is prophesied that [BM] is a witch'. Prosecutions for the assaults on BM resulted in three convictions and prison sentences totalling fifty years.

In August 2017 a 3-year-old girl was taken to Whipps Cross Hospital, Waltham Forest, with injuries to her genitalia. The doctor had medical experience in Sudan and suspected the injuries to be female genital mutilation (FGM), but the parents claimed that their daughter had fallen on to the sharp edge of a kitchen door, an account at first supported by the young victim and her 8-year-old brother. Both children were taken into care and, after three months with a foster family, the girl stated that she had been cut by a witch while her parents held her down. When the family home was searched, police found some cow tongues fixed together with nails and screws. They also found limes with names of individuals written on paper inside them. These items, now exhibited in the Crime Museum, were a witchcraft practice to prevent people talking about the offence and to silence the investigating officers, the then DC Lauren Brady and DC Laura Welham. A prosecution using forensic, medical and mobile telephone evidence was commenced at the Old Bailey on 14 January 2019, the mother's conviction being the first in the UK for FGM.

The diary of Heshu Yones was that of a 16-year-old Muslim girl killed by her father on 12 October 2002 because she had a Lebanese boyfriend who was a Christian and the father's attempt to arrange a forced marriage failed.

When police arrived at a block of flats in Acton to answer a call about a man who had jumped from a balcony, they found Abdullah Yones lying injured on the ground. In the family flat, his 16-year-old daughter Heshu lay dead in the bath, having been repeatedly stabbed. The knife used had been bent by the attack. Abdullah claimed that Al-Qaeda had murdered his daughter because he had given information to the security services, but traces of his skin were found under her finger nails. At his trial, Abdullah pleaded guilty, but claimed that he had reacted to information that his daughter had become a prostitute. The family had fled to Britain from Kurdistan to avoid persecution, and he believed that he would not have been punished in Kurdistan.

Heshu's diaries revealed that she often complained of being beaten by her father and had been destined for an arranged marriage against her will. She had felt unable to go to a police station because of the shame that this would bring on her family. Heshu had been taken to Kurdistan five months earlier to be married to a man she had not met, but the transaction failed.

Heshu's diary revealed that she had a Lebanese boyfriend whom she had to keep secret from her family. He was a Christian; they were Muslim. Abdullah's beliefs were taken into account by the trial judge who controversially reduced the tariff for his life sentence, when many would have regarded it as aggravating rather than mitigating the offence.

The orange of a young boy's shorts in the River Thames near the Tower of London caught the attention of a passer-by on 21 September 2001. The police consequently recovered the mutilated remains of an African boy apparently aged between 4 and 7 years. The victim was given the name 'Adam' in the absence of any other identification. It is thought that the murder had been carried out in relation to black magic rituals. Analysis of Adam's stomach contents and pollen from his lungs indicated that he had only been in London for a few days. The remains of a West African potion were found in his stomach. The body can retain indications of the origin of soil in which food was grown and these indicated a Nigerian source. Substantial inquiries in Nigeria failed to trace Adam's parents, but a Nigerian woman who had fled from a Yoruba cult via Germany claimed that her son had also been the subject of an attempted murder. Connections traced from this woman led police to investigate Kingsley Ojo who was jailed for four years in 2004 for unrelated child trafficking.

The London scene is enriched by people who come from many different origins and cultures around the world, but sometimes practices from abroad suddenly present new and different aspects of crime. The attitudes with which families from some cultures regard their female members and arrange, or even force, their daughters' marriages can range into illegality. Forced marriages are now a specific offence under Section 121 of the Anti-Social

Behaviour, Crime and Policing Act of 2014. Jurisdiction is sometimes complicated by the fact that families can travel with their daughters to and from their country of origin in preparation for the crime. Since November 2008, victims can seek protection through the Forced Marriage Civil Protection Act. By the end of 2011, 414 forced-marriage protection orders had been issued by UK courts to protect vulnerable girls and young women. Some minority communities can exert much pressure on victims not to report the illegal activity to police.

Cannibalism is mercifully rare and can be associated with severe mental health and sexual perversion. Born in London, in 1969, to West Indian parents, Peter Bryan was a well-built teenager who used his strength to commit robberies, spending the proceeds to feed his drug habit. In 1987, he tried to throw a fellow resident from a sixth-floor window of a block of flats in east London. In 1993, believing that his former employer owed him money, he beat a shop owner's daughter – 20-year-old shop assistant Nisha Sheth – to death with a hammer as she worked in her family's clothes shop in Chelsea. He jumped from a nearby block of flats, broke both ankles and was sent to Rampton secure hospital. Staff at the hospital later judged that he was making progress in his mental state and he was transferred to other units, given more responsibility and, by 2003, it was thought that he did not present any major risk to the public. The drugs that kept him under control had a side effect of causing his breasts to grow and he avoided taking them when he was free to do so.

In 2004 he was moved back to an open psychiatric ward at Newham Hospital after assaulting a 16-year-old girl near to his residential hostel, but in February that year he walked out of the hospital and killed his friend, Brian Cherry. Police were called after neighbours heard screams, and found Cherry dead, with both arms and one leg severed from his body. Bryan was cooking his victim's brain in the frying pan, now an exhibit in the museum's collection. Bryan was sent to Broadmoor Hospital after this murder, and whilst there murdered a fellow patient – 60-year-old Richard Loudwell. Bryan said that if he had not been interrupted he would have eaten his victim's flesh.

A serious and unusual case by any standards, Bryan was diagnosed as a paranoid schizophrenic, probably associated with drug misuse. He had engaged in frotteurism (rubbing against non-consenting people for sexual gratification), sadistic bondage, 'piquerism' (piercing a victim's skin) with a screwdriver, and was a self-confessed cannibal. He was jailed for life for the murders of Brian Cherry and Richard Loudwell, his mental condition making any future release unlikely. He was very manipulative and had at one stage been under the supervision of an inexperienced social worker with no mental health training. His medication had been reduced after Bryan had complained about it and he had been allowed to self-medicate.

On 30 May 1980, a dismembered body, later identified as Patricia Marina Berkley, alias Malone, a 22-year-old prostitute, was discovered in Epping Forest. It was likely that the killer had been one of her clients and the police undertook research into those who had been using her services, and how the parts of her body had come to be dumped there. Three months later, Peter George Swindell was arrested and questioned. He had been in the habit of picking up prostitutes in the King's Cross area and taking them back to his home in Walthamstow where his fetishes included the use of bondage, masks, hoods and various other items. He would photograph his victims trussed up and sometimes crucified by being tied to a cross. There was a considerable quantity of pornographic images found in his possession. It seemed likely that Patricia Malone had died at his home whilst being engaged in his fantasies and her body then dumped in the forest. Swindell, a former police officer, was charged with manslaughter, obstructing a coroner in his duty and preventing the burial of a dead body. He was acquitted of manslaughter and sentenced to five years' imprisonment for disposing of the dead body.

Bath

THE BATH WAS an exhibit in the trial of George Joseph Smith for the murder of Alice Smith (née Burnham). It was brought down to London by Inspector William Drabble. In 2013, his great-grandson, Gordon Lonsdale, told the museum staff of the family story that Inspector Drabble had marked the bath with his initials, and, on examination of the object, this proved to be quite correct.

It was a report in the *News of the World* about the tragic inquest of Margaret Lloyd – a bride who had drowned in her bath in Highgate a week before Christmas 1914 – that prompted a Mr Charles Burnham and a Mrs Crossley to go to the police, and which brought Divisional Detective Inspector Neil to investigate a complicated case of a series of bigamies and murders. Burnham was a Buckingham fruit grower whose 25-year-old daughter, Alice, had married George Smith in Portsmouth in November 1913, despite parental objections. The couple went on holiday to Blackpool where Crossley had been their landlady. Alice had drowned in the bath on 12 December 1913, not long after her wedding in October of that year. The police agreed with Burnham that the two cases were likely to be linked. The probate issues from Margaret Lloyd's will were being administered by a solicitor and, when the 'grieving husband', John Lloyd, attended an appointment to receive money due to him, the police were waiting for him. He admitted that his real name was George Joseph Smith and that he was the same man who had married Alice Burnham.

DATE:
1915

EXHIBIT:
The bath in which Alice Smith died in Blackpool

The year before Alice Burnham's death in Blackpool, Bessie Munday had died, on 13 July 1912, whilst taking a bath in Herne Bay where she was staying with her husband, Henry Williams, whom she had married in Weymouth in August 1910. 'Henry Williams' also transpired to be none other than George Smith. Inquiries showed that Smith had conducted no fewer than seven bigamous marriages between 1908 and 1914. He apparently had a 'masterful', 'hypnotic' way with some women, a trait that was only exceeded by his ruthlessness in acquiring their money.

Inspector William Drabble marked the bath with his initials

Smith's complex series of relationships started in January 1898 when, at the age of 26 and using the name of George Love, Smith had married, legally and for the first time, 18-year-old Caroline Thornhill in Leicester. They moved to London and she worked as a maid for a number of employers, stealing from them under her husband's tuition. Caroline was arrested in Worthing, trying to pawn some silver spoons and she was sent to prison for twelve months. On her release she incriminated her husband, who was then jailed for two years in January 1901. On his release, Caroline fled to Canada. In June 1908, Smith met a widow from Worthing, Florence Wilson, and married her, bigamously, three weeks later. By 3 July he had left her after taking the £30 she had withdrawn from her savings account. On 30 July 1908 he had undertaken a second bigamous marriage, to Edith Pegler in Bristol, who had replied to his advertisement for a housekeeper. The third, in October 1909, was when he married Sarah Freeman, using the name of George Rose. He later married Alice Reid in September 1914, using the name of Charles Oliver James.

When Smith appeared at the Old Bailey, charged with murdering Alice Burnham, Bessie Munday and Margaret Lloyd, Detective Inspector Neil demonstrated to the jury the method of drowning his victims by raising their knees whilst they were in the bath. His assistant, a nurse in a bathing costume, required artificial respiration after the courtroom demonstration and Smith was duly convicted.

Smith's trial took place during the dark days of the First World War and the judge, Mr Justice Scrutton, remarked that '... while this wholesale destruction of human life is going on, for some days all the apparatus of justice in England has been considering whether one man should die ...' The jury returned their guilty verdict in twenty-two minutes, and Smith was executed on Friday, 13 August 1915 at Maidstone prison.

Caroline Thornhill, whom Smith had married legally, was now a widow and she married a Canadian soldier the day after Smith's execution.

The bath in which Margaret Lloyd died in Highgate was returned to its owner who controversially sold it to Madame Tussauds.

In 2015 the bath from Blackpool was loaned out to the Galleries of Justice in Nottingham as part of their *World War 1: Heroes and Villains* exhibition.

40 Picture of Drain

WHEN A COMPANY attended to a complaint about the drains next to No. 23 Cranley Gardens, Muswell Hill, in 1983, they discovered that the reason for the blockage was connected to human remains. They called the police, who took samples for specialist examination that confirmed that the remains were indeed human. Detective Chief Inspector Peter Jay then called on the top-floor flat, where the occupant was Dennis Nilsen, an executive officer at a Job Centre in Kentish Town with a record of previous employment in public service, including a few months as a Metropolitan Police officer and fourteen years as a cook in the army. Peter Jay told Nilsen that he had come about the drains, and when Nilsen's flat was searched, the police found two half torsos, several severed arms and two heads, one

DATE:
1983

EXHIBIT:
The drain outside Dennis Nilsen's flat

of which had been boiled. Under an upturned drawer in the bathroom, a pair of legs was found. A large pot on the kitchen cooker, today an exhibit in the Crime Museum, had been used for boiling body parts.

Nilsen's account of his activities contained an admission to killing twelve men at a previous address in addition to the victims found at Cranley Gardens and that he had, at one stage, six bodies under his floorboards. Nilsen had positioned one body in a chair as if it was watching television. He had bathed other victims after their death and taken other bodies to bed with him for company. He had picked up men, some of whom were homeless, apparently because, in addition to his mental disorder, he felt himself to be lonely. He apparently murdered his victims rather than face the prospect of them leaving him.

At his trial at the Old Bailey, he tried, unsuccessfully, to persuade the court that he was insane, and was sentenced to life imprisonment. The cooker remains an exhibit in the Crime Museum, with knives, the bath and the collar from Nilsen's Border collie dog, Bleep, who had to be put down after Nilsen's arrest when it became ill.

Thumb mark

Mr Farrows Cash box.

Cash Box with a Thumbprint

THE CASH BOX had a thumb mark that provided identification for a robbery and murder.

When Scotland Yard's Fingerprint Bureau was about four years old, a murder occurred in one of George Chapman's Oil and Colour shops at No. 34 High Street, Deptford. William Jones, one of George Chapman's employees, went to the shop shortly after 9 a.m. on 27 March 1905 to find out why it was still not open for business. He gained entry from the back of the building and found the 71-year-old shopkeeper, Thomas Farrow, dead in a pool of blood. Upstairs, Thomas' wife Ann, 65, was dying on the bloodstained bed. In the middle of the room was a cash box with a bloody thumb mark. The assailants had apparently been wearing masks, and a length of rope with a lead ball seemed to be the murder weapon.

Detective Chief Inspector Fox and a team of detectives traced a number of witnesses, some of whom had seen local thieves Alfred and Albert Stratton (brothers) in the vicinity. In keeping with the fashion of the day, Albert Stratton had been wearing a bowler hat. A milkman and his boy had seen two men leaving the premises at 7.15 a.m. that morning. Detective Inspector Charles Collins searched the fingerprint collection but could find no print that would match the mark from the crime scene. The police arrested the two Stratton brothers on suspicion, but neither the milkman nor his boy could pick them out from an identification parade,

DATE:
1905

EXHIBIT:
The cash box that bore the incriminating thumbprint

165

and the brothers denied the murder, despite a considerable amount of circumstantial evidence pointing to their involvement. The chances of solving the case or mounting a successful prosecution were becoming remote. At Blackheath Road police station Charles Collins took the fingerprints of the prisoners, and the police investigation was transformed when he found that Alfred Stratton's right thumb matched the mark found on the cash box.

At the Old Bailey, the prosecuting barrister, Richard Muir, explained the new science of fingerprints to the jury, one of whom had his fingerprints taken so that the rest of the jury could examine them. Charles Collins gave evidence that there were eleven points of agreement between an enlarged photograph of Alfred Stratton's thumbprint compared with a photograph from the thumb mark on the cash box. There were also other points that he had not marked and numbered. There were 90,000 sets of fingerprints in Scotland Yard's collection at the time and he stated that he had no doubt that Alfred Stratton had left the mark. On that basis Alfred Stratton was convicted, and Albert Stratton was also found guilty because they had acted jointly. Both were sentenced to death, and executed on 23 May 1905, in the first murder trial in Britain where fingerprint evidence had been used.

Marcello Malphigi (1628–94), an Italian anatomist, was probably the first to describe how the papillary ridges of fingerprints form part of the structure of the skin. Dr Nehemiah Grew (1641–1712), from Britain, also described fingerprints in 1684. They begin to form when a baby is a 6-month-old embryo in the womb. The belief that fingerprints could uniquely identify an individual was suggested in 1823 by Czech physiologist Jan Purkenje, who described nine different patterns that could arise. In 1859, William Herschel, a civil servant, took fingerprint signatures to prevent fraud by Indian soldiers collecting their pensions, and demonstrated from his records that fingerprints do not change with age. In 1879, Dr Henry Faulds, a Scottish physiologist and medical missionary, assisted the Tokyo police with the case of a burglar who had left his finger marks on a whitewashed wall. Faulds proved that the man in police custody could not have been the one who left the finger marks, but they did match the marks of a prisoner that the Tokyo police arrested some days later. Faulds mentioned the case, the first crime in the world to be solved using fingerprints, in the October 1880 edition of the journal *Nature*. Francis Galton, a cousin of Charles Darwin, calculated that the odds against any two individuals having identical fingerprints was one in 64,000 million and, by 1895, had devised a classification system according to whether the fingerprints had arches (5 per cent of prints), loops (60 per cent), whorls or composites (35 per cent).

The introduction of fingerprints for police use was first considered as a means for identifying whether prisoners in court had any previous convictions under a different name. The authorities wanted something more scientific than the memories of police officers, who would visit prisons to try and identify those who were in there under false identities. In 1880, Alphonse Bertillon invented a system in Paris for systematically measuring various parts of a prisoner's body, and he did include fingerprints as one of his identifying features. In 1894, Scotland Yard introduced a similar system of 'anthropometry', which used five of the criteria of measurement of particular bones used by Bertillon, but also added the colour of the eyes – and fingerprints. Instruments for measuring the anatomy of prisoners under the 'Bertillonage' system can be seen in the museum.

But there was no method of classifying and quickly retrieving identities from a police fingerprint collection until Edward Henry, on leave from police service in India, conferred with Francis Galton and then, on his return to India, worked out, with Hemchandra Bose and Azizul Hacque, a practical method of classifying and retrieving them. They allocated a score, from 8 to 0 to each digit, according to a set sequence and whether each had a whorl or composite pattern or not, and then put the resulting scores of each digit into pairings (e.g. left thumb and left forefinger). The two thumbs and eight fingers created ten such scores.

These were paired together into five sets of two numbers each, arranged as if they were fractions. The five scores above and the five scores below each line were then added together to create a two-figure total, which would then classify any person's fingerprints into one of 1,024 numbered categories. This immediately gave the police an enormously reduced number of cases in their collection on which to base their detailed comparisons. Edward Henry was later appointed as an assistant commissioner at Scotland Yard and introduced the Fingerprint Bureau, based on his system and Indian fingerprint forms, on 1 July 1901. The first crime solved in Britain by the new system was a burglary at Denmark Hill in June 1902 when a dirty thumbprint on a freshly painted windowsill was photographed and found to match that of 41-year-old labourer Harry Jackson. By 1903, Edward Henry had become commissioner and noted in his annual report for 1904 (published mid-1905):

> The fingerprints of criminals left on bottles, glasses, articles of plate, cash boxes, &c., have, during the past year, been the means of enabling the investigating officers (in many cases of burglary, housebreaking, and in one of murder) to place before the Courts, both in London and in the Provinces, most valuable corroborative evidence.

In the Stratton brothers' trial, Charles Collins quoted how many fingerprints were in Scotland Yard's collection and the number of points of comparison he had found. In 1920, Scotland Yard introduced a standard requirement of sixteen points of resemblance, with no feature different. These could be reduced to ten if more than one finger was involved. In 1953 this was adopted as a national standard for the introduction of fingerprint evidence in court. Other countries adopted different numbers of points of reference. In 1973 the US Standardisation Committee of the Association for Identification recommended abandoning a formal standard, as they believed that a minimum requirement had no scientific validity. In the 1990s, moreover, the sixteen-point standard was relaxed in Britain, partly because of the number of finger marks found at scenes of crime that matched a suspect, but were too small in size to yield the number of comparison points required to meet the sixteen-point standard; the new procedure would, instead, allow the prosecution to introduce evidence with fewer points of comparison, provided that it was accompanied by a suitable explanation by an expert fingerprint officer.

One of the more bizarre fingerprint cases was that of William Mitchell, who, during the course of a burglary in September 1909, climbed over a 3m-high gate in Clerkenwell. As he placed his feet on the crossbar of the inside structure of the gate, he slipped and a ring worn on his right little finger was caught on one of the spikes on top. As he fell, his finger was torn away, leaving it behind. A police officer collected and preserved it, with the ring still attached, for examination. The following month, Mitchell appeared under the name of Harry May at Lambeth court, charged with pickpocketing at the Elephant and Castle, claiming to the police that he could not have committed such a crime because he had a heavily bandaged finger stump. However, the missing finger had been identified as his by the Fingerprint Bureau, thus he faced an additional charge and was sentenced to twelve months' hard labour. The fingertip, which had been preserved in a glass jar, featured in the 1946 National Police Exhibition at Brighton, where it was on loan from Commissioner Sir Harold Scott.

A similar fate befell a Robert Garry, where Crime Museum records show that he tore his finger off on a corrugated iron fence after a burglary. The finger was preserved in a bottle in the museum after being brought to Scotland Yard and identified from its fingerprint pattern.

42 Albert Bowes' Criminal Record File

SIR EDWARD HENRY had been commissioner at Scotland Yard since 1903 and had succeeded in revolutionising criminal records by means of his system for classifying fingerprints, but he himself would be the victim of an attempted assassination that would require one of these records.

DATE:
1912

EXHIBIT:
Criminal record file of Albert Bowes

On the evening of 27 November 1912, Sir Edward Henry arrived back at his Kensington home. As he opened the front door he was approached by 25-year-old Albert George Bowes, who said he wanted to speak to him. Henry replied that he was busy and that the man should call at his office in Scotland Yard, but Bowes pulled out a five-chambered Webley revolver, that is now in the museum, and fired three shots at the commissioner. Henry was wounded in the right groin and leg; the other bullet missed. It transpired that Bowes had been refused a licence to drive a motor omnibus because of a conviction he had received for being drunk and disorderly in March 1912. The Metropolitan Police were responsible for granting these licences and the commissioner would consider appeals against these decisions, but Bowes had become seriously aggrieved at the decision. Henry's

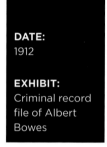
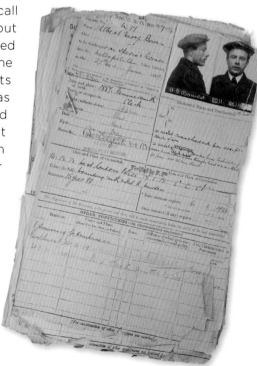

driver, Albert English, seized Bowes and detained him with the help of a nearby porter and a decorator, and was awarded the King's Police Medal for his bravery.

Albert Bowes was later convicted at the Central Criminal Court for attempted murder. The commissioner, whom William Hartley sketched in court, had a well-developed humanitarian spirit and made a personal plea for mercy on Bowes' behalf. The judge therefore reduced Bowes' life sentence to fifteen years' penal servitude. In 1919 a special remission was granted to Bowes and he was released from prison. Sir Edward Henry paid for his passage to Canada to make a new start, but his new life lasted only until 1924 when Bowes was killed in Florida by a bullet through the head from a sheriff's pistol after he had shot and wounded a man. Henry was perhaps the only commissioner able to report on an attempted murder on himself in his annual report for 1912.

The family's relationship with commissioners took a turn for the better when PC Ken Moxley, a grandson of Albert Bowes' sister, was presented with a community award a century or so later.

In November 1922 another security lapse might have led to the loss of life of another commissioner, Brigadier General Sir William Horwood. After lunch one day he started to sample a box of Walnut Whip chocolates that had been sent to him, thinking that they were a present from his daughter. He immediately felt ill but examined the sweets with a magnifying glass and concluded that they had been poisoned. They turned out to have been laced with weedkiller and several other senior police officers had been sent similar parcels. The investigation led to the arrest of Walter Tatam who was found to be insane and was sent to a mental hospital.

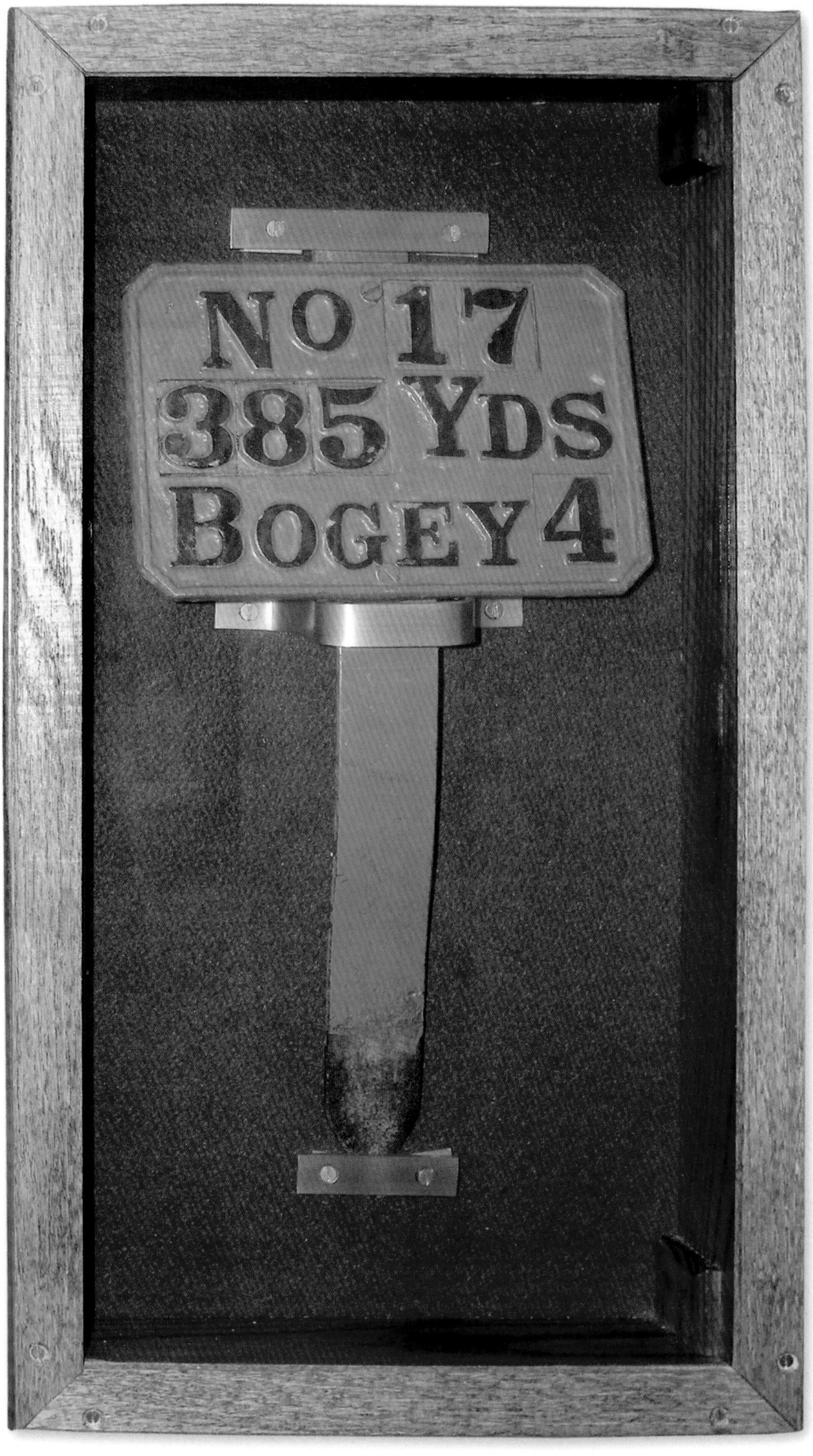
NO 17
385 YDS
BOGEY 4

Golf Course Tee Marker

THE PAPILLARY RIDGE patterns on human fingers also apply to human palms and, therefore, the possibility of identifying criminals from their finger marks became extended to palm marks left at the scenes of crimes. In this example, the palm mark was left on a metal marker from a golf course.

When the body of Mrs Elizabeth Currell was found on 29 April 1955 on Potters Bar golf course, it became apparent that the murder weapon was a heavy iron tee marker. The wound to Currell's skull displayed green paint from the marker and could be matched by an exact 'mechanical' fit. There was a partial palm print found on the tee marker, but it did not match any in Scotland Yard's collection. The offender was believed to be a local man, so, after careful consideration, the police launched a public appeal and invited male occupants of homes in the area to provide their palm prints for elimination purposes. By the middle of that August, four months later, 9,000 palm prints had been taken when a member of a special squad of fingerprint officers found the print that was a match for the mark found at the crime scene. The palm print belonged to a youth named Michael Queripel who lived with his parents close to the golf course. Queripel first admitted only to finding the body, but then admitted the complete crime and was detained 'at Her Majesty's pleasure'. He was the first to be convicted as the result of a mass palm-printing exercise.

DATE:
1955

EXHIBIT:
The tee marker bearing the palm print (no longer visible)

The precedent for the public appeal for elimination prints had taken place in 1948. A particularly traumatic murder case occurred on 14 May that year when 4-year-old June Devaney was found to be missing from a children's ward at Blackburn's Queen's Park Hospital. She was later found battered to death in the hospital grounds. Detective Chief Inspector Colin Campbell, head of the Lancashire Fingerprint Bureau, found marks made by stockinged feet on the hospital ward floor, but there was a second clue that came in the form of a finger mark on a 'Winchester' bottle that must have been moved by the perpetrator. It was a time-consuming task to take the fingerprints of all the hospital staff who might have touched the bottle for legitimate reasons, and the mark did not match any in Scotland Yard's national fingerprint collection. The mass public fingerprinting exercise proposal gained the support of the local population, who were encouraging of any efforts to catch the man responsible. With the assistance of the notable fingerprint expert Frederick Cherrill, the police undertook the enormous task of taking the fingerprints of all the male population of Blackburn to eliminate them from their inquiry. This exercise took weeks, and more than 46,000 sets of fingerprints were taken without any positive result. It was the era of post-war rationing and records of the issue of ration books were then compared with the national registration numbers recorded on the fingerprint forms, and the police realised that there were 200 men who had not yet been seen. Priority was then given to tracing these men, amongst which was set number 46,253 that provided, at long last, a match with the mark on the bottle. The fingerprints belonged to Peter Griffiths. He was hanged on 19 November 1948; two weeks after, all of the other elimination prints were destroyed.

It was in the case of John Egan in 1931, prosecuted for a series of burglaries, that palm-print evidence was first produced in a prosecution in a British court. There had been a clear palm print left by the burglar at one of the crime scenes, and when Egan was arrested on other evidence, Frederick Cherrill, then a detective inspector, went to Brixton prison and took Egan's palm prints for comparison purposes. One of Egan's prints matched the mark left on a glass table at the crime scene. This gave fresh impetus to the collection of palm prints, since at the time Scotland Yard had only a very limited collection – it was generally only fingerprints that were taken routinely from prisoners. Egan pleaded guilty, but the judge called Cherrill to the witness box to inform the court about the development and as an assurance that palm print identification was as reliable as fingerprints.

By 1942, Scotland Yard had collected 4,000 palm prints and Cherrill was a detective superintendent. When a 71-year-old pawnbroker named Leonard Moules was murdered in east London, Detective Chief Inspector Ted Greeno called in Cherrill to examine the scene for finger marks. Cherrill found a palm print inside a safe that matched neither the victim, nor his assistant nor any of those in Scotland Yard's collection. In an inquiry reminiscent of the Stratton brothers' case, one witness recalled that he had seen two men near the scene whom he knew vaguely as 'George' and 'Sam'. This led to the men being identified as George Silverosa and Sam Dashwood who were then arrested as suspects. Their palm prints were taken, and one of Silverosa's matched that found in the victim's safe. Both prisoners blamed each other and refused to give evidence at their trial, which was the first contested trial involving a palm print. They were convicted, and executed at Pentonville prison on 10 September 1942.

Plaster Casts

PLASTER CASTS OF shoe prints and knee marks with a trouser crease became important evidence in the inquiries into the murder of Ruby Keen.

Ruby Keen, aged 23, lived with her widowed mother, her sister and her older brother in Leighton Buzzard, Bedfordshire. She was a vivacious blonde who worked at AC Sphinx works in Dunstable, and at one stage had a regular boyfriend, Leslie Stone, a labourer who joined the Royal Artillery and was posted to Hong Kong in 1932. This caused the affection on Keen's part to fade, and her letters to him petered out. In Stone's absence, Keen saw a good deal of other men, including two young police officers and then became engaged to one of them. In December 1936, Stone was medically discharged from the army and returned home to Leighton Buzzard. On 3 April 1937, he saw Keen in the company of another man and spoke to her the following evening when he bought her a drink in The Golden Bell public house and suggested that they should go out one evening 'for old time's sake'.

A week later, Keen went to The Golden Bell and met up with Stone, who was wearing, for the first time, a new blue serge suit. After a few drinks, they moved on to other places and Stone was overheard trying to persuade Keen to break off her engagement and to marry him instead. Their conversation caused some curiosity and, as the couple left the pub, they were seen to walk off into a lover's lane known as The Firs.

DATE:
1937

EXHIBIT:
Plaster casts of Leslie Stone's knee and shoe marks

A married couple later walked past Keen in the arms of a man they took to be a police officer.

The following morning, 11 April 1937, Keen's body was discovered by a railway worker at about 7 a.m. She had been strangled with her own silk polka-dot scarf (now a museum exhibit). Most of her clothing had been forcibly removed. There was no sign of sexual assault, but there were marks on the ground indicating that a desperate struggle had taken place. That afternoon, Stone called at a local police officer's house and asked the constable's wife to telephone Leighton Buzzard police station because he had been with Keen the previous evening and he wished to help the police with their inquiries. At the time, the police suspected that one of the two police officers had been involved because of the description given by the married couple, but they had probably mistaken Stone's blue suit for a police officer's uniform. Detective Chief Inspector Barker from Scotland Yard interviewed the two officers concerned, but Keen's fiancé had been on police duty the previous evening.

At the crime scene, the police took plaster casts of depressions in the ground where the killer had apparently knelt down to attack Keen. When Sir Bernard Spilsbury examined these he noted the clear mark of the crease of trousers and the marks created by the cloth of the trousers. The police examined the trousers of the three suspects and found that Stone's suit trousers had been cleaned or brushed so hard that the nap of the cloth had been completely worn away. Spilsbury found specks of dirt in the remaining weave of the cloth and similar dirt marks in the trouser turn-ups. In a pioneering case, the dirt was compared under a microscope with samples of the sandy soil at the murder scene and found to match. Heel marks at the scene matched Stone's right shoe. There was a silk fibre in the lining of Stone's jacket that matched Keen's slip, and fibres on her dress that matched Stone's suit. Leslie Stone denied any attack on Ruby Keen, but was charged with her murder.

At his Old Bailey trial, Stone admitted being in the lane with Keen, and said that they had quarrelled, that when she had struck him he had retaliated and pulled at her scarf, then grabbed the front of her clothes as she had fallen down. He had been in a rage and had left her, believing that she was stunned rather than dead. The jury did not believe his story, apparently considered that Stone had killed her whilst trying to rape her, and convicted him of murder. Stone's appeal was dismissed and he was hanged at Pentonville prison on Friday, 13 August 1937.

The Leslie Stone trial took place only about two years after the establishment of the Metropolitan Police Forensic Science Laboratory under the leadership of its first director, Dr James Davidson, and it illustrates the careful crime scene management and analysis that was progressively being developed. As the years passed, the forensic scientists applied the principles of science with increasing effect to confirm or disprove the guilt of suspects. One of the areas in which these advances were made was in blood grouping.

Early in the twentieth century, Karl Landsteiner had begun to discover the importance of blood groups and the First World War taught doctors that it was dangerous to make blood transfusions of the wrong group. In 1925, scientists realised that blood groups could be determined from some people's secretions such as saliva and urine and, by 1932, the evidence in the murder of Annette Friedson included the fact that blood of the same group as the victim, contained in only 3 per cent of the population, had been found on the suspect Maurice Freedman's razor.

In 1949 a case involving Donald Hume and Stanley Setty demonstrated progress in this field. Both the men were involved in car thefts – Hume stealing them and Setty selling them on – but they were far from friends. On 4 October 1949 a fight broke out after Setty had refused to leave Hume's house, and this resulted in Hume killing Setty, cutting up his body, then taking the remains in a hired aeroplane from Elstree Airport, where he was well known as a pilot, and throwing them into the English Channel near the French coast. He landed at Southend Airport because of a shortage of fuel and took a taxi home for which he paid with £5 notes stolen from Setty. Setty had withdrawn £1,000 from a bank shortly before his death, but most of these had become too bloodstained for Hume to use.

On 21 October, just over two weeks afterwards, part of Setty's body was washed ashore in Essex. A skull was also found, now an exhibit in the museum, that was first thought to be relevant, but was soon confidently classified as too old to belong to a modern murder victim.

Hume was linked to the murder because the police traced the serial numbers of the banknotes he had used for the taxi fare to the batch issued by the bank to Setty. Bloodstains from group O were found in Hume's flat, corresponding to Setty's, but the extent of scientific knowledge at the time could not trace this blood more specifically than a group owned by 40 per cent of the population. At his trial, Hume was acquitted of murder, but sentenced to twelve years' imprisonment for disposing of the body. After his release in 1958, he sold his story for £2,000 to the *Sunday Pictorial* stating that he had committed the murder. At the time, it was not possible to reopen a murder prosecution once a defendant had already faced trial. A dagger, apparently used by Hume to embellish his newspaper account of the murder, is in the museum collection. Hume later went to Switzerland where, whilst escaping from an armed robbery, he killed a taxi driver in January 1959. He was sentenced to life imprisonment and was later returned to Britain and sent to Broadmoor Hospital.

By the mid-1960s, the work of forensic scientists Margaret Pereira and Brian Culliford had advanced forensic science to the point where they could link the identity of a suspect with a bloodstain to a much higher degree of accuracy, taking into account a number of subgroups and rarity factors. In 1968, for instance, when Bernard Josephs returned to his Shortlands home to find his wife Claire lying dead, there were signs of her having been disturbed from cooking to receive an unexpected visitor. The detectives, led by

Detective Superintendent John Cummings, suspected Roger Payne, the husband of one of Claire's friends, who bore scratch marks on his hands and a bruise to his forehead that he blamed on injuring himself whilst repairing his car. Claire Josephs' blood group was found in 0.6 per cent of the population of Britain and Roger Payne's in 4.4 per cent. Bloodstains from both groups were found on Payne's handkerchief. Bloodstains from Claire Josephs' group were found in Payne's car.

The forensic science case against Roger Payne involved blood groups, but also the examination of fibres, since Claire Josephs had worn a bright cerise woollen dress made of very distinctive and unusual fibres that were an exact match to residue found on Roger Payne's hat, coat and jacket. Payne had previously visited the flat, which later became the murder scene, but at that time Josephs had been wearing different clothes. During the examination of the clothes of the victim and suspect, but before Payne's arrest, the laboratory staff found a number of distinctive rayon fibres on both sets of clothing, mostly red, but others with permutations of red, black, pale yellow and blue. They speculated that they might have come from a garment similar to a tie. After Payne's arrest, several ties, a cravat and a scarf were seized. One of the scarves was in a very frayed condition, made of rayon and matched the fibres exactly. The fibres in this case were very distinctive. The dress fibres had a fluorescent character and were found, using ultraviolet light, on Payne's suit in the interstices of the cloth after it had been cleaned. Payne was convicted because of a systematic and thorough forensic science investigation, and he was sentenced to life imprisonment.

Probably the culminating case for identifying a suspect by the use of blood groups was the tragic 1983 murders in Sheffield of three members of the Laitner family at a family wedding reception. A bloodstain found at the scene would arise, on average, once in 50,000 people, and the laboratory already had a record of a local criminal, Arthur Hutchinson, who had that same blood group. His palm print was also found at the scene and he was duly convicted of the murders.

45 Ear mark on Goddard and Phillips' Window

A PRESERVED AND framed pane of glass shows the faint but distinct mark of an ear that had been apparently pressed against the windowpane of an office at No. 118a Highgate Road, NW5, the premises of Goddard & Phillips Ltd, which suffered a burglary in December 1968. Their safe was blown open with explosives. Major Wilson, one of Scotland Yard's explosives officers, concluded that the substance used was plaster gelatine, a commercial blasting explosive that had, since 1967, contained aluminium. The explosive had been placed

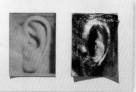

DATE:
1968

EXHIBIT:
Photographs of ear mark, window and Joseph Purton

into the safe's keyhole, and then muffled with a raincoat and a desk placed against it as the detonation took place. Just under £400 in cash was stolen.

There were no significant developments in the case until the night of 6–7 March 1969 when police officers were keeping observation near the premises of G.H. Buttle and Co., in Buttles Yard, Castle Mews, London, NW1. This was the location of a second business premises burgled with a safe being blown open by the same method and with exactly the same type of explosive. Detective Sergeant Miles was in the area very quickly and stopped Joseph Purton in the street, searched him and found a brace tool in his possession. Another, younger, man, James Phillips, perhaps Purton's apprentice, was nearby and was also arrested. This time just over £200 in cash had been stolen, along with thirty-three cheques and some postage stamps.

Both men appeared at the Old Bailey in July 1969 and admitted the second burglary, but not 'aggravated burglary', a new offence under the Theft Act 1968 that had just been introduced. They admitted to breaking in, but denied any connection with the explosives, a factor that was likely to lead to a greatly increased sentence because the possession of explosives would make the offence 'aggravated'.

The prosecution case linked Purton to the original offence at Goddard & Phillips by means of a partial verbal admission made by Purton to the effect that 'you can put that one down to me but I am not signing anything', the unusual coincidence of the same explosive being used and the ear print, which was consistent with Purton's left ear.

Purton had rather unusual ears and a Mr Fuller from the Metropolitan Police Forensic Science Laboratory examined the ear mark and found that it was consistent with an impression that Purton's ear would have made. It was not identical, but the difference could be explained by pressure against the glass distorting the shape of the ear. The ear mark was 54in from ground level, and Purton's ear, whilst he was standing normally, was 56in from the ground, the difference being accounted for by how a person would lean away from the vertical towards the window if listening for sounds from inside the premises.

Unlike fingerprints, there was no database for human ears, so Fuller collected the details of 100 specimens, mostly from laboratory staff and police officers. This study showed that only 3 per cent had ears similar to the shape of Joseph Purton's when the shapes were compared using the tragus of the ear as a reference point. The dimensions of different parts of the ear can be measured and compared using eighteen measurements between different parts of the ear's features. The human ear has highly individual characteristics and retains the same basic shape throughout life notwithstanding that it continues to grow, especially in the lobe. The evidence was treated by the court as indicating that the ear mark could have been made by Purton's ear. It would have been corroborative of Purton's partial confession, like the similarity of the unusual explosive used in the other safe-blowing case. In the end, the jury convicted Purton and Phillips of the second burglary, but not the ear-print case. Had modern advances in DNA technology been available then, it might well have been DNA that would have confirmed or disproved Purton's involvement with a greater level of certainty. It was a fine attempt, however, to apply scientific methods in an unusual case. The caseload of explosives officers moved dramatically away from safe blowing – a crime method then rapidly dying out – towards terrorism cases.

On 7 May 1996, 94-year-old Dorothy May was found murdered in Huddersfield, apparently by an intruder whose ear mark was found on the glass of a transom window that had been forced open. There had been other recent burglaries where entry had been effected by a similar method. Mark Dallagher was arrested and convicted for the burglaries but, whilst in prison, talked about the murder of May and disclosed details that otherwise were known only to the police. He was, therefore, arrested and charged. Two specialists, Cornelis Van Der Lugt from Holland, and Professor Vanezis from Glasgow, testified that they were satisfied that Dallagher's ear print matched that

on the glass from the murder scene and Dallagher was convicted of murder at Leeds Crown Court on 15 December 1998. In 2002, an appeal considered further evidence about the level of certainty that could be given to an expert opinion that two ear prints appeared to be from the same person, particularly when there was no large database of ear prints from which to base research conclusions. The court directed that Dallagher, who had given alibi evidence, should have his appeal allowed and given a fresh trial. Meanwhile, advantage was taken of the advances in forensic science technology and a DNA sample obtained from the ear print was reported as indicating that Dallagher was not the person who had left the print at the scene, so the Crown Prosecution Service did not pursue the case against him further.

Deoxyribonucleic acid (DNA) carries the genetic information of each individual human and provides an absolutely unique 'signature' for each person, based on heredity. Samples can be taken for analysis from flesh, bone, hair roots and body secretions, such as sweat and blood. It is only identical twins who share each other's DNA (but their fingerprints will be different).

The structure of DNA was discovered by Jim Watson and Francis Crick in Cambridge in 1953, but it was in September 1984 that Dr Alec Jeffreys and his team at Leicester University – who were researching gene evolution and heredity in illness – realised that the complex patterns in the X-ray films of their tests were like bar codes that could therefore be used systematically to record and retrieve information. Jeffreys, later knighted for his work, collaborated with David Werrett and Peter Gill of the Forensic Science Service to demonstrate the possibility of extracting DNA from crime scenes, and these techniques then superseded blood groups for crime scene investigation. Initially, a company called Cellmark Diagnostics undertook Scotland Yard's DNA analysis until the Met's forensic science laboratory opened their own unit in 1988. It is overwhelmingly DNA developments that have led to successful solutions to cold cases. The techniques for extracting DNA have seen much progress in the twenty-five years or so since the system was first developed.

It was appropriate that it should be in Leicester – Alec Jeffreys' local force – where the first criminal case would be determined by DNA. In 1983, 15-year-old Lynda Mann from Narborough had been murdered and in 1986 another 15-year-old girl, Dawn Ashworth from Enderby, was also killed. A 17-year-old kitchen porter, Richard Buckland, came under suspicion for Dawn Ashworth's death, which was being investigated by Detective Superintendent Painter. Buckland had admitted being with Dawn Ashworth shortly before her death and gave numerous accounts of what had happened, but retracted some parts of his story. He demonstrated knowledge of the incident that was consistent with details otherwise known only to the police and admitted responsibility for Ashworth's death. Buckland, not surprisingly, was charged with the murder. Blood samples were taken to confirm or disprove his confession, but also to check whether he had been responsible for the earlier unsolved murder of Lynda Mann.

DNA testing proved that the same offender had committed both murders, but, rather dramatically, demonstrated that the offender was not Richard Buckland, who was then released. The police undertook a nine-month exercise in taking mass DNA samples and, by September 1987, had amassed 4,583 cases for elimination. The case was eventually solved when a man named Ian Kelly admitted to having given his DNA to police in place of Colin Pitchfork, who had persuaded Kelly to stand in for him. Colin Pitchfork was then arrested. His DNA matched the samples from the crime scenes and he admitted his responsibility for both murders. He was sentenced to life imprisonment at Leicester Crown Court on 22 January 1988. DNA had demonstrated both innocence and guilt in a landmark case.

The application of DNA to crime scenes had not been recognised when the system was first discovered. There is a possibility that a DNA paternity test was responsible for the criminal conviction of a man for unlawful sexual intercourse at the Old Bailey in the late summer of 1987, as mentioned in *The Blooding* by Joseph Wambaugh (Bantam, 1989), but the case most frequently acknowledged as the first DNA-based conviction involved

Robert Melias, a heavy drinker with a number of convictions for burglary, who was arrested in August 1987. A sample of DNA taken during the course of his arrest was found to match a sample taken in January that year from a rape scene in Bristol. Forensic scientists calculated that the chances the sample had not come from Melias was one in 4 million of the male population. Melias decided to plead guilty and was jailed for eight years on 13 November 1987, two months before the conviction of Colin Pitchfork. The officer in the case, Constable Clive Tippetts, had concluded a worldwide pioneering case solved by DNA.

When Lorraine Benson was found murdered in Raynes Park on 19 December 1988, traces of saliva were found on her body, but they could not be blood-grouped. The new DNA unit did, however, find that a man's handkerchief found at the scene was stained both with Benson's blood and with mucus from a man's nose, from which a DNA profile was obtained. A Vauxhall car at the scene had some strange scratches on it, some of which corresponded with the zip of Benson's jacket, but otherwise there were few clues that could lead to an arrest.

In February 1989, John Dunne, who lived near the murder scene, was arrested for an attempted rape after his fingerprints had been found at that scene. Following a pattern that has led to many subsequent cases being solved, the prisoner's DNA taken on arrest was compared with the DNA profile from a murder scene weeks beforehand, and was found to match. The chances of Dunne not being the person who had used the handkerchief was calculated as one in 1.5 million. An impression of Dunne's teeth matched a bite mark on Benson's arm. He pleaded guilty to the murder and was sentenced to life imprisonment. This was the first case solved with DNA by the Metropolitan Police Forensic Science Laboratory, and the first time that DNA had been obtained from encrusted nasal secretions.

As the DNA database accumulated more records and analysts gained more experience, DNA profiles were identified that were not exact matches but were so close that the suspect must have been a relative of a person whose DNA profile was on record. This was a distinct advantage over fingerprints where heredity does not necessarily generate similar patterns.

In March 2003, Michael Little, a lorry driver, died from a fatal heart attack after a brick had been thrown through the windscreen of his cab from a bridge over the M3 motorway in Surrey, causing him to crash. Detective Chief Inspector Graham Hill from Surrey police was able to establish that DNA from the brick matched DNA found in a nearby Renault car that somebody had tried to steal. A search of the DNA database revealed that a close relative of Craig Harman had similar DNA and that led to inquiries with his family and Harman's subsequent arrest. A voluntary sample from Craig Harman was found to be an exact match, and, faced with this evidence, he pleaded guilty to manslaughter and was sentenced to six years' imprisonment.

Operation Sapphire is a project for reviewing cases of rape and serious sexual assault where there is sufficient DNA evidence to identify the perpetrator. The advances in DNA techniques and the expanding DNA database have sometimes transformed the chances of identifying offenders from the samples taken from crime scenes in the past. These are searched on the database in case a prisoner has given a matching sample in the intervening period. If there is no such match, the crime scene sample details are recorded against the eventuality that future samples given by perpetrators will then link them to past crimes. The match sometimes provides a link with an offender whose apparently respectable background and lifestyle might make such an accusation unbelievable.

In 2001, a DNA sample was given by Nick Keall – a 41-year-old minicab driver from Winchmore Hill, London

– after his arrest for an assault. That sample matched the DNA from a rape that had occurred in May 1989, twelve years earlier, when a man had dragged a female au pair into the grounds of a church, punched her, tried to choke and raped her. The incident had a profound effect on the victim, who had suffered a nervous breakdown. She did, however, have the opportunity to see her attacker sentenced for the assault and the original rape offence when he was jailed for eight years.

After a 77-year-old woman was sexually assaulted by a man who had broken into her sheltered housing flat in Holloway in 1989, she was too traumatised to make a full written statement to police. Nine years later she died, from natural causes, at the age of 86. In 2003, officers from Operation Sapphire reviewed the case and submitted the samples from the crime scene in order to establish a DNA profile of the offender and this in turn led to the identification of Carl Junior Fridye as the offender. He was duly arrested in the West Midlands and pleaded guilty to the offence fourteen years afterwards, notwithstanding the victim having meanwhile died. The victim's family had given up hope that the person would be caught, but the case is an example of how perseverance and the advances in forensic science technology can bring an offender to justice many years later.

Anthony de Boise was an apparently respectable married father with two children, working as an architect for Wandsworth Borough Council. His sister accused him of stealing from his father's estate and during the police investigation, a DNA sample was taken. Although the theft charge that initiated his arrest was later dropped, the DNA sample matched those taken from a series of victims who had been subjected to horrific sexual assaults between 1989 and 1996 by a man dressed as a tramp, who had attacked young girls in the Surrey area – sometimes at knifepoint – creating enormous public fear and huge but unsuccessful police investigations. A scar on de Boise's knee was identified by one of the victims and he was jailed for thirteen years after admitting six counts of indecent assault.

MR SOLLY
JOEL
TELLS
HIS
STORY

MR JUSTICE PHILLIMORE PRESIDES

MR VACHELL K.C
COUNSEL
FOR
THE
PRISONER

WH
'08

FRANZ VON VELTHEIM GIVES EVIDENCE

VON VELTHEIM IN THE DOCK

Courtroom Sketch of Franz von Veltheim

THE COURTROOM SKETCH from William Hartley shows Franz von Veltheim, a colourful German character, who also used the name Franz Ludwig Kurt. A naked body, with hands tied and apparently strangled, found in the River Thames in 1897, was thought to be Franz von Veltheim at one stage because his wife, Maria Louisa von Veltheim (née Yearsley) identified the body several weeks later, after it had been exhumed. Two other women came forward also claiming to be married to him.

But, at the time, von Veltheim was in South Africa as a member of the Cape Mounted Police. He was involved in fomenting rebellion against the Transvaal President Paul Kruger in the events preceding the Boer War and had shot and killed the brother of Solomon Barnato Joel, who was involved in business connected with the Witwatersrand Gold Rush. The jury members were Boers who apparently acquitted von Veltheim through a mixture of antisemitism and antagonism towards the British. Later, von Veltheim sent a series of letters to Solomon Joel that were a mixture of threats and demands for £16,000, and was brought back to stand trial from Paris by Detective Inspector Pentin of the City of London police. Von Veltheim claimed that his letters were a prearranged code whereby his expenses for political subversion were being claimed, but he was convicted and sentenced to twenty years' penal servitude. Franz von Veltheim was released from prison on licence in May 1918 and deported from a repatriation camp in Spalding on 14 February 1919.

DATE:
1908

EXHIBIT:
Hartley's sketches of characters in the von Veltheim trial

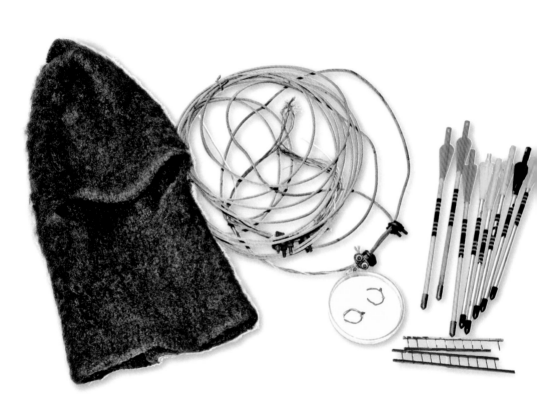

Black Panther Tools

THE EXHIBITS AND part of a courtoon model relate to the case of Donald Neilson, known as the 'Black Panther', who kidnapped Lesley Whittle in the 1970s.

On the morning of Tuesday, 14 January 1975, Mrs Dorothy Whittle, who lived in the village of Highley in Shropshire, went to her 17-year-old daughter's bedroom and found her missing. She had checked on Lesley at about 1 a.m. and found her fast asleep, but now her bed was empty and there was no sign of her in the house. Lesley's clothes were still in the bedroom. Her late father, George, had established a successful coach business but died five years earlier. Dorothy and Lesley lived alone in the house, whilst Lesley's married brother, Ronald, lived elsewhere and ran the business. Dorothy tried to telephone her son, but found that the line did not work, so she drove to Ronald's house. The telephone line had in fact been cut. Ronald drove round the village looking for his sister while his wife, Gaynor, checked the house. Gaynor found a message with strips of letters made by a Dymo tape machine that demanded a £50,000 ransom. The demand instructed that the money should be ready for delivery according to instructions that would be telephoned to one of three public boxes at the Swan shopping centre in Kidderminster that night. The message threatened to kill Lesley if the instructions were not followed precisely, or if police were called in.

DATE:
1975

EXHIBIT:
Balaclava, tethering wire and other items from the Donald Neilson case

There had been some publicity three years earlier when George Whittle's former wife had taken legal action to secure payment from his estate after years of being told that he could not afford to increase her small allowance. (George had not been legally married to Dorothy.) The coach business was successful, but the family did not have wealth on a scale that would normally be at risk from this sort of crime: there were far wealthier and better known families in the area. There was £300 in cash in a briefcase due to be taken to the bank that had been left untouched by whoever had abducted Lesley.

Gaynor went to Ronald's office with the news that Lesley had been kidnapped, and he in turn phoned West Mercia Police. Detective Chief Superintendent Bob Booth gave orders that inquiries were to be low-key and unobtrusive, and that a news blackout should be imposed. Some aspects of the ransom demand seemed amateurish and the police at first speculated whether the case could be a student prank, possibly connected with Lesley's boyfriend who was studying at Sheffield University. Specialist officers from Scotland Yard and surveillance equipment were brought in to help with the investigation, which was a very rare event for anywhere in Britain – even taking into account the Hosein brothers' kidnap of Muriel McKay in 1969 (described from p. 198). Under police supervision, Ronald Whittle took two suitcases of money to the Kidderminster shopping centre to comply with the directions. A freelance journalist had heard about the operation and publicised the kidnap; the police refused to confirm or deny the story. This resulted in news of the police operation being broadcast on television in advance of the arranged rendezvous for ransom pay-ment instructions. Out of concern for Lesley's safety, Ronald Whittle was recalled and Bob Booth gave a press conference to try to control the information given out by the media. Although the telephone boxes were not attended because of the police operation being publicised, monitoring of the lines revealed that those telephones had all rung around midnight.

The ransom note demanded that if there had been no contact, the exercise should be repeated the following evening, and Ronald Whittle again waited by the call boxes on the Wednesday night, accompanied, unfortunately, by press and onlookers whom the police tried to keep from the scene. A telephone call was received at the Whittles' home demanding that the money be taken to a subway in Gloucester, 50 miles away. within ninety minutes. Ronald Whittle drove there, but this call was fake, made by a couple in need of money who had seen the Whittle telephone number publicised and wanted to make some cash for themselves. (A woman was later sentenced to four years' imprisonment.)

That same Wednesday evening, a security guard was shot outside a goods depot at Dudley, 13 miles away, after he had challenged a man acting suspiciously. Bullets recovered from the scene were matched with ammunition found at the murders of two sub-postmasters: one at Higher Baxenden near Accrington, Lancashire, in 1974, where Derek Astin was killed; the second, in November 1974, at Langley, near Oldbury in the West Midlands, where Sydney Grayland lost his life. There had been a series of murders at sub-post offices, a third having occurred at Harrogate in February 1974, when Donald Skepper had been murdered. The Harrogate and Higher Baxenden cases had involved a night-time intruder breaking into the premises. These and other burglaries between 1971 and 1974 involved the suspect gaining entry by using a brace and bit, and were starting to be linked by the police forces involved.

The implications of these offences and any link to the kidnapping of Lesley Whittle were not realised until Thursday, 23 January 1975, a week after the security guard had been shot, when an abandoned Morris 1300 car in a nearby car park was reported to the police, who discovered that it had false number plates and had been stolen. It also contained rope, a torch, envelopes and a cassette tape. The envelopes, all numbered, contained Dymo tape instructions that set out the ransom trail that Ronald Whittle would have followed on the Tuesday and Wednesday nights. The tape (later found to be a duplicate) played Lesley Whittle's voice giving instructions to go to a telephone box near junction 10 of the M6 motorway. The car and the material found in it linked the shooting of the security guard and the kidnapping of Lesley Whittle to a dangerous criminal – the 'Black Panther'. The name came from his masked burglaries and murders carried out at night. The sub-post office offences had involved a masked and armed intruder waking up a member of the family in the early hours of the morning and demanding money. It therefore seemed likely that Lesley Whittle had been abducted in this way. She was wearing only her dressing gown and slippers.

Meanwhile, on the Thursday evening, the night after the security guard had been shot, a telephone call had been received on the Whittles' home number at 11.35 p.m. by Len Rudd, the transport manager of the coach company. Lesley's recorded voice gave instructions to go to Kidsgrove post office telephone box. Ronald Whittle then set off on a complicated 50-mile drive to Kidsgrove, in the Staffordshire police area, and after much searching, found the Dymo tape message that directed him to Bathpool Park, near Kidsgrove. After half an hour's search, he went home, as he could not follow the instruction trail. It later became evident that these instructions had been prepared hastily after the kidnapper had abandoned his stolen car with his original pre-prepared instructions in the Dudley car park. There were no further calls from the kidnapper.

Ronald Whittle could not be blamed for not being able to follow the clues to deliver the ransom in the dark. Two schoolboys eventually found a torch placed on top of a drainage shaft that had been referred to in the instructions and a taped message that said, 'Drop suitcase into hole.' On 6 March, a police officer entered the shaft with a torch and climbed to the bottom, where he found a Dymo tape machine. After further searches of what transpired to be a network of tunnels and shafts, Detective Constable Philip Maskery found a blue dressing gown and then the naked body of Lesley Whittle, with a wire noose tethered around her neck like a collar. There were no signs of sexual assault or other violence. The wire tether was 5ft long, but it had caught on a piece of metal and the extra tightness had prevented her feet reaching the floor of the tunnel below the platform on which she had been standing. This had caused extensive pressure on the vagal nerve and the carotid artery in her neck, which in turn caused her heart to stop.

The Staffordshire chief constable called in Commander John Morrison of Scotland Yard, who took up the investigation. He was assisted by Detective Chief Inspector Wally Boreham, but tracing the Black Panther was a difficult task. The police had partial fingerprints, but few other clues about his identity. It was not until nine months later, on Thursday, 11 December 1975, that the case was solved by the actions of PCs Tony White and Stuart Mackenzie, who followed their instincts by stopping and questioning a man in Mansfield Woodhouse, Nottinghamshire. The man threatened the officers with a sawn-off shotgun and forced them to drive their police car at gunpoint towards Sherwood Forest. The officers acted calmly and complied with his demands until they took their chance at a road junction. As they asked the gunman which road they should take and his attention was distracted by a road sign, PC Mackenzie braked hard and PC White knocked the man's shotgun away, injuring his hand as the gun fired. The suspect was eventually overpowered and taken to Mansfield police station. He was interviewed overnight but gave very little information about himself.

The prisoner's fingerprints were taken and found to match the Black Panther's prints that had been circulated, so Detective Chief Superintendent John McNaught rang Commander Morrison to tell him that they believed they had him in custody. His true identity was later established as Donald Neilson, and when the police searched his house in Grangefield Avenue, Bradford, they found an arsenal of weapons, ammunition, survival equipment, rope and wire. After some hours of being reluctant to admit what he had done, Neilson eventually made a long confession, admitting the post office murders and the abduction of Lesley Whittle, but denying responsibility for her death.

Neilson's trial began at Oxford Crown Court on 14 June 1976, where he pleaded guilty to kidnapping Lesley Whittle and to blackmail charges, but disputed the murder indictment: the issues being how she had fallen off the platform and how much harm Neilson had intended to inflict on her. The prosecution argued that he would have feared her seeing his face, as she would have been able to identify him as her kidnapper. Neilson was convicted of murder rather than manslaughter and was sentenced to life imprisonment. He died aged 75.

The Lesley Whittle case demonstrated that media publicity can affect the chances of the police being able to conduct a monitored rendezvous and that it can severely reduce the chance of a kidnap victim being released unharmed. It also showed the difficulty of one individual family member trying to make sense of complex instructions in the dark without company and support. It was a very difficult judgement to make about whether to risk anybody being seen to be waiting for a telephone call once the media had broadcast details of the operation. Separate crimes and crime scenes linked in hindsight to the case were invariably occurring in different police force areas. Sometimes sheer chance and bravery results in an arrest that hours of detective work have failed to produce.

Since the Lesley Whittle case, kidnap cases have been resolved successfully with the media voluntarily agreeing not to publicise details of the police operations. The responsibility for Lesley Whittle's death lay fairly and squarely with Donald Neilson, who had killed previously when he was at risk of being identified, but nobody will ever know for certain whether things that could and should have been done differently might have made a difference to Lesley being released alive.

In 1969, Alick McKay was deputy chairman of the *News of the World* and was temporarily using the company Rolls-Royce normally used by the chairman. Arthur and Nizamodeen Hosein, two Trinidadian brothers from Hertfordshire, were observing the car with the intention of kidnapping the wife of Rupert Murdoch, and holding her for ransom. Just before 8 p.m. on 29 December, Alick McKay returned to his Wimbledon home and found his wife Muriel missing, but her handbag, now an exhibit in the museum, had been left behind. After midnight, a telephone call from 'Mafia M3' was received at the house demanding a £1 million ransom, not realising they had the wrong victim. There were debates about whether it was a publicity stunt and whether publicity would help towards the safe return of Mrs McKay. In the event, the case caused enormous publicity, and the McKays' telephone was soon besieged with calls from reporters and hoaxers. A second call was received from Mafia M3 referring to a letter that would be in the post, and, on the Wednesday morning, a letter duly arrived, apparently from Muriel, but with no ransom payment details. On 1 February instructions arrived for the McKays' son, Ian, to go to north London, where further messages would be left. A police officer posing as Ian McKay then received a call at a public telephone box that he should leave a suitcase of money by the roadside at Dane End, Hertfordshire, at a spot marked by paper flowers. The officer went to the destination, but the police surveillance operation frightened off the Hosein brothers.

A second operation to leave money for the kidnappers was also aborted when a member of the public who was concerned about the suitcase called in the local police, who had not been informed about the operation. Eventually the repeated sightings of a Volvo car owned by the Hosein brothers led to police calling at their address in Rooks Farm, Hertfordshire, and to their arrest. Nizamodeen was identified by an officer as having been driving the Volvo near the money pick-up scene and an exercise book was found that matched the paper used for the letters from Muriel McKay. No trace of Muriel McKay was ever found.

Both Hosein brothers were convicted at the Old Bailey of murder and sentenced to life imprisonment, despite no trace of their victim's body ever being found. There was speculation that she may have been murdered, dismembered and disposed of at Rooks Farm, where there was a meat grinder used for pig feed and in which two spots of human blood were found. It was the first kidnap and ransom case ever to have been committed in Britain, a distressing catalyst for improving police techniques for the future, and a rare example of a conviction for murder where no body was found.

On 5 July 1984 a group of men seized Umaru Dikko in his garden in Porchester Terrace and manhandled their struggling victim into a van with blacked-out windows. Umaru Dikko was an important member of the Nigerian government led by his brother-in-law, President Shehu Shagari, but had fled to London in 1983 when a military coup overthrew the government. The new Nigerian government accused him of corruption and embezzlement. Umaro Dikko's secretary called the police and a search was launched. As part of that search, customs officers at Stansted Airport became suspicious of two large crates that were due to be loaded on to a Nigeria Airways aircraft as diplomatic baggage. One of the crates gave off a 'medical smell'. Despite the presence of Nigerian diplomats, the crates had not been labelled correctly as diplomatic baggage, and customs officers insisted on opening them.

Inside one crate was a heavily sedated Umaru Dikko with Israeli anaesthetist Dr Levi-Arie Shapiro, who had been given the task of keeping Dikko alive and sedated during the flight. The second crate contained a Nigerian diplomat and a second Israeli. Dikko was taken to hospital but found to be uninjured. Four people were convicted of abducting him and imprisoned for periods of between ten and fourteen years. Those involved were Major Mohammed Yusufu, who had planned the operation from the Nigerian High Commission, Dr Shapiro, Alexander Barak and Felix Abithol. The Nigerian government denied any involvement, and later requested Dikko's extradition, which failed. Umaru Dikko later returned to Nigeria when the government changed. He died, aged 78, in 2014.

One early Sunday evening, on 24 March 1996, George Fraghistas, a member of a Greek shipping family, was set upon by four men in Maida Vale as he parked his car, bundled into the boot of another car and driven off. He may have been mistaken for his cousin, also named George Fraghistas, who was much wealthier. Thirty-six hours later, his family in Athens received a multi-million-pound ransom demand. Members of the family then flew to London to undertake negotiations, which involved more than fifty calls with the kidnappers. The police were able to make a number of arrests on the night of 2 April. Two men were conducting ransom negotiations from a car in Golders Green, one man was arrested outside a house in Hogan Mews, Paddington, where George Fraghistas was being held, and a further suspect was found inside that house.

George Fraghistas was found in a cupboard where he had been held for the nine days hooded, blindfolded and forced to wear earplugs. He was shocked and distressed, but otherwise physically unharmed by his ordeal. He appeared at a press conference soon after his release, thereby giving the media a more authentic story in return for their silence whilst the operation was in progress. Two Greeks, Constantinos Korkolis and Thanassis Zografos, and two Frenchmen, Jean-Marc Mereu and Djemel Moussaoui, were convicted of the kidnapping; the Old Bailey jury rejected their imaginative defence that the incident was no more than an elaborate plan to extort money from his own family. They were sentenced to sixteen years' imprisonment.

48 Crossbow

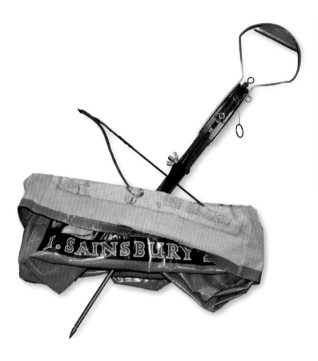

DATE:
1998

EXHIBIT:
Crossbow with remote firing device used to threaten supermarket customers

THE CROSSBOW, WITH its concealing bag, was used to threaten Sainsbury's supermarket customers.

In December 1994, six branches of Barclays Bank received booby-trapped explosive packages. Later, Sainsbury's supermarket branches were also targeted, receiving a total of thirty-seven devices, ranging from dangerous to lethal. They were invariably accompanied by a calling card marked 'Welcome to the Mardi Gra Experience'. Individual customers of Sainsbury's were also targeted and incidents continued to occur until 28 April 1998. Thousands of plastic cards capable of being used in cash dispensers were distributed through one edition of *Exchange & Mart* magazine. This special offer was in fact a response made at the request of the criminal and his attempts to extort money from major businesses. An associated PIN was published in a code.

In an operation led by Detective Superintendent Jeff Rees, police officers were able to close in on the suspect very quickly at an automated cash dispenser in Whitton, south-west London, assisted by a computer program that alerted police to a particular transaction being attempted. The offender, Edgar Pearce, had been attempting to use random cash machines to withdraw the money he was extorting, but was defeated by a technological enhancement to computer systems operating the dispensers. Pearce had made thirty-six explosive devices, some of which had injured staff and customers. He was found to have a specially adapted briefcase to carry a crossbow with which he had threatened customers, and a large number of photographs of Sainsbury's consumers. Pearce, then 61 years old, was jailed for twenty-one years in April 1999, his defence making a plea that he was suffering from a degenerative brain problem called Binswanger's disease.

Large companies who rely heavily on maintaining a good reputation amongst their customers can appear to be vulnerable to demands for cash in return for not disrupting their business, but collaboration between those organisations and the police, determination and sophisticated methods of tracking can lead to detection of the offender.

In 1988, Heinz (the food company) and Pedigree pet foods had both been threatened by an anonymous person who claimed their products would be contaminated unless they agreed to pay out a large sum of money (also through a bank's automated cash machine system). The threat was backed up by a jar of baby food being contaminated with caustic soda. Some payments were made to the perpetrator and this revealed an apparently random pattern of using cash machines in different parts of the country, but the offender was eventually caught by a large police observation operation whilst he was withdrawing cash in Woolwich. He turned out to be Rodney Whitchelo, a former CID officer, who was sentenced to seventeen years' imprisonment on 17 December 1990. The case led to companies reviewing their design of tamper-proof food containers.

Mauser Pistol

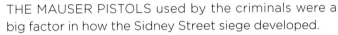

THE MAUSER PISTOLS used by the criminals were a big factor in how the Sidney Street siege developed.

This famous incident originated from the murder of three City of London police officers on 16 December 1910 when they disturbed a gang of Latvian immigrants breaking into a jeweller's shop in Houndsditch. Sergeants Charles Tucker and Robert Bentley, and PC Walter Choat were killed by the burglars' gunfire, and two of their colleagues were seriously injured. The incident was one of the most serious in British history for loss of life of officers by criminals. The gang escaped, but one of them, George Gardstein, died from gunshot wounds accidentally inflicted by one of his own side. A manhunt then ensued for the gang, including one known as 'Peter the Painter'.

On 2 January 1911 the Metropolitan Police responded to information that two of the gang were hiding at No. 100 Sidney Street. Overnight, the police quietly cordoned off the area and evacuated residents from neighbouring buildings. The owner of the second-floor flat was a Mrs Betty Gershon. The gunmen took her skirt and shoes to prevent her from leaving the building, but she was allowed to go to the ground floor and it was from there that she was rescued by the police. At dawn on 3 January, Detective Inspector Frederick Wensley, who was in charge of Whitechapel's CID, knocked on the door, but received no reply. He then threw pebbles at the window to try to start communications with the two

DATE:
1911

EXHIBIT:
Mauser pistol
with stock, from
Sidney Street
siege

men inside, but was met with a hail of gunfire. Wensley's assistant, Sergeant Ben Leeson, was wounded, and Wensley, himself unarmed, arranged for Leeson's evacuation across rooftops, but was pinned down behind a chimney stack by gunfire from the men, who were identified as Fritz Svaars and a man known only as 'Josef'. The Mauser pistols used by the men were capable of rapid, accurate fire up to 1,000m, and were far better than the police's mixture of bulldog revolvers, shotguns and .22 weapons normally used on the rifle ranges.

The commissioner, Sir Edward Henry, was not in London, so Deputy Commissioner Major Frederick Wodehouse took charge and asked for military reinforcements to provide better firepower. This request went through the Home Secretary, Winston Churchill, who attended the scene himself just before 12 p.m. He was probably the only Home Secretary to have taken personal charge at an operational incident and arguably should have taken a more detached role, but Churchill was forthright and did not shrink from leadership situations. It is also possible that a government minister should have been on hand when both military and police forces were being deployed. In modern times, the government would set up the Cabinet Office Briefing Room (COBRA) to co-ordinate the response of different government departments.

At 10.45 a.m., twenty-one marksmen from the Scots Guards had arrived the short distance from the Tower of London. They took up positions and started to return effective fire against the gunmen. This drove the gunmen from the second floor to the ground floor. About 500 officers were needed to keep back the large crowds that had gathered. Winston Churchill decided that heavier firepower was required and called for a Maxim gun, but before this arrived, the house caught fire – possibly due to gunfire, but also perhaps started by the gunmen as a diversion. One of the men, probably Josef, put his head out of the window and immediately fell back, apparently shot by the soldiers. The shooting from the house then slowed and the fire took a firmer hold; Churchill ordered the fire service not to risk their lives trying to extinguish it. The last shots from the house were heard shortly after 2 p.m. The roof of the house collapsed and it was clear that nobody could be alive inside. The fire was then extinguished, but a senior fire officer, Charles Pearson, was killed by a falling wall as he inspected the damage inside the house. Two bodies were found, one of whom had been killed by gunfire, the other by the effects of smoke.

This large-scale armed siege suddenly became an unexpected crisis for the police to resolve, and a challenge for detailed investigation to support a prosecution.

The police eventually caught the surviving members of the gang responsible for the Houndsditch jeweller's shop burglary. They had a mixture of extreme left-wing political views, but were united in their belief in theft of property and using violence. The prosecutions were complicated by language difficulties and piecing together the criminals' chaotic lifestyles, so only one conviction was achieved, itself overturned on appeal.

The incident led to a review of the firearms available to the police and better training for the officers using them. On the block of flats now standing on the site is a small red plaque that records the loss of life of Charles Pearson, whose death is often forgotten in relation to the incident.

The Mauser pistol was an exhibit in the Sidney Street case and was presented to the Crime Museum in 1987 by an assistant chief constable of Sussex, following the death of a Lewes magistrate who left instructions that it should be returned to the police after his death.

Balaclava and Hat

ON SUNDAY, 28 September 1975, three men, one armed with a double-barrelled sawn-off shotgun, the others with handguns, attempted to rob the managers of the Knightsbridge Spaghetti House restaurant of the week-end's takings (amounting to about £13,000). They wore balaclavas and hats to disguise their faces, and forced nine Italian staff members into the basement, but one man had managed to escape and raise the alarm. The incident then became the first test of contingency plans for sieges that had been drawn up by police and government agencies.

A cordon was established to keep road traffic and the public well away from the premises. The gunmen claimed to represent the 'Black Liberation Front' and demanded that they should be released and flown to another country, but this was refused. The gunmen had access to the radio, and news programmes were allowed to broadcast details of official decisions that no concessions would ever be made to them. One of the hostages, who appeared to be unwell, was released on the afternoon of the first day.

In order to reassure the hostage takers and to encourage them to surrender, the Italian ambassador wrote to them: '[I am] aware that the Italian hostages have received so far no maltreatment by you and your friends. I declare on my honour that I am fully prepared to bear witness of this in court, so that it may be taken

DATE:
1975

EXHIBIT:
Improvised balaclava and hat used at Spaghetti House siege

209

into consideration by the Authorities.' That letter is now in the museum, with the weapons involved.

The leader, a Nigerian named Franklin Davies, was identified, and the police arrested an associate of his. The *Daily Mail* suppressed their hard-won scoop about this development at the personal request of the commissioner, Sir Robert Mark, and when a false message was passed to Davies that this associate had been selling information to the newspapers, it completed a demoralisation process and led to the peaceful surrender on the sixth day of the incident.

Although, in hindsight, it was regarded as a robbery that went wrong rather than a politically motivated siege involving terrorists, it provided valuable experience for the police.

A few months later, there was a siege in Balcombe Street, London.

The IRA terrorist campaign in London in 1974–75 had created a great deal of fear in the city and across the country, as well as a list of murder victims that included Ross McWhirter, Professor Gordon Hamilton Fairley, PC Stephen Tibble QPM and explosives officer Captain Roger Goad GC, BEM. Although there was no predictable pattern to the attacks, which comprised a variety of methods involving bombs in shop doorways, doorstep shootings, car booby-trap explosive devices and drive-by shootings, the police mounted Operation Combo to provide a rapid and effective response to future attacks in central London.

This operation culminated on 6 December 1975, when the occupants of a Ford Cortina passed Scott's restaurant in Mayfair and one man from the car fired two shots at the restaurant. Another occupant tried, unsuccessfully, to fire a Sten machine gun but it jammed. Two plain-clothes officers from Operation Combo made a note of the car registration and circulated details of its description as it travelled towards Oxford Street. Inspector John Purnell and Sergeant Philip McVeigh were posted in plain clothes in Oxford Street and saw the Cortina; they fulfilled a London taxi driver's dream by introducing themselves and ordering him to 'follow that Ford Cortina!' McVeigh radioed a commentary of the car's movements, but the terrorists became suspicious and stopped in a side turning. Purnell and McVeigh then left their taxi and approached the Cortina, but the terrorists, hearing police sirens in the distance, left their car on foot, broke into a run and fired their guns at the pursuing, unarmed, officers. Eventually police reinforcements intercepted them and an exchange of gunfire developed between the terrorists and Special Patrol Group officers. A Flying Squad car arrived and a chase on foot resulted in the terrorists running into the quiet Balcombe Street and forcing their way into a first-floor flat, No. 22b, belonging to John and Sheila Matthews, who had been quietly watching television. The gang took the couple hostage with the intention of bargaining their way out of the situation.

The police cordoned off the area, and screens were erected so that police activity could not be broadcast by the media. Negotiations were conducted with the terrorists by (later Commissioner and Lord) Peter Imbert and others, which eventually, after nearly six days, resulted in the sudden surrender of the men, shortly after the police discreetly leaked the information that SAS units were being called in. They had been discussing a plan to break out of the flat using Mr and Mrs Matthews as human shields. Detective Chief Superintendent Jim Nevill later displayed to the media the great array of weapons that had been used by the gang.

The terrorists, Hugh Doherty, Martin 'Joe' O'Connell (the bomb maker), Eddie Butler and Harry Duggan were arrested and later convicted of multiple counts of murder. They were sentenced to life imprisonment, putting an end to a particularly prolific and violent spell of terrorism. They served twenty-three years in mainland British prisons before being transferred to Portlaoise prison in Northern Ireland. They were released in 1999 under the Belfast Good Friday agreement. The Commissioner's Annual Report for 1977 mentioned the crucial role played in the prosecution case by thirty-six identifications made by Scotland Yard's fingerprint experts. John Purnell, Philip McVeigh and Henry Dowsell were awarded George Medals for their courage during the incident.

51 Note to the SAS

THE PIECE OF notepaper signed jointly by Deputy Assistant Commissioner John Dellow and the commander of 22 Squadron of the Special Air Service (SAS), Lieutenant Colonel Michael Rose, was a formal recognition that the control of this famous incident was being transferred to the SAS by the Metropolitan Police to be resolved by force rather than by negotiation. In military terms, it was 'aid to the civil power'. The events that took place directly after the piece of paper was signed were recorded on television, and did much to enhance the reputation of the SAS throughout the world as foremost specialists in ending sieges with the least possible loss of life of hostages. All but one of the terrorists involved were shot dead by SAS officers.

The incident started at 11.32 a.m. on an otherwise quiet Wednesday morning on 30 April 1980, when PC Trevor Lock, an officer of the Diplomatic Protection Group, was standing in the hallway of the Iranian embassy in Queen Anne's Gate, London. Trevor Lock saw a man with a gun in the entrance hall and tackled him, in an unsuccessful attempt to disarm him, and was overpowered

DATE:
1980

EXHIBIT:
Note transferring authority to deal with siege to the SAS

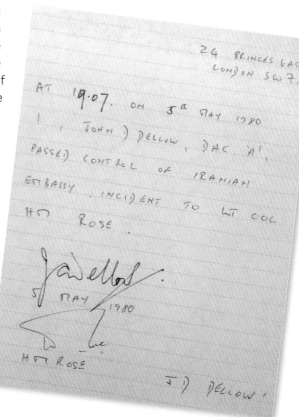

by five other armed accomplices who rapidly took over the embassy building and seized a total of twenty-six staff and visitors at gunpoint. At that time, Metropolitan Police officers on armed protection duty wore their gun holsters underneath their ordinary uniform jackets. A gunman rapidly patted the officer's uniform as a form of search, and noticed the bulge of his concealed firearm, but PC Lock told him that it was his notebook and other documents required for police work. For the remainder of the subsequent siege until its culmination in the attack by the SAS, Trevor Lock did not use his gun, fearing that if he initiated any attack, he would only be able to kill two of the terrorists at best, and the lives of many more hostages would be lost. Except for one occasion, he, therefore, kept his uniform jacket on throughout the incident and restricted his drinking so as not to require the toilet and the risk of supervision from the terrorists that might reveal his firearm. He displayed great initiative, restraint and courage throughout the six days of the siege, acting as a mediator and a conduit for messages between the terrorists and police, at one stage forcefully silencing one of the hostages, Abbas Lavasani, whose vehement arguments with the terrorists was endangering the lives of all the others.

The first senior officers to attend were Chief Superintendent Les Clark from Gerald Road police station and Chief Superintendent Roger Bromley of the Diplomatic Protection Group. Bromley made initial contact with the terrorists and heard that they were demanding the release within twenty-four hours of ninety-one prisoners held in Iran, an end to Iranian political murders and an aircraft to fly them, with their hostages, out of the country.

The police established control rooms in nearby buildings, firstly to enable the most senior officers from the various services involved in intelligence, crime investigation and uniform operations to confer together and to ensure that police operations outside the embassy were consistent with the messages delivered by negotiators, and secondly to ensure that the details of uniform police operations maintaining a cordon around the building were properly controlled. The Cabinet met at Downing Street and supported the recommendation of Commissioner Sir David McNee that no concessions should be made. The government's Cabinet Office Briefing Room co-ordinated further details of Whitehall's actions.

It was a period of political volatility in Iran with various factions regularly organising demonstrations on the streets of London, and a protest soon developed next to the police cordons, complicating the situation significantly by their noise, chanting of political slogans, and sporadic acts of violence. The demonstrators were marshalled into a confined area and allowed to leave, but not return. This provoked protests from some Iranians throughout the world and the police had to be careful about the implications for American hostages then being held in Iran.

As tension periodically rose and fell, the negotiators endeavoured to calm the situation without making immediate concessions to the main demands. The telephones were disconnected, provision of food negotiated and the release of five of the hostages achieved at various stages, usually because of medical problems. Gradually, the background to the terrorists became clearer: they were members of the Democratic Revolutionary Front for the Liberation of Arabistan, campaigning for independence for a southern Iranian region, also known as Khuzestan, where Iranian revolutionary guards had opened fire on a demonstration in 1979, killing around 220 people and injuring approximately 600 more. Gradually the police put together a list of the people held in the embassy, the hostage takers and where they were located within the building. On the sixth day, the situation deteriorated, shots were heard from inside the embassy and the body of Abbas Lavasani was dumped outside the building. It was unclear as to whether another hostage had been killed, and the police decided they should hand the operation over to the SAS, who had been quietly preparing for this eventuality.

SAS officers abseiled from the roof of the building, broke through windows and released stun grenades to create fear, temporary paralysis and an opportunity to take rapid control of the building. The SAS shot five of the six terrorists dead; the sixth, Fowzi Nejad, mingled with hostages being rushed into the embassy garden but was later identified, separated from the hostages and arrested. All the remaining hostages were released alive. The stun grenades used by the SAS started a fire that gradually took hold and burnt out most of the building in a period in which there was uncertainty about the safety of fire service officers. Prime Minister Margaret Thatcher attended an informal debriefing session of the SAS officers involved to congratulate them on their success.

Fowzi Nejad was convicted and eventually paroled in 2008, and Trevor Lock was awarded the George Medal for his bravery.

Collating the evidence from various witnesses and background intelligence was a major operation in itself. The siege represented an enormous achievement for the Metropolitan Police despite some regret that it had not been possible to achieve the ideal of a peaceful surrender by the terrorists through negotiation, as had been achieved earlier with the Spaghetti House and Balcombe Street sieges.

In his annual report for 1980, the commissioner, Sir David McNee, wrote:

Many people were involved in this difficult and complex operation from local residents to Cabinet Ministers and all made their contribution. The keynote was co-operation but I would like particularly to mention the courage and resourcefulness of Police Constable Lock. The hostages spoke afterwards of the comfort they drew from his calmness and steadfastness over the six days. His actions were magnificent and were a powerful illustration of the latent qualities to be found in the ordinary London bobby. We are lucky to have such men who seem to rise to every occasion.

Yvonne Fletcher's Hat

THE UNIFORM HAT belonged to Yvonne Fletcher: the 25-year-old officer who was murdered by 'diplomats' from the Libyan embassy. Her hat marked the place she had fallen and remained on the eerily empty roadway of St James's Square for some days as a poignant symbol of the frustration and dangerous stalemate that occurred as the embassy was surrounded by the police. The hat is displayed in the Crime Museum with the helmet of PC John Murray who was on duty beside Yvonne Fletcher and who has campaigned ever since for action to be taken against any surviving people responsible.

On 17 April 1984, Yvonne Fletcher was part of a group of officers sent to police a demonstration in St James's Square organised by opponents of the regime of Colonel Gaddafi. The Libyan embassy was known as the 'Libyan People's Bureau' and was staffed by Gaddafi extremists rather than conventional diplomats.

At 10.18 a.m., whilst the noisy, but peaceful protests were in progress, shots rang out, apparently from the first floor of the bureau, injuring several demonstrators and fatally striking Yvonne Fletcher in the back. She was rushed to Westminster Hospital but died soon after arrival, accompanied by John Murray, who promised her as she died that he would ensure her assailant was brought to justice.

It was clear that the 'diplomats' had murdered Yvonne Fletcher, and the police then cordoned off the embassy

DATE:
1984

EXHIBIT:
The uniform hat of Yvonne Fletcher

217

to prevent any of the occupants from leaving. The siege lasted eleven days, during which attempts were made to persuade the occupants to surrender. The police organised their operations according to established practices and experience of other sieges, and were guided by the Whitehall's Cabinet Office because of the serious nature of this diplomatic incident. Gaddafi made protests about the refusal of British authorities to allow his diplomats to leave the embassy. In Libya, the British embassy in Tripoli was besieged, six British nationals were held as hostages and there was a risk of further reprisals against many British citizens living there. A decision was made by the UK government that they had no choice but to respect the law of diplomatic privilege, and, on the day of Yvonne Fletcher's funeral, accompanied by much media protest, the 'diplomats' were escorted from the premises and expelled from the country. Michael Winner shared his outrage at the opinion, apparently expressed by a member of the government, that the incident involved 'only a police officer', and instigated the Police Memorial Trust, a charity that erected a memorial at the location of Yvonne Fletcher's death.

Diplomatic relations between Britain and Libya were severed, and two years later American aeroplanes bombed Libya from British airbases. Later, the British government undertook a series of negotiations with Libya during the premiership of Tony Blair. This resulted in the surrender of two men who then stood trial for the destruction of Pan Am flight 103 at Lockerbie, compensation to US (but not British) victims of Libyan-sponsored terrorism, the end of Libya's nuclear and chemical weapons programme and an end to international sanctions imposed on Libya. In 1999, Colonel Gaddafi accepted Libya's responsibility for the death of Yvonne Fletcher and offered compensation. In June 2007, British detectives visited Libya and were allowed to interview the two main suspects in Yvonne Fletcher's murder and, by 2009, a legal opinion had been reached that there was sufficient evidence to prosecute two prominent members of the embassy staff.

In 2011, an uprising in Libya against Gaddafi was backed by NATO and Gaddafi was murdered by his fellow countrymen. Many influential Gaddafi supporters were killed or fled the country, and the overthrow of the government gave fresh impetus to hopes that court proceedings might be possible against those responsible.

Salah Eddin Khalifa, who escaped from the back door of the embassy, later admitted to firing shots but was subsequently killed in Libya. Abdulmagid Salah Ameri was named in a British newspaper as a potential suspect gunman. In November 2021, thirty-seven years after the incident, the High Court considered John Murray's application for £1 damages against Saleh Ibrahim Mabrouk and heard much of the evidence that had been accumulated by the Metropolitan Police and which thereby reached the public domain. In February 1984 the Libyan People's Bureau was run by four individuals: Maatouk Mohamed Maatouk, Abdul Qadir Al-Baghdadi, Omar Sudani and Saleh Mabrouk. Mabrouk and Sudani objected to police civil staff beginning to erect crowd barriers to control the demonstration, and Mabrouk was heard to threaten any proposed demonstration with guns. Mabrouk and Sudani were arrested and taken to Vine Street police station for obstructing police, and despite their being in police custody when the shots were fired from the embassy, Mabrouk was held to have been partly responsible for the incident not least because he would have received instructions from Gaddafi for the bureau staff to act violently to those opposed to the regime. John Murray was duly awarded the damages he sought, a decision that resulted in applause from those attending the court hearing.

Yvonne Fletcher's hat was removed from the street under the windows of the embassy during the siege, at the risk of further potential gunfire, so that it could be placed on her coffin at her funeral, a courageous act by a junior officer that reflected the outrage felt by so many people that 'diplomats' could murder a police officer on the streets of London and escape justice.

53 Roger Casement Warrant

ROGER CASEMENT WAS born in 1864 in Dublin and joined the diplomatic service on behalf of Britain, as it was before Irish independence in 1922. He was a champion of human rights, compiled a notable report about abuses in Congo, served in Peru, where he also reported on similar abuses, was knighted in 1911 and resigned as a diplomat in 1913. In August 1914, just after Britain had declared war on Germany, he arranged a meeting with a German diplomat in New York, proposing that Germany should sell arms to Irish rebels so that they could mount an insurrection and divert British troops from the First World War. He wrote a letter to the *Irish Independent* urging Irishmen to fight against England rather than Germany. He later travelled to Germany and made attempts to recruit an 'Irish brigade' from Irish prisoners of war to support a war of independence from Britain. The head of Special Branch, Superintendent Patrick Quinn, ordered a search of Casement's London address, where three private diaries, a notebook and a ledger were found. The diaries related to Casement's observations as consul in the Congo and Rio de Janeiro as well as time spent in the UK and France, but they also revealed details of his homosexual activities

DATE:
1916

EXHIBIT:
Arrest warrant for treason issued by Bow Street court on 13 May 1916

(then illegal). Claims have been made that the diaries were forgeries aimed at discrediting Casement.

In April 1916, the Germans transported 20,000 rifles, machine guns and ammunition in a German ship, *Libau*, disguised as a Norwegian vessel, but the ship was intercepted by HMS *Bluebell*, assisted by the fact that Royal Navy codebreakers had intercepted details of the voyage. The German crew were treated as prisoners of war and the ship was scuttled on 22 April. Casement had travelled separately, in a German submarine, and was put ashore in Tralee Bay, County Kerry, but was arrested on 21 April. The Easter Rebellion (or Rising), organised by the Irish Republican Brotherhood, was an armed insurrection against British rule in Ireland and started three days later, on 24 April 1916.

Sir Basil Thomson interviewed Casement at Scotland Yard where he denied that his proposed Irish Brigade would fight against Britain, but his defence was not helped by the German code book found in his possession. He was prosecuted for treason despite legal argument over whether the terms of the Treason Act 1351 applied to acts undertaken abroad, and he was convicted and executed at Pentonville prison on 3 August 1916.

The widespread loss of life in the Great War polarised loyalties, and it was little wonder that Casement was regarded as a traitor in Britain. His knighthood was withdrawn. After nearly fifty years, and the passage of much history, Casement's remains were repatriated to Ireland in 1965 where he was given a state funeral and honoured as an Irish hero.

54 Torch Battery

A TORCH BATTERY with a hidden storage compartment was one of a number of such items used to conceal miniature microfilms of secret UK defence documents.

Around 1960, the British authorities were becoming aware that secrets were being passed to the Soviet Union from the Naval Underwater Weapons Establishment in Portland, Dorset, so Detective Superintendent George Smith from Special Branch was appointed to lead the police investigation team.

DATE:
1960–61

EXHIBIT:
Torch battery with hidden compartment for microfilm

Items of false information were fed to Portland through official channels and these were detected as reaching the Soviet Union. MI5 suspected two employees at the base, Ethel Gee and Harry Houghton. They also obtained access to the flat next door to one occupied by Gordon Lonsdale, a man apparently earning his living renting jukeboxes to pubs and clubs. They became convinced that Lonsdale was using a short-wave radio transmitter. Smith took out a warrant and obtained a briefcase that Lonsdale had deposited in a bank for safe keeping, whilst Lonsdale was on holiday. The contents of the briefcase not only revealed cypher pads and transmission schedules, but also led to the identification of Peter and Helen Kroger, who had arrived in Britain in 1955 on forged passports and ran an antiquarian book business. In January 1961, after a ten-month period of surveillance, they were all arrested.

The Krogers had radio equipment with which to communicate with the Soviet Union, but would also include microdot photographs of documents obtained by Gee and Houghton hidden within the contents of the books. Gee and Houghton would meet Lonsdale in Waterloo and exchange their photographs of documents for money.

When the Krogers were interviewed, Helen Kroger tried to conceal a handbag that contained three microdots and a code pad. The Krogers' house was searched and more microdots were found, despite their miniature size being comparable to dead flies. Other items were found that were specially adapted for concealment: a table lighter, torch batteries, a hip flask and a picture with a hidden compartment.

On conviction in March 1961, Lonsdale was jailed for twenty-five years. The Soviet Union had constructed his false identity by using the passport of a dead man whose Finnish mother had been married to a Canadian citizen, Arnold Lonsdale. The Krogers received twenty years' imprisonment whilst Houghton and Gee were jailed for fifteen years each. In 1964, Lonsdale was exchanged for Greville Wynne, a British man jailed by the Soviet Union for contacts with Oleg Penkovsky. The Soviet authorities then disclosed Lonsdale's true identity as a KGB agent named Konon Molody.

John Vassall's Bookcase

WILLIAM JOHN CHRISTOPHER Vassall was born in 1924, worked as a photographer for the RAF during the Second World War and afterwards as an Admiralty clerk who became attached to the naval attaché's staff in Moscow in 1952. Vassall was befriended by a Polish man named Mikhailsky, who worked at the embassy, and was introduced to Moscow's gay underworld. In 1954, he was lured to a party secretly organised by the KGB, encouraged into drunkenness and was then photographed in compromising positions with a number of men. Homosexuality was then illegal and Vassall was blackmailed into becoming a spy for the Soviet Union. He transferred details of several thousand classified documents relating to British radar, torpedoes and submarines that contributed to modernising the Soviet naval fleet.

In 1961, Anatoly Golitsyn defected to the USA and revealed the existence of a spy in the Admiralty. Another Soviet defector, Yuri Nosenko, also reported the existence of a spy, but was unable to identify him, and this information led to the inquiry that ended with Vassall's arrest.

After months of surveillance by MI5 and Special Branch, Detective Superintendent George Smith stopped Vassall on his way home from work on 12 September 1962 and searched his flat. Information led Smith to concentrate on searching the bookcase, which was found to contain a cache of incriminating film. Vassall made a full confession of his activities, pleaded guilty and received eighteen years' imprisonment.

DATE:
1961–62

EXHIBIT:
John Vassall's bookcase with its hidden compartment

225

Victorian 'Infernal Machine'

A VICTORIAN BOMB with a timing device reminds us that explosions in London are not a new phenomenon: indeed, Guy Fawkes and others put barrels of gunpowder in the cellars of the Houses of Parliament as long ago as 1605. Inspector Maurice Moser was sent from Scotland Yard to Liverpool in 1883 where a consignment of explosives was expected. He spent three weeks trying to look inconspicuous in Liverpool docks and eventually found a pile of casks supposedly containing cement. The company named on the address details did not exist, and Moser found that each contained a 'fully charged infernal machine' with clockwork mechanism and dynamite.

The phrase 'infernal machine' may have been coined by Colonel Sir Vivian Majendie, one of the first bomb-disposal experts and the Chief Inspector of Explosives from 1871 to 1898. He defused a number of bombs that had a clockwork timing mechanism, designed to fire a pistol into detonators to trigger the main explosion, sometimes called a 'Majendie bomb'. Majendie believed in trying to dismantle and investigate bombs when it was reasonable and safe to do so. His courage, shared with many explosive officers to follow, saved many lives.

The Irish Republican Brotherhood (IRB), forerunner of the Irish Republican Army (IRA), had gained experience of using weapons and explosives from the American Civil War and started to plan a terrorism campaign on the British mainland for Irish home rule.

DATE:
1884

EXHIBIT:
Bomb planted at Ludgate Hill station by Irish Republican Brotherhood

227

The year 1867 saw an armed attack on a Manchester prison van and the murder of Sergeant Brett during the course of setting Thomas Kelly free, one of the IRB leaders. This was followed by the Clerkenwell explosion, which killed six people when the IRB tried unsuccessfully to release 'Colonel' O'Sullivan Burke and his accomplice, Case, from the prison. The explosion destroyed about 60yds of prison wall, killed six people and injured 126, but the prison governor had moved the two prisoners to a different part of the prison after receiving information that an escape attempt would be made.

By 1883, Scotland Yard had established the Special Irish Branch, later named Special Branch, to investigate terrorism, particularly a series of bombs left in railway stations. Between March 1883 and early 1885 there were thirteen bombings, culminating in 'Dynamite Saturday', on 24 January 1885, when a bomb exploded in the Tower of London where James Cunningham was arrested. Cunningham's accomplice, Harry Burton, planted the bomb that exploded that day in the Houses of Parliament as it was being carried away by PC William Cole. PC Cole was awarded the Albert Medal in gold for his courage, the only police officer to receive such an award. Cunningham and Burton were arrested because PC Thomas Gallagher locked the gates of the Tower of London immediately after the explosion to prevent anybody from leaving. Detective Inspector Frederick Abberline rushed to the scene, questioned everyone and was suspicious of a man who gave his name as James Gilbert. Gilbert was investigated and found to be James Cunningham using a false name, and a search of his lodgings then led to the arrest of Harry Burton.

The IRA planted bombs in London during the Second World War, when, in 1939, the famous Detective Inspector Robert Fabian was awarded the King's Police Medal for bravery for dismantling a bomb left in Piccadilly. As the bomb makers developed their skills and technology developed, the design of IRA bombs became ever more complex. They included anti-handling switches and other mechanisms to trigger an explosion when the bombs were being moved or when explosives officers were taking obvious steps to dismantle them.

57 Timers and Bombs

DATE:
1975–98

EXHIBIT:
Timing device
used by the IRA

WHEN THE IRA terrorists did not have a supply of commercial explosive, they would create an explosive mixture from industrial or agricultural chemicals that would not be as concentrated, and which would, therefore, need to be transported in a motor vehicle rather than by hand because of the weight involved.

In 1973, a Ford Corsair with a J registration plate caused suspicion when an experienced police officer recognised that the registration did not fit the year of manufacture of the car that had been parked outside the post office opposite New Scotland Yard. The car contained 150lb of explosive, made up from 'co-op mix' and gelignite. (Co-op mix comprised sodium chlorate and nitrobenzene, which could be obtained from legitimate sources to create a powerful explosion if sufficient bulk could be achieved and a primary explosion started with a small quantity of commercial explosive.) The Ford Corsair also contained a timing device, a battery and an electronic detonator that would have been used for the initial gelignite explosion. Two other similar car bombs parked outside Great Scotland Yard and the Old Bailey did in fact explode that day, killing two people and injuring 200. The Provisional IRA (PIRA) had been formed in 1969 after a cessation of terrorist activity by the 'official' IRA and sent ten of its members from Northern Ireland to London the day before. They were due to fly back to Belfast before the explosions took place, but the police arrested the ten at Heathrow Airport, their air tickets having been bought all at the same time. Nine of the ten, including Marion and Delours Price, were convicted at Winchester Crown Court and sentenced to life imprisonment.

The aptly named Memopark timer was made in Switzerland to help motorists with the amount of time left on their parking meters. The association with PIRA started in 1975 when a Roman Catholic priest, Father Ryan, started to travel to Europe under a false name, visiting arms dealers and travelling to Switzerland to buy materiel for PIRA. He would pay in cash and collect the items ten days later. On 27 July 1976 his girlfriend was stopped at Heathrow simultaneous to him being stopped at Geneva. The cash and invoices in their possession led to him admitting his role with PIRA and being deported by the Swiss. The Memopark timer became known as a Time and Power Unit (TPU) and was first used by PIRA on the British mainland for a bomb at Oxford Circus on 13 February 1976. They continued to use them for twenty-three years, until 1998.

Libya, under Colonel Gaddafi, supplied PIRA with 6 tons of Semtex H explosive between July 1985 and October 1986, just over half of which has been accounted for by various raids and bomb use in Northern Ireland, Britain and other parts of Europe. Semtex H is made from two explosives, RDX and PETN, and, after stores of commercial gelignite were made more secure against theft, it became a major component of PIRA bombs. It was a light, reliable and powerful explosive that PIRA used to kill and injure many hundreds of people. Semtex H was first found on mainland Britain on 19 January 1987 when stores of it were found in sealed dustbins in Delamere and Macclesfield forests. The first explosion on mainland Britain carried out by PIRA was on 2 August 1988 at Inglis barracks, Mill Hill, and it was also the explosive that brought down the airliner Pan Am 103 over Lockerbie on 21 December 1988.

Another PIRA car bomb exploded on Saturday, 17 December 1983, next to Harrods department store in an area containing the pre-Christmas bustle of shoppers and children waiting to see Father Christmas. A member of PIRA drove a blue Austin 1300 the wrong way down a side street, Hans Crescent, in Knightsbridge, into a parking space that was being vacated by one of his accomplices, and started the timing mechanism of a car bomb. The central London branch of the Samaritans received a bomb warning and officers from Chelsea police station attended the scene, identified the car and started to evacuate the area, but it exploded before the evacuation could be completed. The blast killed three officers – Inspector Stephen Dodd, Sergeant Noel Lane and WPC Jane Arbuthnot – and two members of the public. Seventy-eight people were injured, including nine children, many police officers from the shift on duty at Chelsea and PC Jon Gordon, a dog handler who lost both legs and whose police dog, Queenie, was killed. The IRA Army Council admitted responsibility, but claimed that it had not 'authorised' the attack. Prime Minister Margaret Thatcher described it as a 'crime against Christmas'.

Two small batteries, Memopark timers and traces of EGDN commercial blasting gelignite were found amongst tons of rubble examined at the scene of the Grand Hotel, Brighton, where a bomb was detonated on 12 October 1984 at 2.45 a.m., killing five people, injuring thirty-one and narrowly missing Prime Minister Margaret Thatcher, who was staying in the hotel that was accommodating many prominent members of the government attending the Conservative Party conference. The bomb killed Sir Anthony Berry MP; Roberta Wakeman, the wife of John Wakeman MP; Lady Muriel MacLean, the wife of Sir Donald MacLean, president of the Scottish Conservatives; Eric Taylor, north-west area chairman; and Jeanne Shattock, the wife of Sir Gordon

Shattock, the western area president of the party. The bomb had exploded in room 629, occupied by the MacLeans, and demolished all seven floors above the blast. Margaret Tebbit, wife of Norman Tebbitt MP, was one of the many injured and was permanently disabled by her injuries.

A month earlier, in the middle of September 1984, a Mr Walsh had occupied room 629. PIRA had developed long-delay timers that could have been used. Fingerprint evidence led to the identification of Patrick McGee, a known PIRA terrorist. On 22 June 1985, a raid was made in Glasgow by anti-terrorist officers under Operation Tricorn where Patrick McGee, three other men and three women were arrested. A large quantity of explosives, bomb-making equipment and weapons were recovered, together with documents indicating that there had been plans to conduct a bombing campaign against seaside reports. On 24 June 1986, seven people were convicted of conspiracy to cause explosions. Patrick McGee, Gerard McDonnell, Peter Sherry and Ella O'Dwyer were sentenced to life imprisonment. Martina Anderson was sentenced to sixteen years. Donal Craig and Una Lowney were each sentenced to ten years. Patrick McGee and others were released in 1999 under the Belfast Good Friday Agreement.

A grey plastic box was noticed under a Mercedes car in Kensington, W8, at lunchtime on 13 November 1989, and turned out to contain a quantity of Semtex H explosive, a detonator, a mercury tilt switch, a power unit, timer and magnets. The bomb was set up to detonate when the car started to move. The Kensington device was probably on the wrong car and intended for an army officer who lived nearby. Five days later, a similar device seriously injured an army staff sergeant and his wife at Colchester. On 20 February 1989, a device fell off a car and exploded, causing damage to an army recruiting office in Leicester and slightly injuring the car driver.

The Conservative MP Ian Gow lost his life when an explosion occurred as he reversed his car from his garage on 30 July 1990 in Hankham, Sussex. A great

hole was created in the floor of the car and fragments of the magnet found at the scene identified the
device as one of this series. This murder was reminiscent of the car bomb that killed Airey Neave, who had
a distinguished military record, was the Conservative
Opposition spokesman on Northern Ireland and a
close associate of the then opposition leader Margaret
Thatcher. A bomb that had been planted under his car
detonated when the tilt switch activated as he drove his
car up the ramp and out of the underground car park of
the Houses of Parliament. The Irish National Liberation
Army, an offshoot of the IRA, claimed responsibility
for the attack, which occurred shortly after the Labour
government, led by Jim Callaghan, had lost a parliamentary vote that led to the 1979 general election.

Briefcase Bomb

DATE:
1982

EXHIBIT:
Reconstructed
bomb found in
Regent's Park

ON JULY 1982, a briefcase, found in a boating lake in Regent's Park, illustrated the composition of a bomb that had exploded under the grandstand where a band of the Royal Green Jackets were playing music to lunchtime crowds. Seven soldiers were killed. Fifty-one soldiers and members of the public were injured. A class of deaf and dumb children escaped injury, but were spattered with flesh and blood as musical instruments, shrapnel and human bodies were scattered over a wide distance. The bomb was also similar to that which exploded at Hyde Park earlier that day.

Another scene of carnage was created when a bomb in the boot of a parked Morris Marina exploded in South Carriage Drive, Hyde Park, just as a mounted troop of the Blues and Royals passed on their way to the ceremony of the changing of the guard at Buckingham Palace. Three soldiers were killed outright, a fourth dying later of his injuries. The other twelve soldiers and two mounted police officers were injured. Seven horses were either killed or had to be put down because of their injuries. Seventeen bystanders were also injured. The explosive comprised 9kg of a commercial explosive called Ever Soft Frangex that had been manufactured in Ireland, and 12.7kg of 4 and 6in nails to create a devastating blast of shrapnel. The bomb was the first on the British mainland to be detonated by a remote-controlled device and had been set off by the terrorist 500yds away, using a signboard as a marker for when

235

he should trigger it. Sefton, a horse that survived the blast, became famous and was awarded a medal. Private Tipper's ceremonial helmet, grievously dented, has been on display but has now been returned to the regimental museum.

Gilbert McNamee, a member of PIRA, was convicted in 1986 of his part in the Hyde Park bombing and sentenced to life imprisonment, but later released under the 1998 Belfast Good Friday Agreement. His conviction was later overturned on appeal because the prosecution had withheld fingerprint evidence that also implicated others in the bomb-making process. In May 2013, John Downey was arrested and charged with his involvement, but the prosecution failed because Downey produced a letter initiated by the government, when Tony Blair had been prime minister, that stated Downey had not been circulated by the police as being wanted for any offence. Whereas it had been known that convicted IRA terrorists were being released early, few people had been aware that a process of giving 'letters of comfort' to 'on-the-run' terrorists had been undertaken, and the implications of this policy. Effectively an amnesty had been granted, apparently without the knowledge of those pursuing the investigation.

59 Mk 10 Mortar Device

DATE:
1991

EXHIBIT:
Large Mk 10 mortar device, with smaller, different mortar also shown

THE MK 10 mortar was used on 7 February 1991 when a van with a hole cut in its roof was parked in a side street off Whitehall, with a timing device set to fire three mortar bombs. The driver of the van then left the scene on the back of a waiting motorcycle. There had been snow and when that was cleared, yellow markings were found that seemed to indicate the position planned for parking the van. A few minutes later, three mortars were fired from the van. The second and third mortars failed to explode, landing in a grassed area behind Downing Street and by the Mountbatten memorial. The first exploded in the garden of No. 10 Downing Street whilst a Cabinet meeting chaired by Prime Minister John Major was in progress, breaking windows and scattering large amounts of debris. The mortars travelled 187m, 207m and 240m respectively. Four people, none of them members of the government, were slightly injured in the attack. The Cabinet meeting resumed at another location.

It was the first time that the Provisional IRA had used mortar bombs on mainland Britain. The preparations for the attack had been made well in advance, and had been set up with the assistance of terrorists who were familiar with the mortar trajectories. Those who drove the van on the day, at greater risk of arrest, were regarded as more expendable. The terrorists went to great lengths to disguise the true identity of the van by grinding away the identification marks on the engine and bodywork, but the registration number was traced: the van had been purchased at an auction in Canterbury on 24 January 1991 by two men who paid £1,060 cash. The commander of the Anti-Terrorist Branch at the time was George Churchill-Coleman.

Three years later, on Wednesday, 9 March 1994, another form of mortar attack was used when a Mk 6 mortar launch platform was found in a Nissan Micra that was burning fiercely in Bath Road, near Heathrow Airport, in a parking area near the Excelsior hotel. One hour earlier a coded message had been given anonymously to Sky television, warning that the whole Heathrow area should be cleared because of a large number of bombs due to be detonated. The platform, now in the museum, had four 780mm tubes welded to a heavy metal base plate and pointing through the rear window of the car. The position of the car directed the mortar tubes towards Terminal 1 at the airport. Three mortar bombs and part of a fourth were found within the runway perimeter about 1,000m from the car, but all had failed to explode. It was the first of a series of such attacks that took place over the next few days.

The following evening, a series of coded calls culminated in a set of explosions that were heard near the Hilton hotel at Heathrow. Four mortar bombs were found near Terminal 4, the launch site being hidden in bramble bushes on wasteland 700m away. On the Sunday morning, another series of coded warnings were followed by four mortars landing in and around Terminal 4. They had been launched from a hole in the ground with a concrete base, which had then been covered over with wood and turf.

The garage in north-west London in which the mortars had been prepared had been rented by Michael Gallagher, who was arrested when he requested the return of his £50 deposit on 28 October 1996. He was convicted of conspiracy to cause explosions, was sentenced to twenty years' imprisonment in 1998 and was released in 1999 under the terms of the Belfast Good Friday Agreement.

Timing devices were part of the incriminating evidence – along with 45kg of Semtex, detonators, six Romanian AKM assault rifles, ammunition and other material – found in a lock-up garage and the Northolt house of 37-year-old James Joseph Canning and Ethel Audrey Lamb, who were arrested. On 13 April 1992, the police raided their home as the result of Operation Catnip that had linked Canning to Bride Lane in London where he left a briefcase that later exploded. When he was arrested, Canning had a Smith & Wesson revolver in his waistband. Ethel Lamb admitted that Canning had acted as quartermaster supplying various bombs that had been detonated over the previous year, and one of the recovered rifles had been used in an attempt to murder the governor of Gibraltar. Canning pleaded guilty to conspiracy to cause explosions and was sentenced to thirty years' imprisonment. Ethel Lamb was imprisoned for three years.

A collection of tools and other paraphernalia, such as spades, compasses and maps (some of which might have had innocent purposes) was revealed in its true light in Operation Airlines when police, under the directions of Commander John Grieve, raided an address in Woodbury Street, Tooting, on 15 July 1996 and found explosive devices primed and ready for being planted. The plot had been to attack electricity installations in the London area and to disrupt power supplies. The police surveillance operation provided evidence that resulted in Gerard Hanratty, Donal Gannon, Patrick Martin, Robert Marrow, Francis Rafferty and John Crawley (all members of PIRA) being sentenced to thirty-five years' imprisonment.

El presente pasaporte incluye a los siguientes miembros de familia del titular:

ESPOSA : ....
                    (Nombre)   (Apellido propio)

                    ....
                         (Apellido del esposo)

HIJOS:

Nombre ....   Edad

....

(Firma del titular)

C Nº 035848   1971   3

FILIACION
PERSONAL DESCRIPTION

FILIACION
PERSONAL DESCRIPTION

Cédula de Identidad ....
Identification Card

Nacionalidad ....
Nationality

Nacido el ....
Date of birth

Estado civil ....
Marital status

Profesión ....
Profeesion

Domicilio ....
Address

Observaciones ....
Notes

....

....

DIGITO PULGAR
THUMB PRINT

FIRMA DEL TITULAR
SIGNATURE OF BEARER

Passports

PASSPORTS AND OTHER documents were part of a trail left by one of the most notorious individual terrorists to have conducted attacks in London.

Ilich Ramirez Sanchez, otherwise known as 'Carlos the Jackal', was born in Venezuela, and then studied in Russia, adopting the name Carlos after he had been sent by the Soviet Union to the Middle East for training in terrorist techniques and had joined the Popular Front for the Liberation of Palestine (PFLP). He is thought to have been involved in the attack on Israeli athletes at the Munich Olympics in 1972. He led a team of terrorists who attacked a meeting of the Organisation of Petroleum Exporting Countries (OPEC) in 1975, when they seized seventy hostages and eventually released them after negotiations. He then undertook several bombings and shootings in Britain and France. In 1973 he forced his way into the home of Edward Sieff, the former chairman of Marks & Spencer, and shot him in his bathroom. The bullet injured Edward Sieff's face but the gun jammed, and Carlos fled. He made a grenade attack against the offices of an Israeli bank in London and carried out bomb attacks against French newspaper offices in Paris.

By 1980, Carlos was the target of intense inquiries by Western countries and retreated to Yemen, from where he became, in effect, a mercenary acting on behalf of Arab extremists. In 1982, a group led by Carlos tried to destroy a nuclear reactor in central France, but failed

DATE:
1972–80

EXHIBIT:
Passports used by 'Carlos the Jackal'

241

when their rocket-powered explosives did not succeed in penetrating the concrete walls. Later that year, the French police arrested Carlos' wife, Magdalena Kopp, and another member of his team. When the French government refused to release them, Carlos embarked on a retaliation campaign against French interests, including a government facility in Beirut, a train in France, the French embassy in Austria, a Paris restaurant and the murder of a French embassy worker and his pregnant wife in Lebanon. When not in Europe, Carlos found a welcome refuge in countries such as Lebanon, Yemen, Syria, Iraq and Libya. Syria eventually expelled him and he went to Sudan, where he remained for a period under the protection of a fundamentalist sheikh. Carlos' lifestyle involved overindulgence in drink and sex, however, and this affronted his protector. This in turn led to Sudanese co-operation with the French authorities, who arrested him in August 1994. He was sentenced to life imprisonment in December 1997 in Paris for three murders, but had been responsible for probably over eighty deaths, many hundreds of injuries and countless damage to property.

A gun and two hand grenades were used in the attempted hijacking of El Al flight 219, on 6 September 1970, on its flight from Amsterdam to New York. Leila Khaled and Patrick Arguello attacked the aircraft as part of the Dawson's Fields hijackings, a series of almost simultaneous hijackings carried out by the Popular Front for the Liberation of Palestine. Leila Khaled forced her way on to the flight deck, armed with the gun and grenade, whilst Arguello threatened the passengers at the rear of the aircraft cabin. In a dramatic few minutes, the pilot seized the initiative and threw the aeroplane into a vertical dive that made the terrorists weightless; Leila Khaled was overpowered and Arguello shot a member of the flight crew before being killed by an Israeli security guard. The aircraft was diverted to Heathrow where the security guards were immediately transferred to another El Al flight out of the country. The police took control and Khaled was taken to Ealing police station. On 1 October 1970, the British government released Khaled as part of an international agreement to secure the release of prisoners from aircraft flown to Dawson's Fields in Jordan.

The PFLP abandoned the tactic of aircraft hijacking in 1971. Leila Khaled later became a Palestinian politician and went to live in Jordan. It is said that she had a fondness for the United Kingdom, which started when her first visitor in prison was an immigration officer who wanted to know why she had arrived in the country without a valid visa!

A submachine gun was one of the weapons used on 20 August 1978 when three men attacked a small coach from which the flight crew from El Al airline were alighting outside the Europa Hotel in Grosvenor Square. One opened fire with the machine gun and another threw hand grenades. An air hostess was killed in the attack and nine other people were injured. One of the attackers was killed by the blast of one of their own grenades and a second was caught and arrested by PCs Neil Aiken, George Kendall and Raymond Wasilo, all unarmed, as the man ran from the scene. The PFLP claimed responsibility for the attack. Israeli jets attacked a PFLP training camp in Lebanon a day later in retaliation.

This last incident had been preceded that year by the death of two Syrian embassy employees when a bomb had exploded in their car. Said Hammami, the Palestine Liberation Organisation's representative in London, had been murdered whilst sitting in his central London office. General Al Naif, the former prime minister of Iraq, had been shot dead outside a London hotel, and a grenade had been thrown at the Iraqi ambassador's car. London is often the destination for dissidents, who have fled their own countries for political reasons, but their grievances and political beliefs have sometimes translated into violence and other crimes committed in England. Sometimes old scores have been settled between rival factions and the reasons for murders have occasionally been related to political events in distant parts of world. Sometimes the grievances that fuel terrorist acts are directed against Britain and other countries in the west. The antagonism between Arab countries and Israel, particularly over the Palestinians, have accounted for many terrorist incidents over the years.

On 3 June 1982, His Excellency Mr Sholom Argov, the Israeli ambassador, was tragically shot in the head at close range outside the Dorchester hotel in Park Lane. Two men were arrested in south London and professed to be part of the Abu Nidhal extremist Palestinian organisation that had a list of Jewish targets. Victims such as Argov endure a heavy and tragic fate because of the importation of fanaticism into a country that espouses liberal democratic values.

More recently, the Islamist movement, including Al-Qaeda, has caused significant problems not only in terms of terrorism in this country, but also in outright civil war in countries such as Syria. It is not directly related to the interests of territorially based sovereign countries, but an ideology claiming a link to Islam: it exploits countries where the formal structures of government are weak. Sometimes the perpetrators have not only grown up in this country, but have been embarking on promising respectable careers, thereby provoking questions about our society. One of the sobering aspects to reflect upon is how the methods of terrorism have changed, particularly suicide bombing where the bombers have been motivated to kill themselves rather than simply leave a bomb to explode on a time delay. Historically, acts of terrorism in London have most often been connected to Irish republicans, but have also been linked to anarchists, and to the activities of the Animal Liberation Front where violence and arson are apparently motivated by revenge for the treatment of animals.

61 Shoe Bomb

DATE:
2001

EXHIBIT:
Reconstructed
shoe bomb
used by Richard
Reid

THE ADAPTED SHOES worn by Richard Reid, born in Britain, contain no metal components so they would not at that time have triggered the alarm of an airport screening device, but they were packed with explosives.

On 22 December 2001 – just over three months after the devastating attack on New York's World Trade Center and the Pentagon by Al-Qaeda – American Airlines flight 63 was in mid-flight from Paris to Miami when the cabin crew noticed a smell like burning matches and found Richard Reid trying to set light to a cord near the tongue of his shoes. Reid was then over-powered by the crew and passengers, and restrained with belts for the rest of the flight. The aeroplane was diverted to Boston where Reid was arrested. His shoes were found to contain PETN explosive, similar to nitroglycerine, with a safety-fuse detonating cord containing black powder that would burn and set off an initial explosion of homemade peroxide explosives. At his trial in an American court, he said, 'I am a member of Al-Qaeda, I pledge to Osama Bin Laden, and I am an enemy of your country ... I used a destructive device as an act of war. I do not recognise your laws ... but I admit I tried to use a destructive device.' He was sentenced to life and 110 years' imprisonment in October 2002.

Reid had converted to Islam in prison in Britain and had attended a mosque in Brixton after being released. He had travelled to Pakistan and on to Afghanistan where he had taken up arms and attended a terrorist training camp. He had spent a week in Paris preparing for his attempt to bring down the airliner and had missed the same flight the previous day because he had been delayed by security checks at the airport by French police, who had been suspicious of him but had not detected the explosives in his shoes. It was the first time that this method of putting explosives on to an aeroplane had been discovered and this case is the reason for subsequent procedures for checking passengers' footwear.

A second shoe bomber, Saajid Muhammad Badat, accompanied Reid at the same terrorist training camp. Badat was provided with shoes adapted in a similar manner to Reid's but decided not to go through with the plan. He was arrested in 2003 and imprisoned for thirteen years in 2005, but freed in 2012 after providing information on up to eighteen terrorist plots covering a six-year period.

62 Burnt Laptop Computer

DATE:
2007

EXHIBIT:
Laptop from which much data was extracted

GAS CYLINDERS, PETROL containers and nails were part of the contents of a car bomb discovered on 29 June 2007 at 2 a.m. when the police were called to a Mercedes parked outside the Tiger Tiger nightclub in Haymarket in the heart of London's West End. An ambulance crew reported smoke coming from the car and explosives officers were then able to dismantle the bomb. There were in fact two 13kg patio gas bottles, plastic containers with 20 litres of petrol, several other gas canisters and no fewer than 675 nails, all of which would have created a devastating explosion. The bomb was designed to be triggered by a mobile phone.

A second Mercedes car bomb had been left in a bus lane in Cockspur Street outside Canada House. After a

traffic warden issued it a parking ticket the vehicle was removed to a car pound at Park Lane and the explosive device inside was discovered there.

The two London car bombs were linked to an incident the following day when, at 4.20 p.m. at Glasgow Airport, a Jeep Cherokee drove at speed through the doors of the main terminal building. It came to rest in the terminal entrance and burst into flames. Two men of Asian appearance were seen in the vehicle, one of them with his clothing alight. The police arrived quickly and, after a struggle, arrested the men, one of whom needed urgent hospital treatment. The jeep contained bomb components that were identical to those found in the two Mercedes cars in London. The police soon arrested a third man and, at a house in Houston, near Johnstone in Scotland, found more bomb-making equipment and documents linking the Glasgow Airport incident to the car bombs found in London. On 17 December 2008 at Woolwich Crown Court, Dr Bilal Abdulla was convicted of conspiracy to murder and to cause explosions. He was sentenced to thirty-two years' imprisonment. His accomplice, Kafeel Ahmed, also in the medical profession, died of his injuries four weeks after the Glasgow attack. A third man, Dr Mohammed Asha from Jordan, was cleared of any involvement but was detained in custody pending deportation.

Two years earlier, personal property found at the scenes of three explosions confirmed suspicions that London had been attacked by suicide bombers on 7 July 2005 – the day after London celebrated the award of hosting the 2012 Olympic Games. At around 8.50 a.m., there were three explosions on Underground trains in tunnels at Edgware Road station, between King's Cross and Russell Square, and between Liverpool Street and Aldgate East. An hour later a further bomb exploded on a No. 20 bus at Tavistock Square. A total of fifty-two people were killed and 700 injured in the four explosions, the largest number of casualties from a terrorist attack on mainland Britain.

As well as the enormous task of helping to rescue the injured and controlling the chaos that ensued, the police undertook the huge exercise of studying CCTV images. The inquiries identified the suspect for the Edgware Road bombing as 30-year-old Mohammed Sidique Khan; for the Aldgate bombing as 22-year-old Shahzad Tanweer; for the Russell Square bombing as 19-year-old Germaine Lindsay; and for the Tavistock bus incident as 18-year-old Habib Hussain. Each explosive device was transported in a plastic container in a large rucksack carried by each bomber. The homemade explosives comprised a peroxide-based mixture known as hexamethylene triperoxide (HMTD). The devices were set off either by a flame-activated fuse cord, or a battery and switch. This meant that the explosions could be detonated with immediate effect by the bombers, in case they were approached by police officers prior to reaching their intended destination.

CCTV pictures showed that the four young men had travelled from Luton railway station, where a blue Nissan car, driven by Tanweer, was still parked in the station car park. When explosives officers searched the vehicle they found a cool box with a number of HMTD bottles and fuses, some with nails included, ready to be used for further bombs. The original bomb 'factory' was then traced to Leeds. The four young men had all been British, but had apparently been indoctrinated into Islamist militancy to the point that they embarked on their journey to London, took their separate routes on to the Underground system (in one case reverting to a bus diverted by the emergency) and then deliberately killed themselves along with the innocent strangers standing near them. It was the first time a suicide bombing had occurred in the United Kingdom.

An entirely separate group attempted to bomb London a fortnight after the suicide bombings on 7 July using 6-litre plastic containers with screws and washers taped to the outside. On 21 July 2005, small explosions occurred at 12.25 p.m. at Shepherds Bush Underground station; at 12.30 p.m. at Oval; at 1.20 p.m. at Warren

Street; and at 1.30 p.m. on a bus in Hackney. The bombers ran away when their devices failed to explode fully. The detonators worked, but they failed to set off the main charge that was made of different explosives from those used a fortnight earlier. This time it was TATP, a mixture of hydrogen peroxide, sulphuric acid and chapati flour, a mixture that can be extremely sensitive and volatile. A fifth device was abandoned by a would-be bomber, who did not attempt to set it off.

Again, CCTV images produced vital evidence. Pictures of the bombers were publicised by the police the day after the incidents. By 25 July the police had identified two of them as Muktar Said Ibrahim and Yasin Hassan Omar, who were arrested within two days. Osman Hussein was arrested in Rome and then extradited back to Britain. Along with Ramzi Mohammed, they were found guilty of conspiracy to murder and were sentenced at Woolwich Crown Court to life imprisonment with a minimum of forty years to be served before their release. Manfo Kwaku Asiedu, 34 years old, who abandoned his device in a litter bin, was found guilty and sentenced to serve thirty-three years before release.

During the search for the suspects for these incidents, officers were faced with the difficulty of challenging and detaining a suspected suicide bomber without giving any opportunity of them detonating the bomb by means of a covert trigger before any meaningful investigation could take place. It was the background to an innocent man, Jean Charles de Menezes, being wrongly identified as one of the suspects, and then shot and killed by the police at Stockwell Underground station on 22 July 2005.

63 Grenade Launcher

DATE:
2000

EXHIBIT:
Grenade
launcher used
against MI6
building

A SOVIET-MADE LIGHT anti-tank RPG-22 rocket-propelled grenade launcher was used against the headquarters of the Secret Intelligence Service (MI6) on 20 September 2000 at 9.46 p.m., by dissident Irish republicans, two years after the Belfast Good Friday Agreement established the process for cessation of terrorist activity. The missile exploded as it hit the exterior wall of the building below the window line. The warhead of the missile turned to molten copper. Part of this copper penetrated through the window frame and the blast effect was funnelled along channels in the building's framework, creating a peculiar damage pattern. Part of the blast was absorbed by wastepaper sacks and a pillar that formed part of the main structure of the building.

A search of the area immediately afterwards found the launcher in Spring Gardens, from where the grenade had been fired across a busy railway line.

This incident was part of a series of terrorist attacks that started in June 2000 when a car bomb exploded in Ealing. The grey Saab was bought from a dealer a fortnight earlier. Six people were injured from flying glass and debris and serious structural damage was caused to nearby buildings. A fractured water main flooded the crime scene.

A blue barrel containing 35kg of ammonia nitrate and sugar was found in a taxi outside the BBC Television Centre in Wood Lane shortly after midnight on Sunday, 4 March 2001 as part of a campaign by the Real IRA, who continued their own activity after PIRA agreed to halt terrorist attacks. The taxi had been bought for cash the day before, and exploded while it was being examined by a remote-controlled device. Windows were broken, but no structural damage was caused to the BBC building.

A third bomb exploded in Manchester on 3 November 2001 in an incident that was similar in many respects, except for the use of a brown, rather than blue, barrel. Five men were arrested shortly afterwards and sentenced at the Old Bailey for these incidents and five other offences in London and Leeds. Noel McGuire and James McCormack received twenty-two years' imprisonment, Robert and Aidan Hulme were given twenty years, and John Hannan was sentenced to sixteen years.

64 CCTV Images of the 'Nail Bomber'

THE CCTV IMAGES from cameras located in various parts of London have often been crucial in providing images that help identify offenders. In this case it was a series of nail bombs that exploded over the course of three weekends in London in April 1999. The first detonated on a Saturday at 5.30 p.m. in Electric

DATE:
1999

EXHIBIT:
CCTV images that helped to identify David Copeland

Avenue, a busy market street in Brixton. The police had been notified of a suspicious cardboard box with a plastic container on top and a clock in it. Another member of the public described a sports bag with a box of nails and batteries. The bag was stolen by a thief, who had apparently not realised the danger he was in. The timing device had not been triggered at this point, but the bomb did explode shortly afterwards. The thief was injured, along with thirty-eight other people, which included the three police officers who responded to the call. The explosive had apparently been removed from fireworks, and various pieces of small cog wheels indicated that a clockwork timing mechanism had been used.

The second explosion occurred shortly before 6 p.m. on the following Saturday, 24 April 1999, in the East End's Brick Lane, also an area with many ethnic minority residents. The owner of a Ford Sierra estate had returned to his vehicle after he had found the restaurant he intended to visit closed. Finding a sports holdall with a box inside it by his car, the man picked it up to take to the nearby police office, which was also closed, and then put it into the back of his car. When the car owner had walked 100yds away, the bomb exploded. He became the second man to have unwittingly picked up a sports bag that had been about to explode!

The third incident was outside the Admiral Duncan public house in Soho, close to an area described as the 'gay community's heartland'. This bomb – also in a sports holdall – had been left behind in the pub by a man who had then walked out. The explosion killed three people, including a pregnant woman, and injured 139, four of them suffering the loss of a limb.

The police had examined many hours of footage from CCTV cameras in Brixton and managed to publicise pictures of the bomber on Thursday, 29 April, just under a fortnight after the Brixton incident. This caused the bomber to bring forward his plan to set off a third bomb by one day, and it was the reason for the Admiral Duncan public house explosion occurring on a Friday night rather than on a Saturday.

Just over an hour before that third bomb was detonated, an electrician from London Underground contacted police with the information that he believed the culprit to be his work colleague, David Copeland. Police investigated the information but it was too late to prevent the third bomb. The police called at Copeland's address in Cove, Hampshire, on Saturday, 1 May and he immediately admitted responsibility for the bombs, claiming neo-Nazi political views. He had apparently acted alone, and his room contained Nazi flags and newspaper stories about bombs. It also contained over 500 items consisting of fireworks, pyrotechnics, firework casings and receipts for holdalls, clocks and nails, along with several terrorist handbooks.

Copeland's trial was noteworthy for having no fewer than six psychiatrists giving evidence about his state of mind. They all diagnosed mental illness. Five of them diagnosed paranoid schizophrenia, the sixth a personality disorder that would not affect his legal responsibility for his actions. The prosecution did not accept his offer to plead guilty to manslaughter and persisted in their attempts to prove murder. He was indeed convicted of murder and given six life sentences. In 2007, the High Court decided that he should remain in prison for fifty years and this was upheld by the Court of Appeal in 2011.

65 Fake Suicide Belt

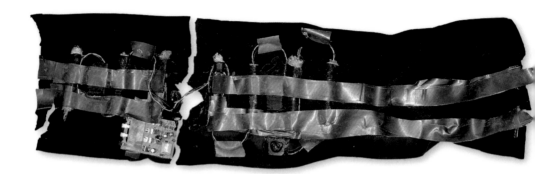

ON 29 NOVEMBER 2019, a Learning Together event was held at Fishmongers' Hall in Upper Thames Street, adjacent to London Bridge, as part of a prisoner rehabilitation scheme supported by the Prison Service. Over 100 people attended the event, including prisoners on day release, people convicted of murder, a judge and Probation Service staff. One of those invited to the event was 28-year-old Usman Khan. Khan had been convicted of preparing acts of terrorism in 2012 and was sentenced to sixteen years' imprisonment. During his first years in prison, he was known as an Islamist extremist who was regularly involved in fights. In 2017 Khan enrolled in the Learning Together programme. His behaviour improved and in 2018 he was released on licence, with conditions that he should wear an electronic tag and not visit London. Khan appeared in a promotional video played at the event in which he stated that Learning Together had changed his life.

Shortly before 2 p.m., Khan went to the toilet and strapped knives to his hands, one of which had 'Allah' scratched upon it. He then murdered Jack Merritt, a Learning Together employee, by stabbing him twelve times. Afterwards he fatally stabbed Saskia Jones, a 23-year-old Cambridge graduate and volunteer for

DATE:
2019

EXHIBIT:
Fake suicide belt worn by Usman Khan at Fishmongers' Hall

Learning Together, in the neck. Two other women stab victims survived. Khan shouted that he had a bomb, and the suicide belt, which later transpired to be fake, could clearly be seen.

Three men bravely tackled him, one with a Narwhal tusk from the wall of Fishmongers' Hall, and one with a fire extinguisher. Police officers arrived and, faced with the threat of Khan exploding his suicide belt, shot him twice at close range. Khan was still alive, however, and perceiving him as a continuing threat, police officers shot him a further nine times, all recorded on the officers' body-worn video cameras. The officers then cleared the area and gave first aid to Khan's victims. An explosives detection dog was sent to check Khan, but did not react, and an explosives officer then examined him and found the belt to be a fake.

The case illustrates the difficulty in assessing whether prisoners are genuinely rehabilitated and the difficult situations faced by armed police, who can very rarely judge whether it is safe or not to shoot a terrorist apparently able to set off an explosion with an unseen trigger. The case resulted in recommendations to improve communication about prisoner risks amongst different services and changes to the law to prevent early release from prison in terrorist cases.

66 Button and Badge

DATE:
1918

EXHIBIT:
The button and badge found at the scene of Nellie Trew's murder

TWO SMALL ITEMS from an overcoat proved to be the crucial clues leading to the conviction of David Greenwood for murder.

When 16-year-old Nellie Trew from Eltham had not returned from Plumstead Library by midnight on Saturday, 9 February 1918, her father reported her missing. Her body was found the following morning on Eltham Common, ¼ mile from her home. She was covered in mud and had been dragged for about 30yds.

Her handbag and the library book lay beside her. In the mud was a replica of the badge of the Leicestershire Regiment and an overcoat button that had been fixed with wire rather than cotton. It seemed that the killer had lost these items during the course of committing the crime. The newspapers published pictures of the items and the case soon became known as the 'Button and Badge murder'.

Ted Farrell, who worked in an aeroplane component factory in Newman Street in central London, knew that his 21-year-old colleague, David Greenwood, wore such a badge, and he drew Greenwood's attention to it, particularly as the item was now missing from his coat. Greenwood told his workmate that he had sold the badge on the Saturday afternoon for 2s to a man he had met on a tram. At Farrell's suggestion, he went to Tottenham Court Road police station to help the police with their inquiries. Detective Chief Inspector Francis Carlin was in charge of the inquiry. He became a member of the famous 'Big Four' senior detectives who each took charge of CID officers and major inquiries in a quarter of London. His counterparts were Frederick Wensley, Arthur Hawkins and Arthur Neil.

The badge was not the only evidence, of course, and Carlin asked Greenwood about his coat, which had all of its buttons missing. Greenwood said that the buttons had been lost for some time and tried to explain a tear in the coat's fabric as being caused by the button being pulled off. The wire found with the button was established as being part of a type of metal spring that was used in the factory where Greenwood was employed.

On this evidence, Greenwood was charged with murder. At his trial, Greenwood claimed never to have liked his overcoat, which had been issued to him when he had been discharged from the Royal Army Medical Corps in 1917 because of shell shock. Despite his defence that he had not been wearing the coat on the day of the murder, and that he was too weak to overpower the victim, he was convicted and sentenced to death. On the eve of his execution he was reprieved and sentenced to life imprisonment, and was released from prison in 1933.

67 Miniature Furniture

A SET OF miniature furniture was used in the trial of Patrick Mahon to clarify the evidence given by him about how his victim had come by her fatal injuries.

By the end of April 1924, Jessie Mahon was worried about the activities of her husband Patrick. She found a cloakroom ticket in a pocket of one of his garments and took it to a friend, a former railway policeman, who then went to Waterloo station left-luggage office and inspected a locked Gladstone bag that was linked to the ticket. By prising the sides of the bag apart, the

DATE:
1924

EXHIBIT:
Miniature furniture used in court to reconstruct a murder scene

former detective could see bloodstained female under-wear and a knife, so he returned the bag to the attendant and the ticket to Mrs Mahon, and informed Frederick Wensley, the CID chief constable at Scotland Yard. On 2 May Patrick Mahon, 35, came to collect his bag and was arrested by Detective Sergeant Thompson. He was later interviewed about the bag's contents by Detective Chief Inspector Percy Savage.

Mahon gave a long account of how he had been having an affair with Emily Kaye and that a fortnight earlier she had attacked him in the bungalow he had rented out at the Crumbles, near Eastbourne. In the struggle, Mahon claimed that she had hit her head on a coal scuttle and had died. It was this account that Bernard Spilsbury and others found unbelievable and was the reason for using the miniature furniture. The jury were apparently not convinced by Mahon's account either. Mahon continued his version by saying that he had then bought a knife and a saw in London, and had returned to the bungalow to dismember the body.

The detectives went to the bungalow and found various parts of the victim's body in a large, locked trunk. Some organs were in a biscuit tin, a hat box and a saucepan, with bone fragments in a heap of ashes in the garden. In a reflection of how ill-equipped the police were at handling bodies in the first part of the twentieth century, the pathologist, Bernard Spilsbury, expressed his surprise at seeing Detective Chief Inspector Percy Savage handling the remains of a dead body with his bare hands. This led to a review of what detectives needed for scene of crime examination and the introduction of the Scotland Yard 'murder bag' to give officers immediate access to better forensic equipment. Bernard Spilsbury tried to recon-struct the body on a table in the back garden. The head and some parts of Emily's limbs were never found.

Mahon had entertained another woman, Ethel Duncan, in the bungalow immediately after the murder. Her evi-dence, expert testimony from Bernard Spilsbury about whether hitting the coal scuttle could have caused death and other details disproving Mahon's explanation of events all contributed to the jury's decision to send him to the gallows, despite important parts of Kaye's body never being found. He was hanged on 3 September 1922.

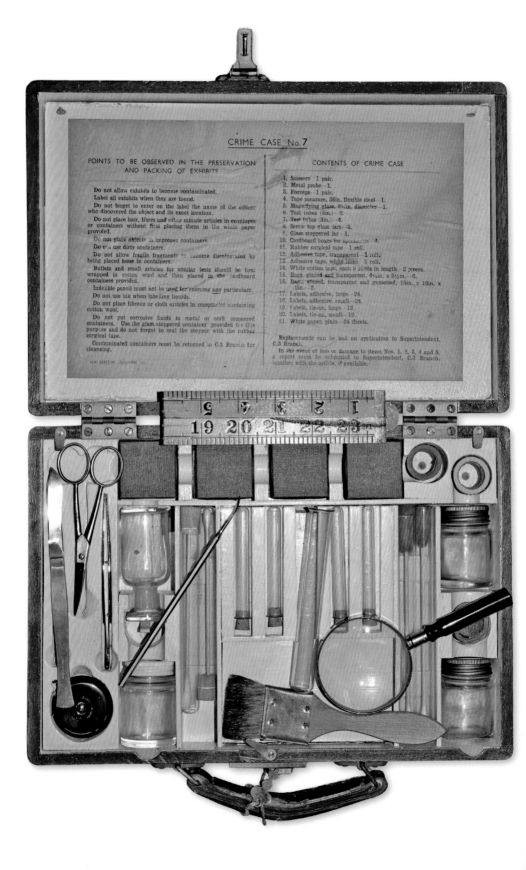

CRIME CASE No. 7

POINTS TO BE OBSERVED IN THE PRESERVATION AND PACKING OF EXHIBITS

Do not allow exhibits to become contaminated.

Label all exhibits when they are found.

Do not forget to enter on the label the name of the officer who discovered the object and its exact location.

Do not place hair, fibres and other minute articles in envelopes or containers without first placing them in the white paper provided.

Do not place objects in improper containers.

Do not use dirty containers.

Do not allow fragile fragments to become disintegrated by being placed loose in containers.

Bullets and small articles for similar tests should be first wrapped in cotton wool and then placed in the cardboard containers provided.

Indelible pencil must not be used for entering any particulars.

Do not use ink when labelling liquids.

Do not place fibrous or cloth articles in receptacles containing cotton wool.

Do not put corrosive fluids in metal or cork stoppered containers. Use the glass stoppered container provided for this purpose and do not forget to seal the stopper with the rubber surgical tape.

Contaminated containers must be returned to C.3 Branch for cleansing.

M.P. 32417.50 July 1946 A.

CONTENTS OF CRIME CASE

1. Scissors—1 pair.
2. Metal probe—1.
3. Forceps—1 pair.
4. Tape measure, 36in. flexible steel—1.
5. Magnifying glass, 2½in. diameter—1.
6. Test tubes (5in.)—2.
7. Test tubes (3in.)—4.
8. Screw top glass jars—3.
9. Glass stoppered jar—1.
10. Cardboard boxes for specimens—4.
11. Rubber surgical tape—1 roll.
12. Adhesive tape, transparent—1 roll.
13. Adhesive tape, white linen—1 roll.
14. White cotton tape, each 9 yards in length—2 pieces.
15. Bags, glazed and transparent, 4½in. x 3½in.—6.
16. Bags, glazed, transparent and gusseted, 15in. x 10in. x 3in.—2.
17. Labels, adhesive, large—24.
18. Labels, adhesive, small—24.
19. Labels, tie-on, large—12.
20. Labels, tie-on, small—12.
21. White paper, plain—24 sheets.

Replacements can be had on application to Superintendent, C.3 Branch.

In the event of loss or damage to items Nos. 1, 2, 3, 4 and 5, a report must be submitted to Superintendent, C.3 Branch, together with the article, if available.

Murder Bag

THE FIRST POLICE officer to attend the scene of a murder, or indeed most crimes, is often the officer on the beat or in a patrol car. Their role is to take steps to save or preserve life, call up medical support, ensure that any suspect does not leave the scene, find witnesses who may be immediately available and to call in the CID. In the early days of the Metropolitan Police, a detective would carry virtually no equipment at all, but this started to change at the beginning of the twentieth century when fingerprint expertise was introduced and crime scene photography became more commonly used. The ability to call in an experienced pathologist to the murder scene was recognised as very valuable, with Bernard Spilsbury being one of the first recognised as a specialist in this field. The local divisional surgeon called in to examine the victim no longer carried out a nineteenth-century post-mortem examination at the scene or nearby; the doctor would simply be called upon to pronounce life extinct.

Spilsbury had worked under Augustus Pepper from St Mary's Hospital at one stage and started to rise to prominence with the Dr Crippen case in 1911. Being a medical man, it was natural for Spilsbury to bring his medical instruments and equipment to a crime scene, and his comments to Detective Chief Inspector Percy Savage at the scene of the Crumbles murder in 1924 started the process of formalising what became known as the 'murder bag', which contained essential

DATE:
1924

EXHIBIT:
Case of crime scene equipment known as a 'murder bag'

crime scene examination supplies and equipment. One of Spilsbury's successors, Professor James 'Taffy' Cameron, later donated his own case to the museum. It would be another decade before the introduction of the Metropolitan Police Forensic Science Laboratory. The police progressively developed methods for collecting, transporting and storing exhibits without risking contamination. Exhibits have become smaller; in the 1960s, items would often reach the laboratory in large sweet jars but, nowadays, evidence may not be visible to the human eye. Scientific instruments and techniques have become more sophisticated and capable of detecting minute amounts of substances such as drugs.

A set of instructions – apparently printed in 1946 – were associated with the murder bags and contained crime scene advice that often aimed to avoid chemical and other types of contamination of exhibits, as well as ensuring that there was clear evidence of continuity to establish exactly where each item had been found. The list was as follows:

Do not allow exhibits to become contaminated.

Label all exhibits where they are found.

Do not forget to enter on the label the name of the officer who discovered the object and its exact location.

Do not place hair, fibres and other minute articles in envelopes or containers without first placing them in the white paper provided.

Do not place articles in improper containers.

Do not use dirty containers.

Do not allow fragile fragments to become disintegrated by being placed in loose containers.

Bullets and small articles for similar tests should be first wrapped in cotton wool and then placed in the cardboard containers provided.

Indelible pencil must not be used for entering **any** particulars.

Do not use ink when labelling liquids.

Do not place fibrous or cloth articles in receptacles containing cotton wool.

Do not put corrosive fluids in metal or cork stoppered containers. Use the glass stoppered container provided for this purpose and do not forget to seal the stopper with the rubber surgical tape.

Contaminated containers must be returned to C3 Branch for cleansing.

The contents of the 'crime case' were also listed:

Scissors
Metal probe
Forceps
Tape measure
Magnifying glass
Test tubes
Screw top glass jars
Glass-stoppered jar
Cardboard specimen boxes
Rubber surgical tape
Adhesive tape
Plain white cotton tape
Transparent bags
Labels
White paper

The protective gloves were not mentioned, but presumably became a natural part of officers' equipment, along with aprons to protect their clothing. In modern times, the public has become used to crime scene examiners wearing disposable suits, having arrived in special vans with specialist equipment on board. In fact, the modern developments in crime scene investigation have often given primacy to the specialist crime scene examiners, who sometimes have to calculate the best sequence of applying various forensic techniques so as to ensure that, for instance, the application of chemicals to illuminate bloodstains does not interfere with the ability to retrieve fingerprints.

Hacksaw

THE HACKSAW WAS used by Norman Thorne to cut up parts of his victim's body.

At Christmas 1922, Elsie Cameron, a 24-year-old London typist, became engaged to Norman Thorne, 22, who owned a poultry farm near Crowborough, Sussex. By 1924, Thorne's attentions turned to another woman, however, and he wanted to find a way of breaking off his engagement. Cameron made visits to Thorne in Crowborough to try to resolve the matter of their future together, and when Thorne disclosed his interest in another woman, Cameron became desperate and claimed to be pregnant. On 5 December 1924, Cameron travelled to Crowborough with new clothes, a new hairstyle and an apparent determination to 'burn her boats' – to live with Thorne regardless and to force the marriage issue.

Elsie Cameron disappeared. Thorne claimed that she had never arrived at his farm, and the local police tried to trace her without success. The police made inquiries with the neighbours and discovered that Cameron had been seen entering Thorne's farm. This development informed their decision to call in Scotland Yard. Detective Chief Inspector John Gillan duly arrested Thorne on 14 January 1925 and a thorough search of the farm commenced. Various items of jewellery belonging to Cameron were found in Thorne's hut. Her attaché case was found buried in the 1-acre farm grounds, and it seemed likely that Cameron might also be buried there.

DATE:
1924

EXHIBIT:
Norman Thorne's hacksaw with a photograph of his hut

At 8 p.m., more than twenty-four hours after his arrest, and after being told that he might be charged with murder, Thorne made a statement to the effect that Elsie Cameron had hanged herself with some washing line from a beam in his hut, whilst he was temporarily absent from the property. He had then cut off her head and legs and buried them on the farm. Thorne told the police where to look and Cameron's remains were found late that night.

Sir Bernard Spilsbury examined the body and it was buried at Willesden, but later exhumed in a dispute over whether a mark from the rope was visible on her neck or not. Spilsbury testified that death seemed to have been caused by shock. There had been a crushing blow to her forehead and several bruises and other injuries that had been inflicted shortly before death, but no evidence of a hanging injury. The defence pathologist, Dr Robert Brontë, whose post-mortem investigation took place a month after Spilsbury's, stated that crease marks on the victim's neck could have been caused by a rope. Spilsbury, on the other hand, claimed that such marks were found naturally on many female necks. The upper beam of the hut had been dusty, with no signs of rope marks; the lower beam was dust free. Thorne was convicted of the murder and executed at Wandsworth on 22 April 1925. One might speculate that he copied Patrick Mahon's attempts to dispose of Emily Kaye's body a few months earlier, and only 20 miles away.

A murderer's disposal of the body can sometimes destroy the evidence of how death was caused, but Thorne's account of hiding a supposed sudden suicide from the authorities was apparently and understandably disbelieved by the jury.

70 Wicker Wastebasket

DATE:
1927

EXHIBIT:
The matchstick (in glass tube) and other exhibits that convicted John Robinson

A SUCCESSFUL MURDER inquiry sometimes depends on small details and in this case a matchstick stuck in a cane wastebasket proved to be the crucial clue that provoked the confession of a murder suspect who had disposed of his victim in a trunk.

On 10 May 1927, the staff at the left-luggage office of Charing Cross station called the police to investigate a trunk that had been left there four days earlier and was giving off an offensive smell. Inside the trunk were five parcels, each wrapped in brown paper and tied with string. The parcels contained various female body parts. Some of the clothing also found in the trunk bore laundry marks, and these were traced to a Mrs Holt from Chelsea. Holt was alive and well, but she had had ten female servants over the previous two years and the police successfully traced all but one of them: Mrs Rolls. Holt identified the head of the victim as belonging to Rolls. A Mr Rolls was traced, who turned out to be an Italian waiter whose name was Bonati. His wife's name was Minnie, a 36-year-old woman given to drink and from whom he was estranged.

A shoeblack at Charing Cross had picked up a left-luggage ticket thrown from a taxi and, as the number corresponded with the trunk, the police then made inquiries of taxi drivers. A cab driver reported to police that he had taken a passenger with a trunk from No. 86 Rochester Row. The building largely comprised legal offices, but there was one second-floor office where the occupant, 36-year-old John Robinson, had gone missing on 9 May. The police made inquiries into Robinson's background. He had left his lodgings in Kennington without leaving a forwarding address, but an undelivered telegram was returned to the lodgings because the addressee could not be identified. The telegram had been sent to the Greyhound Hotel in Hammersmith where the police found a Mrs Robinson, who was not a guest but who worked there. Detective Chief Inspector George Cornish, who had been making background inquiries, had a serious talk with Mrs Robinson, who was surprised to be informed that her 'husband' had in fact already been married to another woman. She, therefore, readily agreed to set up a meeting, accompanied by the police, to challenge her 'husband' at a pub in Walworth. The conversation with Mrs Robinson was the least of John Robinson's worries as he was instead arrested on suspicion of murder. When interviewed, Robinson denied all knowledge of the trunk and was not identified in a parade by any of the witnesses. He was, therefore, temporarily released.

On 21 May 1927, at a conference that reviewed the inquiry and the evidence that had been obtained, Cornish asked for a grimy and bloodstained tea towel found in the trunk to be washed, a process that revealed the word 'Greyhound' written on a thin tab, thus establishing a connection to Robinson. Revisiting the previous inquiries, the police undertook a further search at Robinson's office in case anything might have been missed. This second search revealed a bloodstained match that had been caught in a wickerwork wastebasket, as if it had been left behind whilst the remainder of the basket had been emptied. It was before the advent of sophisticated blood-grouping techniques, or indeed the establishment of forensic science laboratories, and matchsticks were common when so many people smoked. But the bloodstains were significant. Robinson was rearrested and, when confronted with this evidence, he admitted using Minnie Bonati's services as a prostitute and disposing of her dead body. He gave the police information that led them to discover a knife buried on Clapham Common, but claimed that Minnie Bonati had died accidentally after an argument when she demanded money for her services that he couldn't pay. Robinson claimed that she became abusive and had tried to attack him. When he shoved her away in self-defence, she hit her head on a coal scuttle as she fell. She was unconscious, so Robinson had left the office, opposite Rochester Row police station, thinking that she had been only dazed and would make her own way home when she recovered. Later, on discovering that she was in fact dead, he bought a knife and dismembered her body, wrapping it in her own clothes and making up a number of brown paper parcels. He had then bought a second-hand trunk, filled it with the grisly parcels, Minnie Bonati's shoes and handbag, and taken the trunk downstairs with the help of a man he had met in a pub. Robinson had then hailed the taxi and deposited the trunk at Charing Cross station. The trunk, tea towel, knife, matchstick and a cushion are also in the museum.

Sir Bernard Spilsbury testified that several bruises on the victim's forehead, stomach, back, arms and legs had probably been inflicted by pressure from a knee before her death; the cause of which was asphyxiation whilst unconscious. Again giving evidence for the defence, pathologist Dr Robert Brontë stated that she might have suffocated because of her face lying against the folds of the carpet or in the crook of her elbow. Brontë also stated that he thought the bruises could have been caused several hours before death. Robinson could not give a satisfactory answer as to why he had not sought help to save the woman's life, however, and he was convicted of the murder. He was hanged at Pentonville prison on 12 August 1927.

71 Coffee Pot

THE DENTED COFFEE pot shows the force that was used by John Donald Merrett to batter his mother-in-law, Mary Menzies, to death.

Donald Merrett had been born in New Zealand in August 1908, and came to England with his mother in 1924. In January 1926, he and his mother moved to Edinburgh where he was registered on a three-year MA degree course at the university. Merrett's proclivity was to pursue girls rather than his studies and he also used his skill with a pen to forge his mother's signature on no fewer than twenty-nine cheques. Because of this, his mother received a letter from her bank manager about the size of her overdraft. On Wednesday, 17 March 1926, at 9.40 a.m., there was a loud bang, after which Donald Merrett ran into the kitchen and told the maid that his mother had shot herself (a crime in those days). Mrs Merrett, still alive, was taken to hospital and managed to give Dr Roy Holcombe an account of what had happened. She told the doctor that whilst she had been writing letters, her son had been standing behind her. She had told him not to bother her and to go away, but then heard an explosion and could remember nothing more. She died two weeks later, on 1 April. In the following months, the situation regarding Mrs Merrett's chequebook and the forged signatures became clear to the police and this led to 18-year-old Donald Merrett being charged with murdering his own mother and with fraud.

The trial took place in Edinburgh in February 1927 with the

DATE:
1954

EXHIBIT:
The pewter coffee pot used as a weapon by Donald Merrett

prosecution arguing that Mrs Merrett could not have committed suicide because it was impossible for her physically to have held the gun at the right angle and distance to avoid black powder marks on her skin. This was disputed by Sir Bernard Spilsbury and firearms specialist Robert Churchill, who gave expert evidence for the defence. The jury found the murder charge 'Not Proven', but did convict Merrett of forging his mother's cheques, for which he was sentenced to twelve months' imprisonment. In his 1959 memoir, the famous pathologist Sir Sydney Smith thought that Spilsbury and Churchill had made a mistake but were too stubborn to admit it.

On his release from prison eight months later in October 1927, Merrett went to live in Bexhill with one of his mother's friends, then known as Mary Bonar, who had taken pity on him and visited him in prison. Five months later, Merrett eloped with Mary's 17-year-old daughter Vera and married her in Glasgow in March 1928. The following year, in August 1929, Merrett inherited a share of the legacy left by his grandfather which he invested so that Vera received income from the interest but the capital would revert to him if Vera died. Merrett changed his name to Ronald John Chesney and he and his wife embarked on an extravagant lifestyle.

Chesney joined the Royal Navy at the outbreak of the Second World War in 1939 and in 1942 spent some months in an Italian prisoner-of-war camp. After the war, Chesney's life was centred on smuggling and black marketeering on the continent and in Germany. He had become estranged from his wife and in 1949 asked her to divorce him for desertion. This meant that Chesney would benefit from the investment he had given her after their wedding. Vera did not agree and Chesney eventually started to make plans to murder her.

In 1954, twenty-eight years after his mother's death, Ronald Chesney made the trip over from Germany to visit Vera, who by that time was running an old people's home in Montpelier Road, Ealing, with her mother Mary, now Mary Menzies, but often calling herself Lady Menzies. Chesney made a plan to murder Vera and to escape detection. He visited her at Montpelier Road, plied her with alcohol and then drowned her in the bath on the night of 10–11 February 1954. Chesney's plan to make Vera's death look accidental went awry when his mother-in-law, Mary, appeared on the scene, and he then attacked Mary with the coffee pot and killed her as well. Instead of one death that might have appeared accidental, the two bodies clearly indicated a double murder.

The case was investigated by Detective Superintendent Edmund Daws, assisted by Dr Lewis Nickolls, the director of the Metropolitan Police Forensic Science Laboratory; Percy Law, the head of the Photographic Department at Scotland Yard; and Jack Livings, then in charge of the Fingerprint Branch. Livings found that the bathroom had, in his opinion, been wiped clean to remove finger marks. Nickolls noted blood splashes and the signs of a violent struggle with evidence that the room had been tidied to remove signs of the violence. A number of hairs and fibres connected clothing known to belong to Chesney with the two victims. Mary Menzies had blood on her fingernails and it appeared that she might have inflicted noticeable scratch wounds on her assailant. The pathologist, Donald Teare, found that the coffee pot was bloodstained and consistent with the weapon that caused the injuries that had killed Menzies. Mary Menzies shared the same blood group, O, as Ronald Chesney, but Vera Chesney's blood was group A.

Chesney did not stand trial for this incident, however, as he fled back to Germany where, on 16 February, five days after the murder, the police found the body of a man, apparently Chesney, who had committed suicide by shooting himself in the head in a wood near Cologne, the pistol he used now being in the Crime Museum. Edmund Daws travelled to Germany with Detective Sergeant Chadburn, who acted as an interpreter, and liaised with Kriminalkommissar Kuhn of the Cologne police. They saw Chesney's body and noted that his right hand bore bruising and scratch marks. The German police took photographs of the injuries but they did not give as accurate a picture as would have been desirable to establish whether they were wounds sustained in the murder, so the German authorities agreed to Edmund Daws' request to remove the forearms, so that he could take them back to London to be properly examined. The body was formally identi-fied by Jack Livings, who matched the fingerprints on the body to those recorded against Chesney. The officers also brought a farewell letter back to London that Chesney had written to Sonia Winnikes, a woman he had been living with in Germany and whom he may have promised to marry. Chesney had also written a letter attempting to make Winnikes the beneficiary of money to be disbursed after his and Vera's deaths.

The inquest into the deaths of Vera Chesney and Mary Menzies on 24 March 1954 heard evidence from a Richard Pickersgill who had met Chesney in prison in 1951. Pickersgill had been offered £2,000 by Chesney to kill Vera and had been given a plan of the house where she lived in Montpelier Road, Ealing. The jury duly found that Chesney had murdered both women, the case illustrating the careful preparation and evidence for a coroner's inquest when no criminal trial would follow.

72 Fake Antique Bowl

DATE:
Unknown

EXHIBIT:
Fake Greek patera libation bowl

THE ART AND Antiques Unit at Scotland Yard perform a very specialised role combatting thefts and other crime involving antiques that can be very sophisticated and lucrative. In 2017, Detective Constable Sophie Hayes received information about a Greek silver bowl that was being put up for auction for more than £80,000 that may have been looted and sold illegally. The officer made inquiries and traced the item to an auction catalogue published by the Timeline company in Essex, and, believing it to have been smuggled illegally from Bulgaria, seized the bowl in order to make further inquiries.

The item is a type of libation bowl, used by ancient Greeks to perform religious rituals involving the pouring out of wine, milk or honey as a mark of personal piety, apparently dating from the fifth or fourth century BCE and therefore perhaps 2,500 years old. The auction house had provisionally estimated its sale value as between £80,000 and £100,000, and was in possession of a receipt from Mr Aleksander Ribnikov stating that he was the beneficial owner and that he had acquired the bowl around 1986–88 from a central London collection.

The Arts Loss Register acts as the main point for due diligence in tracking the loss or theft of antiques. They sent copies of documents provided by Ribnikov that suggested he had bought it from a Roy Thomas in Swansea in 1987. Contrary to the statement in the auction catalogue, they had not issued an Arts Loss Register certificate because they had not been satisfied with the provenance.

DC Hayes found that a Mr Thomas had never lived at the address given in Swansea and took the bowl to the British Museum, who found it to be a fake, partly because the pattern around the outside of the bowl indicated a different period from the interior. None of the patterns had been made with antique tools.

When Hayes arrested Ribnikov, she found a notebook containing a receipt purporting to be from a Roy Thomas in 1987, but she established from the barcode of the notebook that it had not been manufactured until 2014, proving that the receipt could not have been genuine. She also found correspondence indicating that Ribnikov had been in contact with Christie's and other major auction houses, who had not accepted the item for auction because of unsatisfactory documentation.

Ribnikov pleaded guilty at Isleworth Crown Court in August 2017 to two counts of fraud by false representation: one against Timeline auctions, and another offence against Christie's in relation to other objects. He was given a two-year prison sentence suspended for two years.

The investigation resulted in a great improvement in collaboration with the Bulgarian authorities and is an example of the serious problem of fraudulent dealing in antiquities.

Burnt Chair

DATE:
1933

EXHIBIT:
The chair on which Walter Spatchett's body was found

THE BURNT CHAIR was in a fire in a large shed that had been set ablaze shortly before 8 p.m. on 3 January 1933. The fire service was called to the fire in a yard in Hawley Crescent, Camden, that was rented by builder and decorator Samuel Furnace. Seated on the chair was a dead body, with most of the facial features burnt away. The police searched an adjacent room and found a note that read 'Goodbye to all. No work. No money. Samuel James Furnace'. Furnace was a 42-year-old married man with considerable financial debts, who could not support his wife and children or pay off his creditors. Furnace's home was about 500yds away in Crogsland Road, and a tenant of his, a Mr Abbot, identified the body as that of Samuel Furnace.

The case was duly reported to the coroner, Sir Bentley Purchase, who was sceptical that a man would set himself on fire and remain seated on a chair. He went to the mortuary to examine the body and found a bullet wound in his back. The teeth appeared to be of a man younger than Furnace's 42 years and the post-mortem examination found a second bullet wound. The dead man's clothing was examined, some of which had laundry marks and the initials 'W S'. A wallet and other charred and waterlogged items were found bearing the name of Walter Spatchett. Walter Spatchett was a 25-year-old debt collector who had been missing since the day before and who had been a regular visitor to the Furnace premises. He was believed to have been in possession of £30–£40 when he had last been seen. Dental records completed the identification, which contradicted the 'suicide note' that had originally suggested the body was that of Samuel Furnace.

It was now vital to trace the real Samuel Furnace. A radio appeal, the first ever made through the BBC (which had been established a decade earlier) was broadcast on 9 January 1933 seeking information about Furnace's whereabouts and stating that he was wanted for murder. This resulted in many reports of sightings, but the most important message to the police came from Furnace's brother-in-law, Charlie Tuckfield. Tuckfield reported that Furnace had sent him a letter asking him to bring a change of clothing on the 10.35 a.m. train from Harringay to Southend, where, if he walked down the road opposite the station, he would receive more detailed instructions. There was no address shown on the letter, as Furnace was worried about his brother-in-law being followed by the police. As Charlie Tuckfield walked along Whitegate Road, he saw a sign with the word 'Sam' written on it in a ground-floor window and went into the house. Detectives under the leadership of Detective Superintendent George Cornish had been observing and, after Charlie Tuckfield had left the premises, they entered the same house from the rear, where they found Furnace smoking a cigarette and reading about his case in a newspaper. After his arrest and on the journey back to London, Furnace confessed to killing Walter Spatchett, claiming that his gun had gone off accidentally. He later gave detectives details to enable them to recover the gun from a building site where he had hidden the weapon in a wall. It later entered the museum. Furnace told the police that after having killed Walter Spatchett he had wrapped the body in a tarpaulin. He then formed a plan to set fire to the premises after the others had left there at the end of the day's work, and to fake his own suicide by using Walter Spatchett's body.

When he was being held in a cell at Kentish Town police station he was allowed to keep his coat on because he felt cold at night. He had, however, concealed a bottle of hydrochloric acid in the lining of the coat and swallowed this. He was rushed to hospital in immense pain but died on 18 January 1933.

The scene of a fire is invariably a dirty and wet environment for an investigation, but the ashes often contain useful clues. The prospect of fire destroying all traces of a person's identity and the means by which a victim may have died is sometimes a temptation for fraud, particularly when news of a similar crime has been publicised in the media. In this case, Furnace may have been influenced by two cases that happened in the previous years.

The 'Blazing Car' murder occurred in the early hours of 6 November 1930 near Hardingstone, Northamptonshire, when two young men found a Morris Minor car ablaze. They had passed a respectably dressed man a few minutes earlier who had commented that it looked as if someone had been having a bonfire. When the fire was extinguished, a dead body, burnt beyond recognition, was found inside, but the car's number plate was intact. The registered owner was 37-year-old Alfred Arthur Rouse, a commercial traveller from north London who had a large number of girlfriends in various parts of the country. When he was interviewed by detectives he said, 'I am responsible. I am glad it is over,' and gave an account of how he had given a lift to a hitchhiker on his way to Leicester. Rouse had stopped the car near Hardingstone to relieve himself and claimed that he had given the hitchhiker a cigar before asking him to fill the car with petrol from a can he kept in the boot. Rouse claimed that whilst he was otherwise engaged with his trousers down, he saw a light, returned to find his car engulfed in a mass of flames and then panicked. The car's carburettor had been tampered with, which contradicted his story.

Rouse was tried for the murder of the unknown hitchhiker at Northampton Assizes in January 1931, convicted and executed at Bedford prison on 10 March 1931. He had apparently seduced as many as eighty women, had several children and had also committed bigamy. Rouse's confession and account of the incident may well have concealed his true motive in seeking a completely fresh start and an escape from his complicated life with so many women. In 2014, a DNA analysis was undertaken on samples from the hitchhiker's body from Bernard Spilsbury's original slides to try to establish whether the victim had in fact been William Briggs, a man who had been reported missing at the time. Northamptonshire Police had been keen to help Briggs' family to establish the truth, but the DNA sample did not match those of family members and the identity of Rouse's victim remains a mystery.

A year earlier, when the German police were called to a green Opel car that had caught fire after a traffic accident in Regensburg, they thought that the registered owner from Leipzig, Erich Tetzner, had been burnt to death in the driving seat. Frau Tetzner identified the driver as her husband and claimed on insurance policies that had recently been taken out. The policies were for a large amount for a couple of modest means and the insurance company became suspicious. This suspicion may have been aroused because Tetzner had previously claimed an insurance payout on his mother-in-law's life, having persuaded her to delay an operation for cancer until he had taken out the policy.

The post-mortem examination on the Opel driver was carried out by Richard Kockel, who noted that the accident victim was smaller than Tetzner. The dead man was about 23 years of age, younger than Tetzner's 26 years. His air passages contained no particles of soot, and blood samples were negative for carbon monoxide, indicating that he would have been dead before the fire started. The 'accident' had occurred on 27 November 1929, and damage to the car was not consistent with injuries to the driver's skull. Part of the victim's brain was found on the road 2yds from the car itself.

The police, under Chief Superintendent Kriegern, decided to keep Frau Tetzner under surveillance, on the basis that her husband was still alive somewhere. She used her neighbour's telephone frequently and a detective was able to recruit the co-operation of the neighbours to intercept a call for Frau Tetzner. He asked the man to call back at 6 p.m., but kept the line open and had it traced to a call box in Strasbourg. When the man telephoned again, police went to the telephone box and found the caller to be an alive and well Erich Tetzner. Tetzner confessed, and it appears that he had murdered the unknown man, probably a hitchhiker, as part of an insurance fraud.

74 Udham Singh's Diary

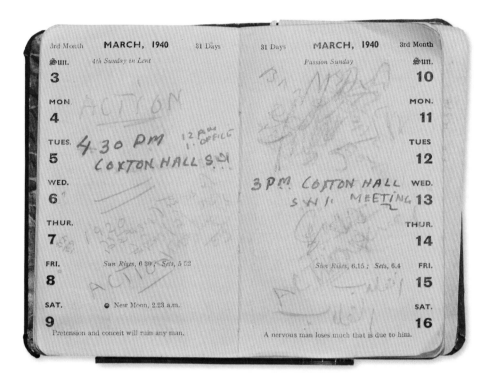

DATE:
1940

EXHIBIT:
Udham Singh's diary, including 13 March 1940

ONE OF THE most notorious incidents in the history of British rule in India was the reason for a revenge murder that took place in London over twenty years later, with a diary entry possibly indicating that the perpetrator was confused about his target.

In April 1919, a large crowd of about 20,000 people gathered at the Jallianwala Bagh garden in Amritsar, Punjab, to protest about the arrest of two leaders for breach of a curfew order. It was the day of a festival, but the British authorities had apparently issued an order banning any such gatherings. The order was not likely to have been well publicised, but the army would have been well aware of it and would have feared public disorder.

General Reginald Dyer attended the scene with fifty riflemen and, despite there not being any disorder, told his men to fire on the crowd, which the soldiers did for ten minutes. This resulted in 379 deaths according to British reports (1,000 according to the Indian National Congress) and 1,100 wounded. This created an understandably enormous sense of grievance against British rule. Sir Michael O'Dwyer was the lieutenant governor of Punjab at the time.

Nearly twenty years later, on 13 March 1940, in wartime London, there was a meeting at Caxton Hall organised by the East India Association and the Royal Central Asian Society, attended by about 160 people. The Secretary of State for India, Lord Zetland, chaired the meeting, which heard a lecture about the position of Afghanistan from Brigadier General Sir Percy Sykes. On the platform were a number of fairly elderly and distinguished men, including the 75-year-old Sir Michael O'Dwyer and the 84-year-old Sir Louis Dane, his predecessor in Punjab. The meeting had recognised the substantial support from the Muslim world for the Allies in the Second World War.

After O'Dwyer had given a short, witty speech and the meeting had ended, a burly Sikh walked down to the front of the hall and fired six rounds at close range from his .45 Smith & Wesson revolver at members of the platform party, the primary target being O'Dwyer. Two shots hit and killed O'Dwyer, one of them entering his heart and right lung, the second passing through his kidney. Sir Louis Dane and Lord Lamington were injured. Lord Zetland was hit in the chest but the bullets were of the wrong calibre and were stopped by his clothing.

The assassin was Udham Singh, aged 37, also known as Singh Azad, from Mornington Crescent, who had survived the Amritsar massacre where his brother had been killed. His diary contained two entries about Caxton Hall meetings. It has been suggested that he confused Sir Michael with General Dyer, who had actually died in 1927, but the diary itself does not clearly support this theory. However, Sir Michael O'Dwyer had voiced his support for General Dyer after the incident. Udham Singh was excitable and spoke English badly, but did express his antagonism more generally towards

Lord Zetland and the British authorities. The murder was described by Clement Attlee as an 'abominable outrage' and Gandhi described it as 'an act of insanity'.

At his trial, Udham Singh said that he had intended to fire shots into the ceiling as a protest about the treatment of the Indian people by the British government and that killing Sir Michael had been an accident. Sir Bernard Spilsbury gave evidence at the trial despite having suffered a mild stroke a few weeks earlier. Udham Singh was found guilty on 5 June, when British forces were reeling from the shock of the withdrawal from Dunkirk, and was executed on 31 July 1940, seven years before India's independence. Udham Singh's gun and knife are also in the museum as reminders of how history changes perceptions about the motivation for crime.

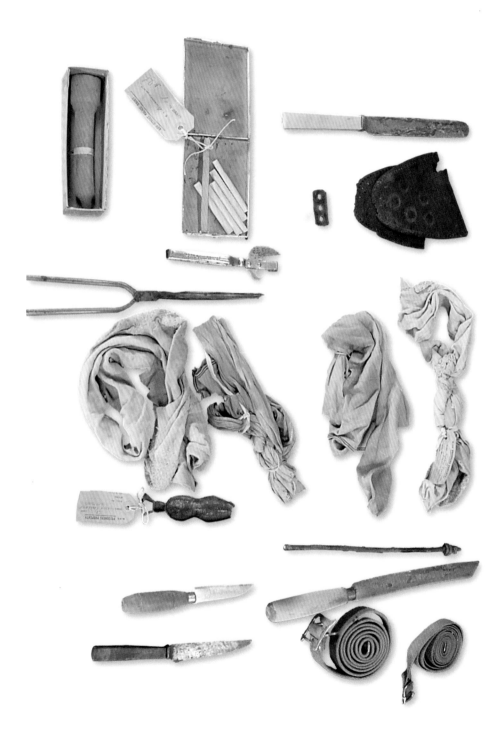

Wartime Stockings

LONDON DURING THE Second World War had to face bombing raids, blackout restrictions and a life expectancy dominated by the uncertainties of war. Ladies' stockings were a luxury, but became the means of strangulation for some of the victims of a man that came to be known as the 'Blackout Ripper'.

In February 1942, four women were attacked and murdered in a space of six days. Evelyn Hamilton, a 40-year-old chemist's assistant, was found strangled in an air-raid shelter in Montagu Place, Marylebone, in the early morning of Sunday, 9 February. Her scarf was wound round her head and her clothing was in disarray, but there was no sign of sexual assault. Her handbag, which had contained £80, had been taken. That night, a 35-year-old former Windmill showgirl Evelyn Oatley (alias Nita Ward) took a client back to her flat in Wardour Street and was strangled to death. Her nearly naked body was found mutilated: her throat had been cut, the lower part of her body sliced open with a razor blade and cut with a tin opener. In the flat, fingerprints were found on a tin opener. The attacker was apparently left-handed.

On the Thursday, 13 February, another prostitute, Margaret Lowe, was found murdered in her flat in Gosfield Street, near Great Portland Street. She had been strangled with a silk stocking, but also cut and disfigured with a knife and razor blade. Detective Chief Inspector Ted Greeno was at the scene, with Detective Inspector Robert Higgins and Sir Bernard Spilsbury, when news of a fourth

DATE:
1942

EXHIBIT:
Stockings and other exhibits in the Gordon Cummins case

murder reached them. Doris Jouannet (32), who was also known as Doris Robson, had been strangled with a scarf and her naked body obscenely mutilated in the flat in Sussex Gardens that she shared with her husband. The murders were occurring with frightening speed.

The breakthrough came on the following evening, Friday, when Mrs Greta Heywood went for a drink and a sandwich with an RAF airman near Piccadilly Circus. As they walked down Haymarket she tried to avoid his physical advances and ran away. The man chased after her and started to attack her in a doorway in St Alban's Street. A delivery boy investigated the scuffling, saw her silk stocking in the blackout and approached to find out what was happening. The man ran away, but left behind an RAF gas mask, which bore his name, rank and number, identifying him as Gordon Cummins (28).

A few hours later, Cummins went to the flat of a prostitute, Mrs Mulcahy, in Southwick Street, Paddington, to whom he gave £5 for her services. Because her flat was so cold, she undressed but kept her boots on. Cummins had just removed his greatcoat and belt when she noticed a strange expression on his face, and the man tried to strangle her. She was able to deliver a hard kick to his shins with her boots and he then left the flat in a hurry, leaving behind his belt.

Ted Greeno traced Cummins to RAF quarters in St Johns Wood, but found that he had been signed in before midnight each night that week but police disproved the alibi by ascertaining that Cummins had left the premises by a fire escape after being officially checked in. Items belonging to his first murder victim, Evelyn Hamilton, were found in a nearby dustbin. A cigarette case belonging to his second victim, Evelyn Oatley, was found in his uniform pocket. Cummins' finger marks were found in the flats of his second and third victims. A fountain pen marked 'DJ', found in his No. 1 uniform, had been taken from his fourth victim, Doris Jouannet, thus completing an impressive set of identification links to the murder scenes. A tin opener, knives, shoe heels, the cigarette case and other items are in the museum.

Cummins was prosecuted initially only for the murder of Evelyn Oatley. He was found guilty and hanged at Wandsworth prison on 25 June 1942.

76 Binoculars

DATE:
1945

EXHIBIT:
The crudely
made
booby-trap
binoculars

THE ORIGIN OF a pair of binoculars, with a spring-loaded spike designed to injure the eyes of a person trying to use them, is not known for certain. It is said that in 1945 a man sent the binoculars as a farewell gift to his former fiancée in Southampton after she had broken off their engagement. They were featured on the poster of Herman Cohen's 1959 film, *Horrors of the Black Museum*, and might have been inspired by a similar booby-trapped weapon that appeared in the plot of the 1943 musical *Oklahoma!* by Rodgers and Hammerstein.

77 Riding Whip

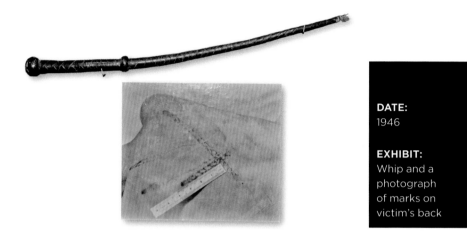

DATE:
1946

EXHIBIT:
Whip and a
photograph
of marks on
victim's back

THE WHIP WAS a weapon used to inflict pain on the victims of a sadistic killer. Unusually, it created a pattern that could be matched to a victim's wound.

It was at the Pembridge Court Hotel in Notting Hill, just after the end of the Second World War, where a 32-year-old woman named Margery Gardner went to a room with a good-looking younger man, the so-called Lieutenant Colonel Neville Heath, 28. Margery Gardner was an artists' model and occasional film extra living a bohemian lifestyle who had briefly met Heath a few weeks earlier and then again on the evening of 20 June 1946. Heath took Gardner back to his hotel in the early hours of 21 June, opening the main door with his key, since there was no night porter, and took her up to Room No. 4. At 2 p.m. on the same day the chambermaid found the room in disarray and the dead body of Margery Gardner, horribly mutilated and with weals across her back that featured a distinctive dia-mond pattern. Gardner had been suffocated to death. There was no sign of Heath, who had gone to Worthing to visit 20-year-old Yvonne Symonds who he had only met a week earlier and became engaged to the day after he had murdered Margery Gardner.

Symonds had served in the Women's Royal Naval Service and was no doubt impressed by the bearing of

Heath, who created the impression of being an authoritative senior army officer. Heath took Symonds out to dinner and told her about the murder in London that had occurred in the hotel room he had been staying in. He told her that he had seen the victim with another man, who must have been a 'sexual maniac'.

He sent a letter to Detective Chief Inspector Barratt at Scotland Yard repeating the story he had told Yvonne Symonds. The newspapers had published the fact that the police wanted to interview him, something that greatly disturbed Symonds' parents, so Heath told her that he would travel up to London to clear things up with the police. In fact, he went to Bournemouth, with the new name of Rupert Brooke and the rank of group captain.

On 3 July he entertained Miss Doreen Marshall with dinner at the West Cliff Hotel, Bournemouth, and escorted her out of the premises at about 11.30 p.m. Doreen Marshall was never seen alive again. The so-called Rupert Brooke was called on to help the Bournemouth police investigate her disappearance and a local police officer, Detective Constable Souter, recognised his similarity to pictures of Heath issued by Scotland Yard and challenged him. Heath denied it, but he was kept at the police station until Detective Inspector George Gates arrived.

Whilst searching Heath's belongings, the police found a railway ticket belonging to Doreen Marshall, a pearl from her necklace and a left-luggage ticket. George Gates used the ticket to reclaim the suitcase, opened it and found several items bearing Heath's name. He also found bloodstained clothing, which still bore hairs that matched those of Margery Gardner, and the bloodstained riding whip that created the distinctive diamond pattern.

Detective Inspector Reginald Spooner from Scotland Yard arrived and took Heath back to London to answer questions about Margery Gardner's murder, but at about the same time as they were leaving for London, Doreen Marshall's body was found in Bournemouth on 8 July, again brutally and sadistically murdered.

Heath went for trial at the Old Bailey where he was found sane and guilty. When he was about to be hanged the prison governor offered him a whisky, to which Heath replied, 'Under the circumstances, you might make that a double.'

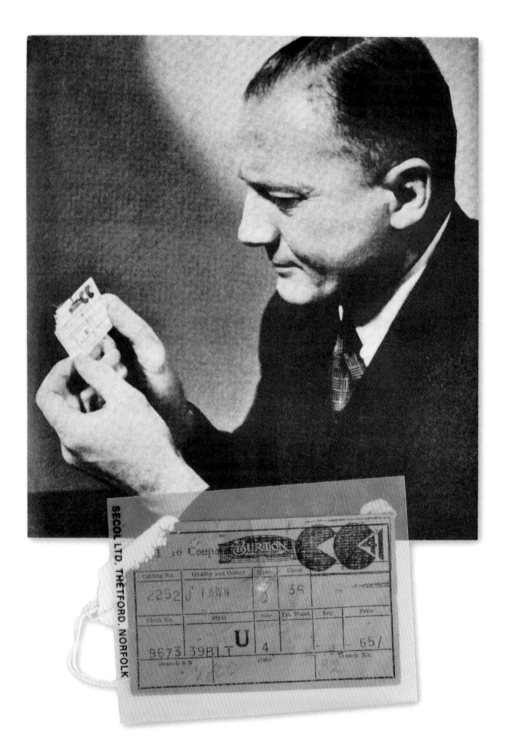

1 16 Coupon **BURTON**

Cutting No.	Quality and Colour	Quan.	Chest	
2252	J FAWN	2	36	
Cloth No.	Style	Size	Trs. Waist	Leg	Price
9673	39BLT	U	4		65/
Branch 8 N		Date		Branch No.

SECOL LTD. THETFORD. NORFOLK

78

Clothing Label

THE COUPON, FOUND in a coat used by armed robbers, was used by Detective Superintendent Robert Fabian to trace the killers of Alec de Antiquis, who had tried to stop their escape from the scene of the burglary. It formed part of the evidence that convicted Charles Jenkins (23), Christopher Geraghty (21) and Terence Rolt (17) of robbery and murder.

When three masked gunmen entered a jeweller's shop in Charlotte Street, near Tottenham Court Road, on 29 April 1947, the director of the company managed to slam the safe door shut, but was fired at by one of the gang. The shot went wide and hit a wall, and the director was pistol-whipped, but the robbers realised that their raid had gone wrong, threw away the gun that had misfired and ran from the shop, only to find that their stolen Vauxhall 14 getaway car had been blocked in by a lorry. They were running down Charlotte Street, wearing masks and waving their guns, when 34-year-old Alec de Antiquis, a father of six children, drove his motorcycle into the path of one of the raiders. He was shot dead. Soon afterwards Detective Superintendent Robert Fabian arrived at the scene and his team started to piece together the evidence of the stolen car, the bullet and the abandoned revolver. Twenty-seven witnesses were interviewed, but their testimonies varied and the police found no finger marks.

Two days later, a taxi driver reported that he had seen men with white face masks going into a building

DATE:
1947

EXHIBIT:
The label, with a photograph of Robert Fabian

in Tottenham Court Road, and it was there, in an empty top-floor office, that the police found a discarded raincoat which had some gloves, a piece of white cloth and a cap in its pockets. Inside the lining of the coat was a 'utility label' that enabled the police to trace the garment to a tailor in Deptford High Street. Because rationing after the Second World War was still in force at that point, the shop had kept records of its customers, and this led the police to Bermondsey. The customer's wife had lent the coat, now in the museum, to her brother, Charles Henry Jenkins. Jenkins was arrested, but was not picked out at an identification parade. Two revolvers were found on the foreshore of the River Thames, near to where Jenkins' parents lived. One of them had fired the fatal bullet; the other had fired the bullet that been found embedded in the wall of the shop. The guns and bullet now form part of the display in the Crime Museum. Two of Jenkins' known associates, Christopher Geraghty and Terence Rolt, were detained. Geraghty had been the one who fired the fatal shot that killed the heroic Alec de Antiquis, and was the first to confess. Then Rolt implicated Jenkins.

All three were tried at the Old Bailey in July 1947. It took the jury only fifteen minutes to return a verdict of guilty. Jenkins and Geraghty were both sentenced to death and were executed at Pentonville prison on 19 September 1947, amidst demands for the abolition of the death penalty. Rolt had been only 17 years old and was sentenced to serve at His Majesty's Pleasure.

Alec de Antiquis was posthumously awarded the Binney Medal for bravery in trying to stop the crime. (The medal is named after Captain Ralph Binney who, in 1944, was knocked down and killed whilst trying to stop a smash-and-grab raider's car near London Bridge. Coincidentally, one of the criminals involved in that case was Jenkins' brother.)

79 False Teeth

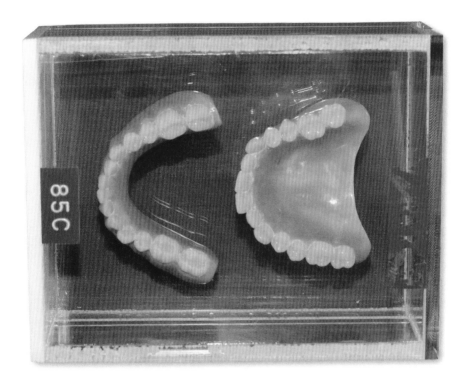

DATE:
1949

EXHIBIT:
Replica of Olivia
Durand-Deacon's
false teeth

IN 1949, JOHN Haigh (40) lived at the Onslow Court Hotel in South Kensington where a 68-year-old widow, Mrs H. Olivia R. Durand-Deacon, was also a resident. Haigh was in debt through gambling losses, but gave the impression of being knowledgeable about business. He invited Mrs Durand-Deacon down to Crawley on 18 February 1949 to take forward her idea of making a new type of artificial fingernails for women. Haigh had a connection with a disused storeroom in the area. There he shot her, put her body into a large 40gal drum of acid and returned to London later that same night. The following day Haigh asked Mrs Constance Lane, another resident at the hotel, whether she knew where her friend Mrs Durand-Deacon was as she had not been at the Army & Navy stores where he had arranged to meet and drive her to Crawley. He had therefore made the trip on his own. Whilst inquiries about Mrs Durand-Deacon were being made at the hotel, Haigh went about the process of selling her watch and jewellery and took her fur coat to be cleaned in Reigate.

On 20 February Haigh accompanied Mrs Lane to Chelsea police station to report Mrs Durand-Deacon missing. The following morning the astute Sergeant Alexandra Lambourne went to the hotel where she formed suspicions about Haigh and discovered that he had been in prison three times for fraud.

When Detective Superintendent Barratt and Detective Inspector Symes later interviewed Haigh, they had already discovered much about his movements around the Crawley and Horsham area, and presented Haigh with the cleaning ticket for Durand-Deacon's fur coat. During a short absence from the interview room of the other two detectives, Haigh asked Detective Inspector Webb about the chances of being released from Broadmoor, said that there would be no trace of Durand-Deacon because she had been dissolved in acid and challenged them to prove murder without a body. He then went on to give details of murdering others, eventually reaching a total of eight other people, using the same method of disposing the bodies (these cases were never verified by the police). He also claimed to have drunk his victims' blood, though this could have been part of an attempt to construct a defence of insanity. It appears he was motivated entirely by financial gain.

Examination of the storeroom in Crawley with pathologist Keith Simpson revealed some blood spots above a workshop bench and a hatpin at the bottom of a metal drum that had once contained acid. The sludge from the acid was taken to the Metropolitan Police Forensic Science Laboratory and found to contain fat, gall stones, part of a foot, eighteen bone fragments, a lipstick container, part of a handbag and a set of dentures that were later identified by her dentist as belonging to Mrs Durand-Deacon.

A gas mask, apron, and the .38 Enfield revolver used by Haigh are also in the Crime Museum, together with replicas of the gall stones. Haigh was convicted of Mrs Durand-Deacon's murder and executed at Wandsworth prison on 10 August 1949.

80 TV Bracket

THE TELEVISION AERIAL bracket was used by Daniel Raven to commit a murder that left many questions unanswered about his motivation.

Daniel Raven was 23 years old and, on Monday, 10 October 1949, had been visiting his wife, Marie, in a maternity home where she had given birth to their first child four days earlier. Raven had driven his parents-in-law, Leopold and Esther Goodman, to the maternity home and gave them a lift back to their own house. Whatever passed between Raven and the Goodmans, who were immensely proud of their daughter and their new grandson, was a mystery, but after they left the maternity home shortly after 9 p.m. that evening, Daniel Raven destroyed his wife's family by battering the Goodmans to death using the base of a television aerial. Television had not become popular at that time,

DATE:
1949

EXHIBIT:
TV aerial bracket used as a weapon by Daniel Raven

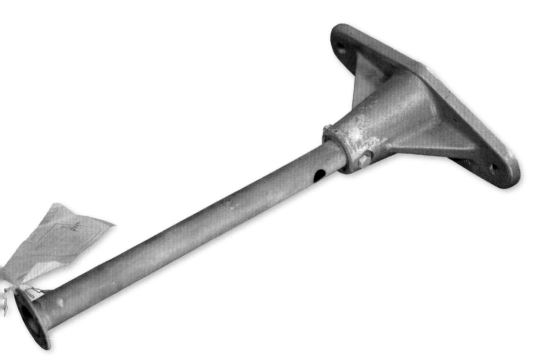

but Leopold Goodman was a partner in a radio business. The attack took place around 9.30 p.m.

At about 9.55 p.m., Esther Goodman's brother-in-law, who was also Leopold Goodman's business partner, called at the house with his wife and daughter to enquire about the new baby. When he received no response, he climbed into the house through an open window and found the murder scene. He telephoned the police and Detective Inspector Diller started the police investigation. The police telephoned Daniel Raven and asked him to come round to the house as they had some bad news. Raven soon arrived from his own home in nearby Edgwarebury Lane, a house bought for him and his wife by his parents-in-law.

There were bundles of banknotes in the house, including some under a mattress and over £2,500 in a safe, so it appeared that robbery was not the motive for the crime. Raven arrived at the house and appeared overcome with emotion. The police noticed that he was wearing a clean shirt and others noticed that he had changed his suit. Raven lamented that he had not stayed longer with his parents-in-law who, he said, were worried about being burgled. He had been present at the house during the crucial time and was asked to come to the police station for further investigation. He was asked to provide the keys to his house, and when Detective Inspector Diller went there he immediately smelt burning. A gas poker was alight in the kitchen boiler, from which the officer managed to retrieve the remains of a suit. Both victims shared a relatively rare blood group, AB, and bloodstains matching this group were found on the suit and on a pair of Raven's shoes. Raven's car seat had been recently cleaned. On this evidence, Detective Chief Inspector Albert Tansil charged him with the murders.

When Raven appeared at the Old Bailey in November 1949 he claimed he had left his parents-in-law alive, but had then called on his cousins, who had been out, so he had returned to his parents-in-law and found the murder scene, which is when he got blood on his clothes. He claimed to have driven to his own home in fear and then burnt his suit and washed his shoes. The unlikely story was rejected by the jury who found him guilty and he was sentenced to death.

Raven appealed and for the first time introduced evidence of mental instability, drawing on his record of having been discharged from the RAF because of 'severe anxiety neurosis' and on a doctor's report that he had been suffering from 'blackouts and brainstorms'. The appeal and a petition seeking a reprieve from the death penalty both failed, and he was hanged at Pentonville prison on 6 January 1950. The burnt clothing and a denture also became museum exhibits.

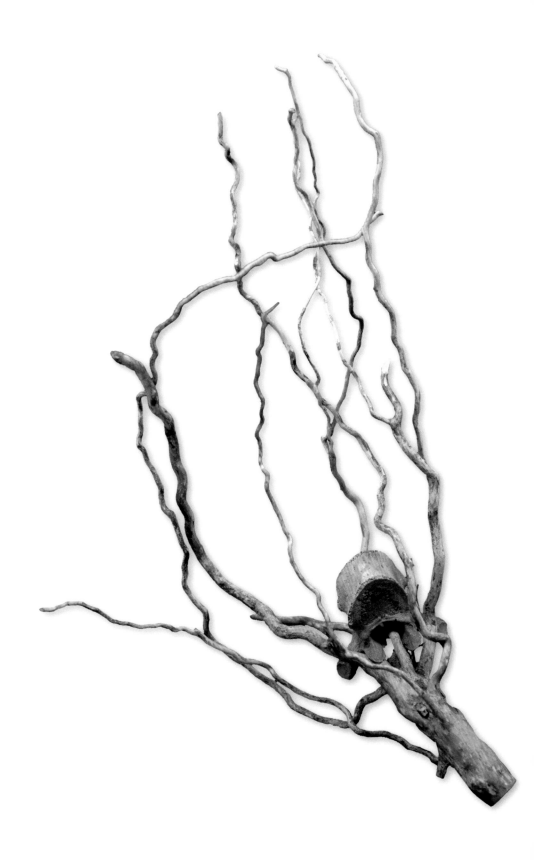

Shrub Root

A SET OF human bones found in the garden of the three-storey house at No. 10 Rillington Place near Ladbroke Grove, Notting Hill, where John Christie was a lodger, was of great interest – not least because one of the thoracic vertebrae, later identified as that of murder victim Ruth Fürst, had a root growing through it. The rate of growth of the root helped to determine the period of time for which the body had been buried. A reconstructed skull of Ruth Fürst showed that one of her teeth had a metal crown with signs of a dental technique not normally practised in Britain. Fürst was an Austrian born in 1922 who had come to England in 1939 and had last been seen alive in August 1943. Other exhibits include a small metal tin containing pubic hair from four of John Christie's murder victims, apparently collected as trophies.

On 24 March 1953, a tenant from No. 10 Rillington Place was pulling away wallpaper in the corner of the kitchen in the ground-floor flat, prior to fixing a bracket for his radio, when he found a wooden partition with a gap in it. Looking through the gap with a torch, he saw a dead body. Another tenant, 53-year-old John Christie, had sold all his furniture and left the flat a few days before; he had gone to live in a Rowton House hostel for the homeless, subletting his flat without the landlord's permission. The landlord discovered the new tenants, evicted them the following day, and had then allowed the other tenant to use the ground-floor kitchen. On the discovery of the body, the police were

DATE:
1943–53

EXHIBIT:
Ruth Fürst's
vertebra
with shrub
root growing
through it

called and started an investigation led by Detective Chief Inspector Albert Griffin. The body was that of 27-year-old Hectorina MacLennan. The police also found two other bodies behind the partition, those of Kathleen Maloney, 26, and Rita Nelson, 25. All three women had been missing for between four and twelve weeks. All had died from asphyxiation and carbon monoxide poisoning, and there was evidence of sexual intercourse having occurred around the time of death.

The discovery of these bodies led to further searches. The body of Christie's wife Ethel, aged 54, was found under the floorboards of the front room. She had been strangled with a ligature, but, unlike the other victims, there was no evidence of gas poisoning nor sexual interference. When the police dug up the garden, they found a large number of bones from which two almost complete female skeletons were reconstructed. One was that of 21-year-old Ruth Fürst whose vertebra had the root growing through it, and the other of Muriel Eady, 31, who had died in 1944. The time in which they had died and were buried there was important.

The police went to the Rowton House hostel to arrest Christie, but he had already moved on. On 31 March 1953, 43-year-old PC Tom Ledger from V Division was patrolling near Putney Bridge when he saw a shabby, unshaven man who had been living rough and questioned him. The man gave a false name, but when the officer asked him for proof of his identity and to remove his hat, he recognised Christie, whose picture had been circulated as wanted for murder, and arrested him. In due course, Christie admitted to killing all six women and was sentenced to death at the Old Bailey in June 1953 despite a defence of insanity. He apparently considered that the more deaths he admitted to, the higher his chances of being found insane. Christie had sexual difficulties and used the services of prostitutes; he became violent and strangled them, sometimes subjecting them to partial gas poisoning by means of a rubber tube connected to a gas pipe, with a bulldog clip to control the gas flow. Christie had been a petty criminal but also served as a war reserve special constable during the war, when he had claimed not to have any convictions and the war-stretched police did not make a thorough check of his fingerprints. He was hanged at Pentonville prison on 15 July 1953.

The major complication of the case was that five years earlier in 1948 a young married couple, Timothy and Beryl Evans, had been tenants in the house. They then had a baby girl, Geraldine, and Beryl became pregnant again in the summer of 1949. This created financial difficulties for them and they discussed an abortion. John Christie persuaded them that he could conduct the operation. (There had in fact been rumours of the house being used for illegal abortions with which Christie may or may not have been connected.) On 8 November 1949, at around lunchtime, Christie, according to his own, possibly unreliable, account, went to the flat upstairs whilst Evans was at work, brought his gas pipe that he claimed would ease the pain of the procedure and then, as Beryl prepared herself for an abortion, attacked and killed her in a sexual frenzy. When Evans arrived home from work, Christie told him the bad news that the abortion procedure had not worked and that Beryl had died from septic poisoning of the stomach. Christie pointed out that Timothy Evans was arguably an accessory to the crime of trying to give his wife an abortion. Christie persuaded him that Beryl's body should be concealed, and that they should tell people that mother and daughter had gone away to Bristol. Christie told Evans that he would make arrangements for his daughter Geraldine to be cared for by a married couple from Acton. In reality, the infant was strangled to death.

Timothy Evans disconsolately disposed of his furniture, left the flat and travelled to Merthyr Vale in Wales to visit his uncle and aunt, telling them that his wife had gone to Brighton. After a few days, he returned to London to try to see Christie, but Christie refused to talk to him. Evans then returned to Wales, under great pressure from family members because different accounts were circulating about his wife's whereabouts. He went to Merthyr Tydfil police station on 30 November 1949 and gave himself up to Detective Constable Gwynfryn Evans for 'disposing of his wife'. His first confession was to the effect that he had given his wife some pills for an abortion that had killed her and had then disposed of her body down a drain. The police in Wales notified

Notting Hill police station, where officers went to the street outside No. 10 Rillington Place and inspected the drain, which was empty. Evans' second statement included Christie's role in procuring the abortion and Christie's promise to put Beryl's body down a drain.

The Notting Hill police searched Evans' rooms and found a stolen briefcase and, in a cupboard, cuttings from four newspapers about the case of Donald Hume who had cut up the body of his victim, Stanley Setty, the previous month in October 1949 (see p. 179). The briefcase had been supplied by Beryl's friends. Detective Inspector Black and Detective Sergeant Corfield went to arrest Evans on a holding charge of handling the stolen briefcase and brought him back to London. Christie was arrested by police but stoutly denied involvement with the abortion, claiming that Timothy and Beryl Evans were constantly arguing and that Beryl had been risking her life by trying to conduct an abortion on herself. Ethel Christie, then still alive, was present when the police searched the wash house where they found not only the body of Beryl Evans, but also the strangled body of little Geraldine. Detective Chief Inspector Jennings confronted Evans with the clothing found on the two bodies, and Evans agreed that he had been responsible for their deaths. A confession, recorded by Jennings in his notebook, recounted how Evans had strangled both his wife and his daughter and then hidden their bodies in the wash house. A later written statement gave more detail and Evans was duly charged with the murders, the charge book being preserved in the museum. The timing of the crime, as given in Evans' statements, was in conflict with the fact that decorators had been working in the wash house when the bodies were supposed to have been left there, but the workmen made further statements that a pile of wood might have been in the wash house and that they might not have noticed the bodies hidden under the wood.

In prison, Evans told his solicitors about Christie's involvement, but this was probably too late. At Evans' trial at the Old Bailey, Christie gave evidence that he had heard a bump in the middle of the night and the sound of something heavy being dragged across the floor. He denied Evans' accusations against him, and probably made a better impression on the jury than Evans. The jury found Evans guilty of killing his daughter Geraldine and he was executed on 9 March 1950.

When Christie's crimes came to light, he confessed to killing Beryl Evans but not Geraldine. Christie was trying to promote a defence of insanity and stated, in partially withdrawing his confession, that the more victims he accounted for, the better his chances of success with this defence. This confession by a second man of murdering the same victim prompted an inquiry by Mr John Scott Henderson QC, who concluded that Christie's confession to killing Beryl Evans had been false. In 1965 the case was reheard by a High Court judge, Sir Daniel Brabin, whose conclusion in 1966 was that 'it is more probable than not' that Evans was guilty of killing his wife and that he did not kill his daughter. As Evans had been convicted of killing Geraldine and not Beryl, he was given a posthumous free pardon in 1966. It was a complex case: there were two arguably unreliable confessions to killing Beryl; one probably unreliable confession by Evans to killing Geraldine; and one unreliable denial of killing Geraldine by Christie.

The case has retained an infamy for many years, not least because Christie appears to have given evidence against Evans and seen him hanged for a crime that he himself later confessed to committing. Had the police investigating the deaths of Beryl and Geraldine Evans dug up the garden when investigating Timothy Evans, they would undoubtedly have found two further bodies, and it is speculation to wonder how that find would have affected the investigation. The case is a reflection of a time when illegal backstreet abortions took place, when the death penalty removed any chance of redressing unsafe convictions and when suspects did not have routine access to solicitors in police stations. It also illustrates the inconsistent and sometimes unreliable verbal and written confessions that defendants can make, especially when they have an interest in retracting incriminating statements, or in increasing the severity of their wrongdoing. This type of case also gives cause for reflection that the criminal justice process does not always guarantee that the truth will be confidently uncovered.

82 Log

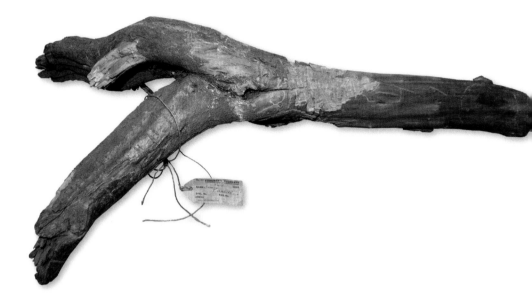

THE LOG OF wood was a weapon used by the 'Beast of Croydon' to inflict serious injury and acts as a reminder not only of the danger that some sexual offenders can represent to women, but also of the immense courage of two female police officers who, before the advent of personal radios, CCTV or the modern technology for raising an alarm, volunteered to act as decoys in order to trap the offender.

The location of the series of sex attacks on women was Fairfield footpath near Croydon police station; a dimly lit path where the police patrolled at various times in uniform and in plain clothes. When the patrols were in place there were no attacks, but when they ceased, the attacks started again, and they were becoming more violent. On 20 February 1955, a man leapt from behind bushes and attacked a 25-year-old woman who was punched in the face, but managed to scream and attract the attention of a passer-by who intervened and caused the attacker to run off. There were five women officers stationed at Croydon at the time, who all volunteered to

DATE:
1955

EXHIBIT:
The log used to attack Sergeant Ethel Bush GM

patrol the path as decoys, knowing that they themselves were at risk of serious assault.

Kathleen Parrott was in plain clothes shortly after 10.30 p.m. on 7 March 1955 when she heard the sound of running footsteps behind her. A man grabbed her from behind with his forearm around her throat. She dropped her handbag and shopping and, as she was beginning to lose consciousness, managed to scream and hit him with her torch. The man told her that he would not hurt her if she stopped screaming, and indecently assaulted her, but she fought back, broke free from the chokehold and turned to face him. He was masked, so she pulled the cloth away from his face in order to obtain a good view of his features. Her courage and resistance led to the man running off.

Parrott had severe bruising to the side of her neck, injuries to her face, thigh and knee, and was confined to bed for three weeks. She was on sick leave for five weeks but then returned to work to rejoin the patrols, determined to catch the offender. It was on Saturday, 23 April that Ethel Bush and a colleague were on patrol in uniform, and noticed a man hiding in bushes whom they immediately suspected of being the offender. Kathleen Parrott had also seen the man and set off on a patrol with one male officer ahead of her and one behind, but the suspect had by then disappeared. About an hour and a half after the initial sighting, Ethel Bush then commenced a lone decoy patrol with a number of CID officers and a police dog handler hidden nearby. She noticed a man coming from the direction of the nearby recreation ground and instinctively knew she would be attacked. Kathleen Parrott was also on the observation and recognised her attacker from six weeks earlier. Ethel Bush continued her walk, assuming an air of nonchalance. The man ran up behind Bush, picked up the log and wielded an enormous blow to her head. She turned and grabbed hold of the man until her colleagues arrived to arrest him, but he punched her so hard in the face that the nearby dog handler heard the crack as if it had been a pistol shot. In the confusion, the man ran off, and, despite police officers surrounding the area, he escaped arrest.

Kathleen Parrott found a fountain pen and pencil at the scene and managed to confirm from Ethel Bush, being treated for her injuries at Mayday Hospital, that they did not belong to her. The CID officers reviewed the case and concluded that a former commando captain, William Barnett, who lived not far from the area, was a likely suspect. When Detective Sergeant Frederick Fairfax GC visited Barnett's house to investigate further, he showed the fountain pen and pencil to Barnett who was with his wife, who immediately identified them as the Christmas present she had bought for her husband. Barnett was therefore linked to the scene and arrested. He was positively recognised on an identification parade and then made full admissions to all the attacks carried out on the footpath. At the Old Bailey on 16 May 1955, he pleaded guilty to assaulting the two police officers and was sentenced to ten years' imprisonment.

In his book *The Brave Blue Line*, author Dick Kirby quotes the words of the judge, Sir Anthony Hawke, to Kathleen Parrott and Ethel Bush:

> I cannot imagine higher courage than you showed along that footpath with full knowledge, with your eyes open, that you might be, as Sergeant Bush was, the victim of a horrible and violent assault. The conduct of the police is always a matter of which we in this country can be proud. I think this country is entitled to be proud of you two officers. I think you have done a very great and gallant thing.

Both officers were awarded £15 cheques from the Bow Street Reward Fund and George Medals from Queen Elizabeth II. Kathleen Parrott and Ethel Bush were the first female officers to be awarded the medal. Both were born in 1916 and lived long lives, dying in 2015 and 2016 respectively.

83 Police Officer's Medals

DATE:
1952

EXHIBIT:
The medals of
PC Sidney Miles

SIDNEY MILES (b. 1910) JOINED the Metropolitan Police in 1930 with military service that entitled him to wear the Defence Medal (centre). He also qualified for the Police Long Service and Good Conduct Medal for twenty-two years' police service (right). The third medal (left) was the King's Police and Fire Service Medal that recognised his bravery on the night of Sunday, 2 November 1952.

It was at about 9 p.m. that evening when 16-year-old Christopher Craig and 19-year-old Derek Bentley were seen climbing the gate leading to the side of Barlow & Parker's warehouse in Croydon. When the police were called and went up on to the roof to arrest the offenders, a series of tragic events unfolded. Detective Constable Frederick Fairfax was one of the first officers to arrive in a police van. PC Norman Harrison attended, as did PC James MacDonald, who arrived in a police wireless car with PC Leslie Miles (not related to Sidney). They and other officers surrounded the building. Frederick Fairfax climbed on to the roof, about 22ft high, by means of a drainpipe, and James MacDonald followed him, but could not negotiate the last 6ft, and had to return to the ground. Fairfax saw Craig and Bentley behind a brick stack, challenged them and grabbed Bentley, but the culprit broke away and Craig shot at Fairfax, wounding him slightly on the right shoulder. Craig and Bentley ran past him, but Fairfax got up from the ground and grappled with Bentley, dragged him behind a skylight and removed from him a knuckleduster and dagger, despite being shot at a second time by Craig.

James MacDonald made a second attempt to climb up the drainpipe and was helped up on to the roof by Fairfax who then called on Craig to drop his gun, but he refused and made further threats. Norman Harrison, meanwhile, had climbed on to a sloping roof nearby and was edging his way towards the gunman with his back to the roof and his heels in the guttering. Craig fired a shot that struck the roof close to his head, but he continued his manoeuvre. A second shot missed Harrison who then found his way behind a chimney stack and joined other officers who had gained access to the roof via a fire exit door. As PC Sidney Miles jumped from the doorway on to the roof, Fairfax shouted a warning but Craig shot Miles between the eyes and killed him. Frederick Fairfax went to bring Miles to shelter and, despite another shot, he and James MacDonald pulled Miles behind the fire escape exit. Norman Harrison threw his truncheon and other missiles as Craig fired at him, but without effect. PC Robert Jaggs then joined the officers on the roof by means of the drainpipe, despite being fired on. Fairfax, with Harrison, then pushed his prisoner, Bentley, through the fire exit door, so that he could be detained by other officers. Fairfax was given a police firearm, returned to the roof and called on Craig to drop his gun. Fairfax advanced towards Craig as they exchanged gunfire and Craig, out of ammunition after twenty minutes of firing at the police, jumped off the roof. He was arrested on the ground and had injured his spine and wrist as he landed.

Craig and Bentley were tried at the Old Bailey in December 1952 before Lord Chief Justice, Lord Goddard, and the case caused controversy that lasted for many years. It was clear from the outset that 16-year-old Craig was too young to be hanged even though he had murdered PC Miles. Bentley, under arrest at the time of the murder, was also convicted of PC Miles' murder as he had called out, 'Let him have it, Chris!' This could have been interpreted either as an incitement to Craig to commit murder, or as telling Craig to surrender his weapon. The jury must have decided – in the seventy-five minutes they took to reach their verdicts – that the words were used to encourage Craig to kill the officer. The police gave evidence that Bentley had otherwise accepted his arrest peaceably and had not tried to escape once rearrested by Fairfax.

Craig, in view of his young age, was sentenced to be 'detained at Her Majesty's pleasure'. Bentley, three years older, was sentenced to death. The Home Secretary, Sir David Maxwell Fyffe, was in office during a time of great concern about crime in the period after the Second World War and decided not to reprieve Bentley, regardless of the fact that the main culprit was not being sentenced to death and that many people would feel the decision to be an affront to their sense of justice. Bentley was executed at Wandsworth prison on 28 January 1953 but a long campaign by his family eventually resulted in a Court of Appeal decision – forty-five years later – that declared the conviction against Bentley to be unsafe. The decision was based on the grounds that the trial judge, Lord Goddard's, summing-up had been unfair, and had completely failed to put Bentley's defence properly before the jury. There had been 'substantial evidence' of Bentley's guilt but it was not overwhelming compared to the evidence in Craig's case. Later paroled and rehabilitated, Christopher Craig expressed, in a dignified way, sincere regret for the trouble he had caused for the families of PC Miles and of Derek Bentley. The case against Derek Bentley, and his life, relied crucially on a reported verbal statement made on a dark rooftop at night, but the main controversy was the hard decisions that were sometimes made when implementing strictly to the law relating to the death penalty.

A police operation on a rooftop and against an armed burglar would undoubtedly be conducted differently today, but Frederick Fairfax, later promoted, was awarded the George Cross, one of only five such awards ever to be bestowed upon Metropolitan Police officers. Sidney Miles was awarded a posthumous King's Police and Fire Service Medal. Norman Harrison and James MacDonald were awarded George Medals. Robert Jaggs was awarded the British Empire Medal. These medals, presented in the first months of the reign of Queen Elizabeth II, still displayed the head of King George VI. The gun, knuckleduster and knife from the case are also in the collection.

The death penalty gave an extra dimension of importance to the sometimes small details of evidence that might assume enormous significance in a contested trial: in a murder trial, such statements might contribute to an execution rather than imprisonment. Verbal statements can be subject to misinterpretation and inaccurate or incomplete recording by police officers; in modern times these would be confirmed in a tape-recorded interview using technology not available to the police until a generation after these cases occurred. Despite the controversy and the concentration on the defendants, the bravery of the police officers has never been in doubt.

PC Nathaneal 'Nat' Edgar was deployed on a special plain-clothes patrol in the Winchmore Hill area on 13 February 1948 as part of an operation to combat a series of domestic burglaries. Edgar challenged a suspect and wrote some details into his pocketbook – 'M Thomas Donald, 247 Cambridge Road, Enfield BEAH 257/2' – but was then shot three times in his back and thigh. Later that evening, he died in hospital. Edgar's note provided a vital clue about his murderer's name and identity card details. Donald Thomas was a 23-year-old thief who had been wanted for deserting from the army since 13 October 1947. The police wanted to enlist public support to find clues about Thomas' whereabouts but did not want the publicity to risk prejudicing the prospect of a fair trial. After advice from Percy Fearnley, Scotland Yard's first public information officer, a famous formula was used for the first time: 'The police urgently wish to interview Donald George Thomas, who is believed to be able to assist them in their inquiries.'

Stanley Winkless of Camberwell responded to the appeal. He believed that his wife Noreen had run off with Thomas. Detective Inspector Thomas Stinton was an important member of the investigating team, who succeeded in requesting newspapers to publish a photograph of Noreen Winkless with the news that police wanted to interview her in connection with the inquiry. This resulted in a boarding-house proprietress from Clapham, Constance Smeed, recognising Noreen Winkless and Thomas as the tenants in her top-floor room. As the result of her information, the police raided the room and succeeded in arresting Thomas after a violent struggle. The four officers who arrested Thomas were each awarded the King's Police and Fire Service Medal for gallantry. The gun that Thomas tried to use against the arresting officers was a Luger, later displayed in the Crime Museum. Seventeen rounds of ammunition were also found with it. Thomas was convicted at the Central Criminal Court and sentenced to death, but was reprieved because of Parliament's decision to suspend capital punishment for five years. Thomas was, therefore, sentenced to life imprisonment.

In May 1948, Sir Harold Scott received a letter from Jan Read who worked for J. Arthur Rank, the film magnate, asking for co-operation in making a film that would reflect the police and their daily work. The project resulted in the influential film, *The Blue Lamp*, which was based on Nat Edgar's story. In turn this led to the long-running TV series *Dixon of Dock Green*.

84 Blazer

AN ORDINARY BLAZER with a small hole in the lapel tells the story of how a bullet, fired from the gun of Günther Podola, killed Detective Sergeant Raymond Purdy on 13 July 1959.

Raymond Purdy had rushed from Chelsea police station with a colleague, DS John Sandford, to catch a man making a call from a telephone box in Thurloe Street, near South Kensington Underground station. The man was ringing a woman in Roland Gardens as part of a blackmail plot after her flat had been burgled a week earlier, with her passport, money and some personal papers stolen. The victim had kept the suspect on the line whilst his demands for $500 were being discussed, thereby enabling the call to be traced to the telephone box concerned.

The officers caught the man as he was still making his call, and Raymond Purdy seized the blackmailer's address book. Then, however, the suspect ran to a block of flats in Onslow Square where the officers caught up with him in the entrance hall. The man pulled out a gun and shot Raymond Purdy at point-blank range. Despite his desire to catch the blackmailer, John Sandford telephoned for assistance and did what he could for his dying colleague. Detective Superintendent David Hislop and Detective Chief Inspector Bob Acott rushed to the scene and began a murder hunt.

DATE:
1959

EXHIBIT:
DS Raymond Purdy's blazer and bullet hole

The address book, at first thought to belong to Raymond Purdy, contained details of 'Little Jack' who ran a shop in Soho where a man had been questioned by police a few days earlier as he tried to sell a suspected-stolen tape recorder. This gave police the name of Günther Podola, a former member of the Hitler Youth movement who had been imprisoned in Canada for burglary after escaping from East Berlin in 1952. The fingerprints from Canada matched those found on a window ledge in the flats in Onslow Square and linked Podola to the crime scene.

On 16 July, Podola was traced to Room 15 at the Claremont House hotel in Kensington. As Flying Squad Detective Inspector Peter Vibart tried to enter his room, the officers thought they heard the click of a gun being cocked on the other side of the door, but nevertheless Detective Sergeant Albert Chambers charged the door with Detective Constable Morrissey, knocking Podola across to the other side of the room in the process. Podola was dazed by his arrest and may have lost consciousness temporarily. He later claimed amnesia as part of his defence at his trial, but the argument was rejected, partly because of a letter he had written from prison that indicated his memory had not been lost. He was convicted, and on 5 November 1959, became the last man executed in Britain for the murder of a police officer. The gun and address book are also in the museum collection.

On 13 July 2019, as part of the continuing work of the Police Memorial Trust, established after the death of Yvonne Fletcher (see pp. 217–9), a memorial was erected in memory of Raymond Purdy in Onslow Square. See thepolicememorialtrust.org/ds-raymond-purdy.

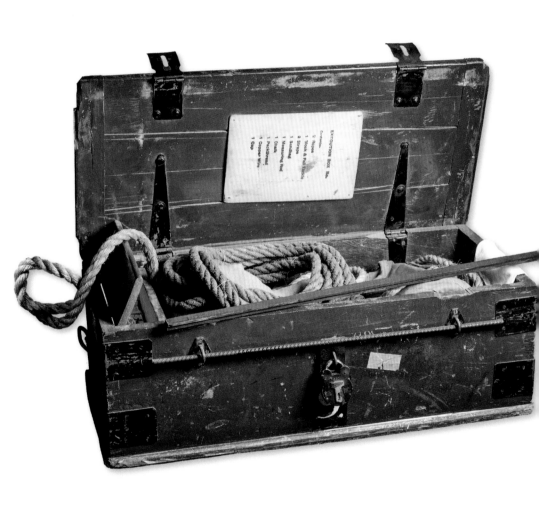

EXECUTION BOX No.

Contents:

2 Ropes
1 Brick & Fall Tackle
2 Straps
1 Sandbag
1 Measuring Rod
1 Chalk
1 Packthread
1 Copper Wire
1 Cap

85 Executioner's Equipment

THE EXECUTIONER'S BOX, from Wandsworth prison, where the last execution took place in 1961, contains a test bag that was filled with sand so that it could measure the strength and elasticity of the rope to be used for hanging the prisoner. A block and tackle was used for the process, and copper wire assisted in marking the upper end of the drop. Following a practice going back at least as far as Henry Pierrepoint – who conducted executions between 1901 and 1910 – a 6ft ruler was provided to assist in measuring the length of the drop, calculated from the height of the person being executed, but most executioners preferred using their own flexible measuring tape. Vaseline was supplied and used over the soft leather section of the rope to ensure the rubber washer would slide as smoothly as possible to tighten the noose. A hood was placed over the prisoner's head when he or she was standing on the trapdoors. Straps for wrists and ankles were available as restraints: the wrist strap was applied in the condemned cell and the ankle strap applied at the trapdoors by the assistant executioner. Another item in the box was some chalk, to make a 'T' mark across the centre of the trapdoors. This would indicate where the feet of the condemned prisoner should be positioned. All execution boxes were transported by rail, as indicated by labels on the exterior of the box. There were never any reports of the boxes being lost or tampered with on these journeys. There were about twenty of the boxes in existence at one time and they were sent out immediately to one of the prisons with execution apparatus after each death sentence was pronounced. Fairly frequent reprieves would mean that the equipment was not needed for every occasion that the boxes were dispatched.

DATE:
1961

EXHIBIT:
Prison service box of executioner's equipment

Old ropes used for executions are also in the Crime Museum's collection. There were used for hanging Henry Fowler, Albert Milsom, William Seaman, John Platts, Amelia Dyer and Mary Pearcey. William Marwood, an executioner, visited the museum and signed the visitors' book on 18 June 1883, not long before he died. Succeeding William Calcraft, Marwood hanged 176 people in nine years, and was paid an annual retainer of £20, plus £10 per execution. Marwood apparently introduced the 'long-drop' method of execution, which broke the person's neck and resulted in a more humane death than by the 'short-drop' strangulation. In 1873, Mary Cotton's executioner, William Calcraft, miscalculated the length of rope required for her execution; it apparently took three minutes for her to die of strangulation. Marwood appears to have changed his mind about donating ropes, having sent an original letter in 1876 refusing to part with any. He was better at executions than spelling:

> aug 20th 1876
> <u>Sir</u>
>
> Pleas this is in Anser
> to your Letter that you Sent
> to me Conserning me to
> Send you my Rope for som
> Purpose or For me to Cut
> a Pees of the Rope for
> you **<u>Sir</u>** i feel very mutch
> Surprised at your Letter
> my Rope i never Let go
> out of my hands to anywon
> and i never Let any won
> of my Ropes to be Cut
> <u>Sir</u> if you would like
> to see you Can by Coming
> to the Prison
> Sir i Remain yours
> Wm Marwood

In 1849, Charles Dickens joined 30,000 others outside Horsemonger Lane prison to witness the public executions of Frederick and Maria Manning after their conviction for the murder of Patrick O'Connor. The travel company Thomas Cook ran excursions for those wishing to attend the spectacle. Dickens wrote a letter to *The Times* deploring the inhumane behaviour, language and temperament of the crowd and made an eloquent plea that executions should in future be undertaken within the privacy of prison walls. This change did not take place for another two decades.

The last public execution was on 26 May 1868 at Newgate and involved Michael Barrett, who had been convicted for his part in the December 1867 Clerkenwell explosion. The 2,000-strong crowd apparently booed, jeered and sang 'Rule, Britannia' and 'Champagne Charlie' during the execution proceedings.

Reynolds News commented:

> Millions will continue to doubt that a guilty man has been hanged at all; and the future historian of the Fenian panic may declare that Michael Barrett was sacrificed to the exigencies of the police, and the vindication of the good Tory principle, that there is nothing like blood

In 1885, John Lee became known as 'the man they couldn't hang'. John Henry George Lee was born in Devon in 1864 and served in the Royal Navy, but had a number of convictions before being found guilty of the November 1884 murder of the woman he worked for, Emma Keyse, in Babbacombe. He was duly sentenced to death in February 1885 but on three occasions his execution at Exeter prison failed, despite the mechanism being tested by the executioner, James Berry, beforehand. Subsequent examination revealed that there was a fault in the trapdoor drawbar that prevented the door from dropping open when weight was placed upon it. The Home Secretary commuted his sentence to life imprisonment and he was released in 1907. A postcard written by Lee is an exhibit in the Crime Museum.

In 1803 an Englishman named Joseph Samuel survived three attempts to hang him in Australia when firstly the rope broke, then the noose slipped off his neck, and finally, on the third attempt, the rope broke again. It was a public execution and the crowd became boisterous, demanding that no further attempts should be made to hang him; the punishment was commuted to life imprisonment. The method of execution used was to stand the prisoners on a cart that was then driven away.

The practical effects of the Homicide Act 1957, which made certain categories of murder liable to attract the death penalty, were illustrated by the murder of Alan Jee in Hounslow on 25 June 1960. Four young men attacked him with the intent to rob him as he walked home on a footpath within a few yards of his front door. Jee was repeatedly kicked in the head. A shoe worn by Francis Forsyth, now an exhibit in the museum, had Alan Jee's bloodstains on it and this formed a vital part of the prosecution evidence. Because Forsyth was just over 18 years old and had intended to steal, it was a capital murder, so he was hanged after being convicted. He was executed on 10 November 1960 at Wandsworth prison. One of his accomplices, 23-year-old Norman Harris, was executed on the same day at Pentonville prison. Terence Lutt had been 17 at the time of the incident, had struck the first blow and was convicted of capital murder, but was detained 'at Her Majesty's pleasure' because of his age. He was released after ten years. The fourth assailant, 20-year-old Christopher Darby, claimed not to have struck Jee at all, but was convicted of non-capital murder and sentenced to life imprisonment.

The last executions in Britain, those of Gwynne Evans and Peter Allen, took place on 13 August 1964 at Strangeways prison, Manchester, and Walton prison, Liverpool, respectively, for the murder of John West on 7 April 1964.

Also in the Crime Museum is a collection of twenty-seven death masks – casts of prisoners' heads taken after their execution. Newgate prison, demolished in 1902, was the location of many of the executions, but some masks came from other places, such as Tyburn, York and Derby. The practice appears to be based on the theory of phrenology expounded in 1796 by the Viennese physician Dr Franz Joseph Gall, who believed that the way in which we think affects the shape of the brain according to seven faculties known as selfish propensities and moral sentiments, and forty-two faculties like combativeness and benevolence. This in turn would affect the shape of the skull and enable a person's character to be determined by the 'bumps' on their head.

In one case, that of Frederick Deeming in 1892, the death mask was taken in Australia and sent to London, allegedly as possible identification evidence, as Deeming had supposedly admitted to the last two of the Whitechapel murders and thereby became a suspect for Jack the Ripper. The confession was denied by Deeming's solicitor. Deeming had immigrated to Australia where he lived with Emily Mather in a rented house in Andrew Street, Windsor, New South Wales. On 3 March 1892, the new tenant complained of a nasty smell in one of the bedrooms, and, when the hearthstone was lifted, the body of Mather was found. Her skull had been fractured and her throat had been cut. This prompted the police in England to examine Deeming's old home in Rainhill, Liverpool, where his former wife Marie and four children were found dead under the kitchen floor.

The collection of death masks, listed in Appendix III, and the execution equipment act as reminders of things that have passed into history: a medical theory, capital punishment, and public attitudes to executions.

METROPOLITAN POLICE

BOOK 25

UNIFORM OFFICERS EMPLOYED — DIARY
IN PLAIN CLOTHES

STATION

DIV.

The Crew of Foxtrot 11

Geoffrey FOX   Christopher HEAD   David Wombwell

Q-Car Diary

THE DIARY FROM F Division's Q-car was one of the standard items used by three officers on patrol before they were tragically shot and killed.

The incident happened in Braybrook Street near Wormwood Scrubs prison. Detective Sergeant Christopher Head, Temporary Detective Constable David Wombwell and the driver, Police Constable Geoffrey Fox, were the plain-clothes crew of F11 Q-car, an unmarked Triumph 2000 with an automatic gearbox, crewed for proactive crime patrol. On 12 August 1966 the officers saw three suspicious men in a Standard Vanguard in Braybrook Street, W12, near Wormwood Scrubs prison, at 3.15 p.m. and decided to investigate. They did not know that the men had in fact been planning to rob a rent collector. It is possible that Geoffrey Fox recognised the driver, John Witney, as a criminal. After questioning Witney about the ownership of the car, Christopher Head pointed out the fact that Witney's insurance certificate had just expired and then asked to look inside a holdall in the car. At that point David Wombwell was leaning in to the car to talk to Witney, when, without word or warning, Harry Roberts, a passenger, suddenly shot the officer through his eye and killed him outright. Christopher Head started to move towards the Q-car for assistance, but Roberts fatally shot him twice in the back, whilst the third man, John Duddy, fired three shots at Geoffrey Fox, the third bullet hitting the officer in the temple and killing

DATE:
1966

EXHIBIT:
Diary for recording the crew's duty hours and arrests

323

him instantly. The three criminals drove away from the scene, where the stationary police car's wheels were still turning with Christopher Head's body jammed underneath it and Geoffrey Fox's foot still on the accelerator. A man driving into Braybrook Street noted the Vanguard's number as it sped away.

It was a day when every officer in the Metropolitan Police knew what they had been doing when they heard the news. An enormous effort was made by great numbers of officers, and offers of help poured in from the public. A passing security officer had made a note of the index number of a Standard Vanguard PGT 726 that he had seen racing away from the scene. It was before the days of the Police National Computer, so arrangements had to be made to gain access to the paper records of the car licensing system to trace the last registered owner of the Vanguard. That owner had sold the car to a dealer and he, in turn, had sold the car to John Witney. Although Witney had not registered his ownership of the vehicle, Detective Inspector Ron Steventon arrived on his doorstep at 9 p.m. the same evening. Witney claimed to have sold the car on to a man in a pub and gave a false account of his movements that day, details that were disproved. Information also arrived about a blue Standard Vanguard being garaged at Vauxhall, and this led to the police finding the car. There were cartridges in it from the gun that had been fired by Duddy and the garage owner eventually identified Witney as his tenant after Detective Inspector Jack Slipper reassured him that he should not allow his fear about receiving stolen lead from Witney to stop him from telling the truth. Witney was charged with the murders and then named the two men who had been with him. John Duddy was arrested five days after the crime, in Glasgow. Roberts went on the run, camping in Epping Forest and, after a long police search and many inquiries co-ordinated by Detective Superintendent Dick Chitty, was arrested three months later.

87 Ketchup Bottle

DATE:
1963

EXHIBIT:
Ketchup bottle
with finger
marks from
Leatherslade
Farm

THE KETCHUP BOTTLE, found at Leatherslade Farm, was one of the articles from the location on which finger marks had not been erased. This led to the conviction of those responsible for an infamous crime.

Robbery of a moving train is virtually unprecedented, but it was the basis of the crime that has become generally known as the Great Train Robbery. On 8 August 1963, the Glasgow to London night mail train came to a halt at a red signal at Sears Crossing, near Cheddington, Buckinghamshire. The green signal had been obscured with a glove, and the red signal illuminated with a red lightbulb and battery without otherwise tampering with the wiring mechanism. The gang boarded the locomotive, struck the resisting driver, Jack Mills, with an iron bar, causing concussion and trauma, and then forced him to drive 1 mile on to Bridego Bridge. The robbers broke into the high-value packages coach, intimidated the Post Office workers with axe handles and then, during thirty minutes of using a human chain, unloaded £2.5 million in used banknotes into their convoy of vehicles, and drove off. It was, at the time, the most valuable cash robbery in British history.

The Flying Squad, under the command of Detective Chief Superintendent Tommy Butler, were immediately called in, and, with assistance from Detective Chief Superintendent Ernie Millen, made inquiries amongst their usual London-based informants for suspects likely to have committed such a high-profile robbery.

The police incident room in Buckinghamshire, under the command of Detective Superintendent Gerald McArthur, was inundated with calls from the public offering information. McArthur arranged for a news broadcast on the radio to the effect that he was concentrating searches on isolated buildings in the area and when a shepherd reported strange activity at Leatherslade Farm, 28 miles from the crime scene, the police found mailbags, tinned food, sleeping bags and other evidence of the gang having spent time there after the robbery, apparently having left in a hurry after the radio news bulletin. Despite an attempt to clean the premises, several finger marks were found and, using the suspects identified by Flying Squad officers, the Fingerprint Bureau made rapid positive identifications.

Roger Cordery was arrested in Brighton, where a landlady mistrusted him and his friend, Arthur Boal, as they had made a large advance payment to her in cash. Cordery had apparently been responsible for interfering with the railway signal. Known association with other criminals then led to the arrests of Jimmy White and Tommy Wisby from south London, and to evidence against Bruce Reynolds from north London, who was eventually arrested in 1968 in Torquay after spending time in Canada and France. Gordon Goody was incriminated by traces of yellow paint on his shoes that matched one of the vehicles that had recently been repainted. Buster Edwards fled to Mexico but later negotiated his return to Britain and was sentenced to fifteen years in prison.

The main trial of the robbers took place at Aylesbury Crown Court in 1964, lasted nearly four months under the eye of Mr Justice Edmund Davies, and resulted in sentences that totalled 307 years, with the main culprits receiving thirty years, undoubtedly influenced by the need to deter any future similar offences. One of those convicted, Ronald Biggs, escaped from Wandsworth prison on 8 July 1965 and moved to Brazil via France and Australia, gaining notoriety for being allowed to remain in Brazil and avoid the attempts of the British authorities to extradite him. He voluntarily returned to Britain in May 2001 when he appeared briefly at Bow Street Court before being returned to prison to complete his thirty-year sentence. His false passport and the letter he sent requesting to return to Britain are also exhibits in the museum, along with a Monopoly game and a number of other items on which finger marks were found at Leatherslade Farm.

There had in fact been an earlier 'Great Train Robbery'. On 15 May 1855 the Victorians were shocked by the theft of £12,000 worth of gold being transported from London to Paris via London Bridge and Boulogne. The gold was transported in three boxes secured by iron bars and kept in safes overnight at London Bridge station where two separate keyholders were required to open their Chubb locks. At various stages on the journey the boxes were weighed. Discrepancies were noted at Boulogne, and when they were opened in Paris, their contents were found to have been replaced with lead shot.

The investigation only really made progress when Edward Agar, an associate of James Saward (or 'Jim the Penman'), had been sentenced to transportation in relation to a cheque offence and wrote to Fanny Kay, the mother of his child, stating that William Pierce, a former rail employee, should have given her £7,000.

Fanny Kay had not been paid this vast amount of money and explained her situation to John Rees, a solicitor investigating the theft on behalf of the railway company. Fanny Kay moved home and lodged, for safety, in the house of Inspector Stephen Thornton of Scotland Yard. In due course, Edward Agar gave evidence against William Pierce, James Burgess and William Tester at the Old Bailey on 5 January 1857. All three were employees of the railway company and had made wax impressions of the safe keys when the lock company had replaced them and Tester, a trusted clerk, had temporary possession of them. They had entered the guard's van during the journey to Folkestone, replaced the gold with lead and then travelled on to Dover before returning to London with the gold. They were sentenced to transportation for fourteen years.

88

Machine Gun

THE MACHINE GUN was in fact a deactivated weapon, supposedly rendered harmless, but brought back into use by a criminal armourer. This gun, in fact, contributed to a debate that led to a tightening of the firearms legislation about deactivated weapons.

On 17 August 1993 Flying Squad officers from Tower Bridge were conducting observations on two men suspected of armed robberies in south-east London. The officers witnessed the suspects robbing a Security Express van in Blackfen, near Sidcup, Kent, where £17,000 in cash was stolen at gunpoint by Steven Farrer, who then ran to a vehicle driven by Anthony Pendrigh. As the Flying Squad car chased the men, Farrer leaned out of the car's window and fired seventeen rounds of machine-gun fire at the pursuing police. One bullet bounced off the windscreen wiper arm, went through the windscreen and into the roof of the car, narrowly missing Detective Constable 'Jumbo' Redford. Another round grazed the head of Detective Sergeant Michael Stubbs, who narrowly avoided death. The machine gun jammed and Farrer continued firing with a magnum handgun, which hit the engine of the police car and immobilised it. Farrer was then seen abandoning the getaway car and fired at two unarmed uniform officers. Farrer and Pendrigh were arrested soon afterwards in a nearby house where the cash was recovered along with three loaded firearms. They were charged with fourteen armed robberies, including five where shots had been

DATE:
1993

EXHIBIT:
Rapid-fire machine gun used in an armed robbery

fired. At the Old Bailey on 2 June 1994, they pleaded guilty and were sentenced to eighteen years' imprisonment. Detective Sergeant Barry Nicholson took charge of the case.

Nine years later, in 2003, Farrer was released. He was not rehabilitated however. On 8 August 2005, a cash-in-transit van was robbed of £68,000 in New Eltham by a suspect with a handgun who was wearing a motorcycle crash helmet. Information led the Flying Squad to search a garage in Greenwich where they found a stolen Vauxhall Astra van, inside which was a motorcycle helmet, a Ruger pistol and some £20 notes with a security dye on them. These were forensically linked to Farrer but the Crown Prosecution Service decided against a prosecution. Farrer would often leave his house at 5 a.m. and would regularly spend hours watching cash-in-transit deliveries. He now worked with a new accomplice, Mustafa Hunter, taking steps to evade surveillance and planning potential escape routes. On Thursday, 19 October 2006, Farrer left his home address very early in the morning, carrying a grey holdall, and drove off in a stolen VW Golf with Hunter following in another car. They later drove to Charlton village. Farrer remained in his stolen car whilst Hunter waited at a bus stop for the arrival of a cash-in-transit van. The security van was, however, unaccountably late in arriving and the two men seemed to be abandoning their plan for the day. With the evidence available of all their preparations, however, the Flying Squad moved in to arrest them. Farrer rammed his car between two police vehicles, but lost control and crashed into a gatepost. Farrer and Hunter were both arrested and their holdall was found to contain a full-face motorcycle helmet, a two-way radio, a scanner to pick up police radio messages, a plastic bottle of flammable liquid, CS gas and a loaded handgun. Both were charged with conspiracy to rob and, on 12 October 2007, were each sentenced to sixteen years' imprisonment.

The disregard for life shown by armed robbers, and the traumatic effect on the families of victims, was also illustrated on 10 November 1976 at 12.25 p.m. when an armed robber walked in to Barclays Bank, Upper Ham Road, Richmond, went to the cashier nearest to the door, pointed a sawn-off shotgun at 20-year-old Angela Woolliscroft and demanded money. She sensibly complied and handed over £2,500 in banknotes, but the man then callously fired the gun at her through the safety glass and killed her. He drove away in an Austin A40 car that he had stolen from Bentall's car park, Kingston, but returned it to the same space in the car park. A coat that he had used to cover the gun was found to belong to the owner of the car.

After extensive inquiries by Detective Chief Superintendent James Sewell, during which information was received that a Michael Hart had been seen to put a shotgun into the back of a car, Hart was arrested, but gave alibi evidence. Shotgun cartridges found at his home were found to be of a different type to that used in the murder, but closer inspection revealed that they did in fact match and had been mislabelled by the manufacturer. Instead of normal birdshot, the cartridges contained heavier trap shot pellets, which penetrated the cashier's protective screen more easily. Hart told the police that he had thrown the weapon into the River Thames at Hampton Court after the robbery. He claimed that the gun had discharged by accident, but ballistics evidence demonstrated that it required 5lb finger pressure to operate the trigger. During his time in custody, Hart tried to hang himself. In November 1977 he was sentenced at the Old Bailey to life imprisonment with the recommendation that he should not serve less than twenty-five years.

The bank screen, ammunition, gun and the coat are in the museum's collection.

89 Wooden Eagle

WHEN AN OFF-DUTY police dog handler witnessed an armed robbery taking place on a Group 4 delivery van in Station Square, Petts Wood, on 15 August 1984, he released his dog, named Yerba, to tackle one of the robbers. The man fired and killed the dog with three shots from a .38 revolver; Yerba's bravery is recorded on a plaque placed on the wall of a nearby building. Flying Squad officers established an incident room in a local police station and soon came to suspect a career armed robber, Anthony Philip Baldessare, of the crime.

DATE:
1984

EXHIBIT:
Wooden eagle found at home of armed robber Baldessare

The 46 year old had three convictions for armed robbery and had a record of taking part in incidents where robbers had shot at police officers.

A nationwide hunt for Britain's 'most wanted' criminal took place, which culminated in police officers surrounding a flat in Gleneldon Road, Streatham, on 24 January 1985. Because of Baldessare's access to guns and his ruthless nature, the police conducted a protracted siege negotiation to persuade him to surrender. Baldessare told the negotiators that he could not face the prospect of another spell of imprisonment. When a shot was heard inside the flat, the police did not know whether it was a trap being laid to lure them into the premises or not. Firearms officers from D11 Branch (later SO19) forced an entry through a wall of the flat, rather than the door or a window, and found that Baldessare had in fact shot himself dead, using the same firearm that he had used to kill Yerba. A search of the flat revealed a pump-action shotgun, a large quantity of money that had been partly burnt and, on top of a bedroom wardrobe, a wooden eagle that Baldessare had acquired as a reminder of his dealings with the Flying Squad.

The Flying Squad, established in 1919 to combat mobile criminals, have specialised in the pursuit of the dangerous and violent armed robbers who have plagued London and other places with their ruthless pursuit of money regardless of the cost to victims' lives. The Flying Squad adopted the eagle as their logo.

90 Millennium Star

THE MILLENNIUM STAR diamond, a copy of which was donated by De Beers to the museum, was the target of an infamous attempted robbery at the Millennium Dome exhibition (now the O2 arena).

Armed robbers invariably face the problem of how they are going to escape from the scene of the crime and evade police officers. In early 2000, the Flying Squad were investigating an attempted robbery of a security van at Nine Elms, Battersea, where a gang had escaped by using a speedboat on the River Thames. Five months later, an attempted robbery had taken place in Aylesford, Kent, where a speedboat was used again, this time on the River Medway, and shots were fired at the police from the boat. The similarity in getaway methods indicated that one gang was responsible for both crimes and a surveillance operation was set up on the basis that it was only a matter of time before the gang struck again.

DATE:
2000

EXHIBIT:
Replica of the Millennium Star Diamond

It then emerged that the next target was the Millennium Dome exhibition where the Millennium Star, valued at over £200 million, was featured in a display organised by the De Beers diamond company.

Under the codename Operation Magician, about 200 police officers were involved, including forty specialist firearms officers. After a dawn briefing on 7 November 2000, officers positioned themselves behind a dummy wall and posed as employees, including cleaners. A further sixty Flying Squad officers were posted at various points next to landing stages of the River Thames, and a further twenty were on duty on river boats. At 8.40 a.m. the robbers arrived, equipped with gas masks, smoke bombs, bottles of ammonia, wire cutters, a nail gun and body armour. They crashed into the Millennium Dome in a stolen JCB excavator with a giant shovel, and then smashed their way into the vault where the diamond was located. The police put their ambush plan into effect and arrested five men, who were later sentenced to terms of imprisonment ranging from four to eighteen years. The robbers made detailed plans and worked on the basis that they could work quickly and escape in an unexpected direction whilst the element of surprise worked in their favour. However, had they succeeded on that morning, they would only have succeeded in making off with a replica of the diamond rather than the real thing.

The world's largest diamond, the Cullinan diamond, originally weighing in at around 3,106.75 carats (or 621.35gm), was found near Pretoria in South Africa, on 26 January 1905. The diamond, presented to King Edward VII, was cut into three large stones and several other smaller pieces, and now forms part of the Crown Jewels. Scotland Yard officers accompanied the ship from South Africa, but they were in fact guarding a replica, whilst the real diamond was sent through the post. At one stage the diamond was stored in a safe at Scotland Yard where Detective Superintendent Frank Froest was just as nervous as anybody else about the security of such a valuable item.

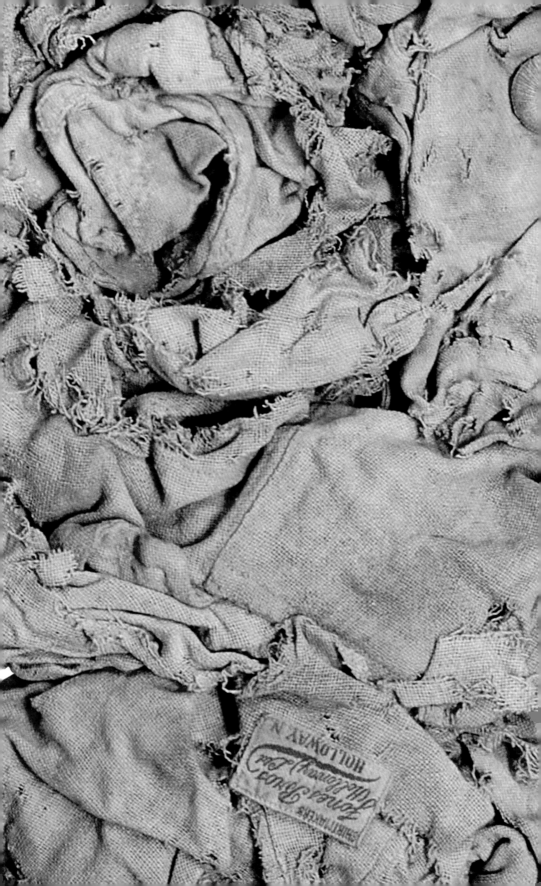

Pyjamas

THE PYJAMAS, SUBSEQUENTLY identified as consistent with those owned by Dr Hawley Crippen, had been used to wrap up the remains of Cora Crippen, which were then buried under the cellar floor. Dr Crippen was in the habit of buying pyjamas in sets of three and the label, from Jones Bros of Holloway, matched two other sets found at his home at No. 39 Hilldrop Crescent. Evidence of the delivery of the pyjamas by the shop to Crippen's home was introduced into his trial to link him with the remains.

The disappearance of Cora Crippen (also known as Belle Elmore), wife of Dr Hawley Harvey Crippen, is one of the most famous cases investigated by Scotland Yard. Crippen was an American doctor who came to England in 1900 to work in a patent medicine company. Cora Crippen had a stage career as a music hall singer but, by 1910, her involvement with the theatre was primarily as the treasurer of the Music Hall Ladies Guild. Cora Crippen was not seen alive after 31 January 1911 when the Crippens had entertained two retired artistes, Paul and Clara Martinetti, for supper. Two days later, her fellow committee members were surprised to receive two letters, apparently signed by Cora: one of them suddenly resigning from her post and the other informing them that she was to go to America to visit a sick relative. The letters were presented to them by Ethel Le Neve, Dr Crippen's secretary, who was later seen wearing Cora's fur coat and jewellery.

DATE:
1910

EXHIBIT:
Dr Crippen's
pyjamas

A little while later, in March, Dr Crippen announced his wife's death, but Cora's friends were troubled by his vague explanations, the fact that they had not been been able to trace her in America and the suspicious status of Ethel Le Neve in the Crippen household. Two of the friends, Mr and Mrs Nash, reported their concerns to Detective Chief Inspector Walter Dew, who started to make inquiries. These revealed that Cora's signature had appeared on cheques for the Crippens' joint bank account up until 22 March, the day before Cora had, according to Crippen, been on her deathbed in America. Walter Dew went to Crippen's house in Hilldrop Crescent, but only found Ethel Le Neve. He took her to Crippen's office and interviewed him there, and back at Hilldrop Crescent, to be told that Cora had left Crippen for another man, leaving him with instructions to cover up any scandal in whatever way he could. For this purpose, she had signed a number of blank cheques. Crippen admitted that he had been having an affair with Ethel Le Neve who, remarkably, told Dew that she had been 'astonished' to hear of Cora Crippen's fate, but that she had not discussed the death openly with Crippen. Dew left Hilldrop Crescent to make further inquiries over the weekend to try to verify or disprove Crippen's account.

By the Monday, Crippen and Ethel Le Neve had disappeared. A search of the house eventually found human flesh and organs under the cellar floor, but no head or bones. The remains were found with Crippen's pyjamas and there were traces of enough hyoscine (a medication used to calm violent patients in asylums) to have caused death. Dr Crippen had ordered five grains of hyoscine from a chemist's establishment twelve days before Cora had last been seen alive. It was estimated that half a grain had been found in the dead body. Professor Augustus Pepper gave expert pathological evidence at Crippen's trial, as did 33-year-old Bernard

The pyjama label

Spilsbury who went on to become a famous witness in many murder trials. Spilsbury testified that one section of a semi-horseshoe-shaped mark found on the flesh was consistent with a surgical scar for an operation that Cora Crippen was known to have undergone to remove her ovaries, despite defence claims that it was only a crease in the skin. Spilsbury had searched for evidence of glands or hair follicles, which would have indicated that it was not a scar, and found none. The other part of the horseshoe mark was indeed a fold or crease in the flesh.

The international search for Crippen and Le Neve was concluded after Henry George Kendall, the captain of a cargo ship, *Montrose*, on a voyage from Rotterdam to Canada, reported his suspicions about two of his passengers to the ship's owners by means of the new Marconi wireless transmitter. Ethel Le Neve had been disguised as a boy, but the captain noted that the male clothes did not fit well, and that the 'son' of 'Mr Robinson' had a voice that began in a low register and became progressively higher. Sir Melville MacNaghten, the assistant commissioner, was asked to authorise Walter Dew and Sergeant Mitchell to travel to Canada by means of a faster ship, *Laurentic*, which was shortly due to leave Liverpool. MacNaghten's decision to send Dew on a transatlantic pursuit would deprive Scotland Yard of its main investigating officer for more than three weeks. MacNaghten's decision to allow the trip was a controversial one not supported by some of his colleagues, until, on the morning of 31 July 1910, news broke that Dew had boarded the *Montrose* and arrested Dr Crippen and Ethel Le Neve.

Ethel Le Neve was grateful to Walter Dew for arranging for some women's clothing and a hat with a veil, which helped to hide her face from the curious crowds and newspaper reporters on her return to England. Crippen stood trial for murder at the Old Bailey in October 1910, was sketched by the courtroom artist William Hartley and was sentenced to death. He was hanged the following month. Ethel Le Neve's lawyers argued successfully for a separate trial and this may have saved her from the death penalty, which was a possible outcome of a joint trial with Hawley Crippen. She was acquitted.

92

Wooden Stool

PETER ARNE (64) appeared in more than fifty films and made frequent television appearances. On 1 August 1983, he was found at his home savagely beaten to death. The murder weapons were a log of wood, a knife and a stool, all of which are in the Crime Museum's collection. A photofit impression of the suspect's face was taken from a witness, and when the body of Guiseppe Perusi (32) was found in the River Thames three days later, the similarity with the suspect was evident. Perusi's fingerprints were found on the murder weapons and his clothes, found beside the river, bore traces of Arne's blood. Perusi had apparently been invited to Arne's home for a cup of tea and had then attacked him.

On 11 May 1812, Spencer Perceval became the only British prime minister to have been assassinated. The Tory premier was walking through the lobby of the House of Commons to attend a committee examining the problem of the recession when he was accosted by John Bellingham, who had fallen into debt after being imprisoned in Russia. The security of the Houses of Parliament was far less strict in those days, not least because the incident occurred before the Metropolitan Police was established. Bellingham had been able to lay in wait, armed with a pair of large-bore pistols, and fire into the chest of Perceval, whom Bellingham appeared

DATE:
1983

EXHIBIT:
The wooden stool used to murder Peter Arne

to blame for his personal situation. Bellingham was detained by a Vincent Dowling and Lieutenant General Isaac Gascoyne MP, aided by other unarmed bystanders who prevented him from committing suicide. A Bow Street officer, John Vickery, searched the prisoner's home and found a number of items relating to firearms. Bellingham appeared at the Old Bailey two days later, on 13 May 1812, was convicted of murder and sentenced to death. The judge, Sir James Mansfield, stated:

> That you be taken from hence to the place from whence you came, and from thence to a place of execution, where you shall be hanged by the neck until you be dead; your body to be dissected and anatomized.

In due course a portion of Bellingham's skin was donated to the Crime Museum. This may have reflected a practice of making use of dead prisoners' skin, such as, for instance, that of William Corder, convicted of the 'Red Barn' murder of Maria Marten in 1827, which was tanned and used as the covering of a book about his case.

William Terriss was an actor famous for playing swashbuckling melodrama and hero roles like Robin Hood, and was also a notable Shakespearean actor. By 1897 he was an actor-manager in London's theatreland but was stabbed to death in Maiden Lane outside the stage door of the Adelphi Theatre, as he arrived to take part in a production of *The Harbour Lights*. He was murdered by unsuccessful Scottish actor Richard Prince. Terriss had taken pity on Prince's situation, had given recommendations to find him work and had lent him money, only to find his kindness repaid with a violent and fatal attack. William Hartley made a court sketch of Richard Prince and the knife used in the attack is on display at the museum. The ghost of William Terriss is said to haunt the Adelphi Theatre and Covent Garden Underground station.

The popular television presenter Jill Dando (38) was shot and murdered on her doorstep in Fulham, on 26 April 1999 at 11.30 a.m. Dando had presented *Crimewatch* and other programmes. A long police investigation led to the arrest and prosecution of Barry George who was alleged to have an obsession with guns and female television personalities. He had once been found in the gardens of Kensington Palace, then the home of Princess Diana, who was not unlike Jill Dando in appearance.

Evidence in the Dando murder included a tiny speck of material that may or may not have been gunshot residue, and George was convicted in July 2001. A first appeal hearing in 2002 concluded that the conviction was not unsafe. In 2007, the Criminal Cases Review Commission referred the case back to the Court of Appeal, the grounds for which included arguments that the particle of firearms discharge residue was not proof that George himself had fired a gun, and that his clothing might have been subject to contamination. George's second trial, which excluded the contentious firearms residue evidence, ended in his acquittal on 1 August 2008. George was paid money by newspapers because of their defamatory coverage of his character, and claimed compensation for wrongful imprisonment. This was rejected, however, by the High Court, following a Supreme Court ruling that a miscarriage of justice must be based on evidence such that *no* conviction could possibly be based upon it; the judges ruled that there was evidence in the case upon which a reasonable jury, properly directed, could have based a conviction for murder.

93

Briefcase with Syringe

THE BRIEFCASE WAS owned by the notorious Kray brothers who, at one stage in their career, told Paul Elvey that he should go to the Old Bailey to kill a witness using this briefcase, which concealed a spring-loaded syringe that would be triggered by pulling a ring mechanism. The device was apparently never used, but the tale would have been effective in spreading the folklore surrounding the Krays and the violence they could organise, thereby increasing their reputation amongst criminals.

Twins Reginald and Ronald Kray were notorious criminals who had an obsession with assaulting others and encouraging each other to greater levels of violence. Their bid to extend their personal power and domination culminated in a serious protection racket in London and a number of murders. The blatant violence and unstable mental condition, particularly that of Ronald Kray, led to intimidation of witnesses and the prospect of their escaping justice until they were arrested with their brother Charles, and convicted by the efforts of a special squad of detectives led by Detective Superintendent Leonard 'Nipper' Read.

The twins were born in 1933 and made their first appearance at the Old Bailey in 1950, where a case of assault against them was dismissed for lack of evidence. In 1952, they marked the start of their National Service by violence, serious trouble with the military authorities and spells in custody. After being released, they commenced a period of increasing control over criminals, pubs and

DATE:
1966

EXHIBIT:
Briefcase
from the Kray
brothers inquiry

345

clubs in the East End of London. On 5 November 1956, Ronald Kray was jailed for three years for assaulting Terence Martin in a gang-related incident, and was diagnosed as suffering from paranoid schizophrenia. His violence worsened after his release.

In February 1960, Reginald Kray was imprisoned for eighteen months for protection-related threats and, whilst he was in prison, Peter Rachman, the head of a violent landlord operation, gave Ronald Esmeralda's Barn nightclub in Knightsbridge. Ownership of the premises served to increase the twins' influence in the West End, and allowed them to entertain 'celebrities' and famous people, rather than East End criminals. They were assisted by Alan Cooper, a banker, who needed protection from the rival Richardson gang from south London.

Christmas 1965 marked a confrontation between the Krays and Richardsons at the Astor Club, when a Richardson henchman, George Cornell, referred to Ronald Kray as a 'fat poof'. A gang war followed and a Kray ally, Richard Hart, was murdered at Mr Smith's club in Catford on 8 March 1966. Ronald Kray took revenge by killing George Cornell in the bar of The Blind Beggar public house, Whitechapel Road. Intimidation prevented any witnesses from co-operating with police.

On 12 December 1966, the Kray brothers assisted Frank Mitchell, known as the 'Mad Axeman', to escape from Dartmoor prison. Mitchell had a long history of violence and prison escapes, but had largely settled down at Dartmoor and become a trusted prisoner allowed out of prison on working parties. He was aggrieved at not having his sentence reviewed, however, and Ronald Kray, who had become friends with him during a previous term in prison, apparently thought that arranging Mitchell's escape would improve the Krays' reputation and publicise Mitchell's grievance. Mitchell became increasingly violent and unstable whilst at large, staying in a flat in Barking Road to avoid a well-publicised manhunt. The Krays had a problem accommodating the increasingly unmanageable prisoner they had helped escape from prison custody.

On Christmas Eve 1966, Mitchell was taken away from the flat and led to a van by Albert Donoghue, supposedly to take him to another 'safe house'. In the van were

Frederick Foreman and Alfred Gerrard who were armed with revolvers. When the van doors closed, they allegedly shot and killed Mitchell, whose body was never recovered. This murder formed part of the Kray brothers' trials but the evidence relied upon the testimony of Albert Donoghue, who was apparently thought to be unreliable by the jury, and so the Kray brothers and Foreman were acquitted of Mitchell's murder. Foreman later recounted that Mitchell's body was wrapped with chicken wire, weighted and dropped into the English Channel.

Ronald gave a gun and £100 to Jack 'The Hat' McVitie with instructions to murder Leslie Payne and the promise of a further £400 when the murder had taken place. Payne remained alive, but it was Reginald who went to collect the £100. He was moved by McVitie's tale of sorrow and gave him £50. This infuriated Ronald and led to a stand off between the Krays and McVitie, culminating in the Krays inviting him to a 'party' in Evering Road, Stoke Newington, where Reginald, egged on by Ronald, tried to shoot him. The gun, now in the Crime Museum having been thrown into the Grand Union canal and recovered by the police, was a Mauser. The gun jammed and Reginald Kray killed McVitie with a knife instead. McVitie's body was another that was never recovered, despite newspaper reports about his body being put into another person's grave. Payne later became an important informant to the police investigation.

The Krays tested Alan Cooper by suggesting that he carry out a murder, and Cooper in turn recruited Paul Elvey to do the work for him. The police found a crossbow at Cooper's house, which the Krays had supplied as a murder weapon. Cooper was at one stage carrying out an errand for the Krays when he was caught at Glasgow Airport with explosives intended to be used against the Richardson gang.

The Kray brothers were arrested on 9 May 1968 and once they were detained in police custody, witnesses slowly started to develop the confidence to give evidence of the truth to the police team. When Elvey was arrested, he confessed, and Cooper then became implicated in three attempted murders.

The trial lasted thirty-nine days at the Old Bailey and the Kray twins were sentenced to life imprisonment, thereby removing a notorious criminal influence from London. Ronald died in prison in 1995. Reginald was released from prison in August 2000 as he was suffering from end-stage cancer, and he died a few weeks afterwards. Charles Kray was sentenced to ten years for helping his brothers dispose of a body, and was released from prison in 1975, only to be sentenced to twelve years for drugs offences in 1997. He died in 2000.

There is a long history of organised gangs operating in London, not least that run by Jonathan 'Thieftaker General' Wild (executed at Tyburn on 24 May 1725), who manipulated both sides of the law with his network of informants, thieves and a system of claiming rewards for the return of the stolen goods. Money, power and influence are at the heart of the motivation for the gang leaders, often with a paranoid concern for their own pride and perceived status. The stock-in-trade of violence can appear to circumvent the law because successful prosecutions for assault normally require the victims to give evidence in a prosecution where the outcome is far less certain than intimidation. The prospect of peacefully run pubs and businesses being disrupted by violence or vandalism can lead to their owners agreeing to pay money to villains for a 'quiet life'. Sometimes gangs use moneymaking opportunities exploiting situations where the law is unclear or poorly enforced (e.g. betting, gaming, prostitution, pornography and drugs). The more established the gang, the greater the chances of the leader being able to remove himself from situations where straightforward, direct evidence could lead to a prosecution. In many cases, therefore, the police have to wait for an opportunity to act on intelligence or to secure the corroborated evidence of accomplices in order to mount a successful prosecution. The problem of gangs has not gone away and many gangs in London are now closely associated with the sale of cocaine and other drugs, often recruiting young teenagers into their ranks with the lure of easy money and a supposedly attractive, powerful lifestyle. Operation Trident, originally set up to deal with murders perpetrated by black gangsters on other black men, has become a permanent squad largely dealing with established and emerging gangs.

94 Electric Torture Machine

DATE:
1966

EXHIBIT:
The Megger
Box, intended
as an electric
torture device

THE BOX WAS used to generate an electric current that would cause electric shocks on sensitive parts of victims' bodies. It would also generate an atmosphere of intimidation.

Charles Richardson was born in Camberwell in 1934 and took up the scrap-metal business. His younger brother Edward, known as Eddie (b. 1936), became involved in supplying fruit machines to public houses. They developed an empire based on protection rackets and fraud, and became known for torturing those who did not comply with their demands. They would stage 'mock courts' and mete out punishments, such as the removal of teeth or toes with pliers.

The escalation of conflict between the Richardson and Kray gangs, especially in the form of the murders of George Cornell and Richard Hart, led to the arrest of the Richardson gang in 1966, and their prosecution in what became known as the 'Torture Trial'. One witness, travel agent Lucien Harris, was tortured because the Richardson brothers wanted information about an associate who allegedly owed them money. Johnny Bradbury, who had been convicted of murdering a man called Waldeck in South Africa, apparently on the Richardsons' orders, also gave evidence against them. Charles Richardson was jailed for twenty-five years, Edward Richardson and Frankie Fraser for ten years.

The police always need to be prepared to mount operations to combat the influence of gangs, and history shows that the Richardsons were by no means the first to try to wield this kind of influence. Arthur Harding was an East End gang leader who helped the social historian Raphael Samuel with his personal reminiscences about crime in London. He was active in the early years of the twentieth century, and grew up near Shoreditch High Street in an area known as The Nichol (replaced around 1895 by the Boundary Estate), where police officers and others entered with great care because of its violent reputation. Harding's gang conducted a feud with a rival group led by Isaac Bogard, a Jewish gangster involved with vice who was dark skinned and, in a reflection of language of the day, was nicknamed 'Darky the Coon'. A series of assaults and reprisals culminated in Harding and his men attacking their rivals as they left Old Street Court. However, they were ambushed and arrested by police officers led by Detective Inspector Frederick Wensley. The direct evidence given by police officers meant that the prosecution was not compromised by intimidation of witnesses. Harding received twenty-one months' hard labour, followed by three years' penal servitude.

Darby Sabini was born in Saffron Hill and took part in boxing. He then turned to crime connected with protection of illegal gaming clubs and controlling betting interests on racecourses with his brother 'Harryboy', Joseph, Fred and George, in competition with other gangs. Based around the Clerkenwell area, they enforced their activities with violence, using various weapons such as razors, guns and hammers. The Sabini gang conducted a form of warfare with Billy Kimber and his gang based in Birmingham, known as the Brummagen Boys. When Darby Sabini was attacked at Greenford on 25 March 1921, he used his gun to shoot his way free, and when prosecuted, even succeeded in getting himself acquitted by pleading self-defence against the rival gangsters. The incident took place before restrictions on firearms were introduced. On the last day of the Derby meeting at Epsom, a pitched battle took place between Kimber's gang and their counterparts from Leeds, who had travelled to Epsom supposedly to join forces against Sabini's followers but had mistaken their enemy. Twenty-three men were convicted and the Flying Squad ensured that the racecourse violence was suppressed.

The Sabinis were involved at one point in a gun battle near The Albion public house in Nile Street, Hoxton, against the Titanics, a gang who had displaced them from a West End gambling club. But, with the death penalty being in force, the somewhat legendary battle was allegedly about intimidation and inflicting wounds rather than committing murder.

Big Alf White led a family gang based in Islington having once been one of Darby Sabini's assistants, and when Sabini was jailed for receiving stolen property and then interned with his brothers during the Second World War, White moved into some of the territory controlled by the Sabinis.

95 Set of Scales

THE SET OF scales was seized from a drug dealer and represents one of the scourges of modern life.

The abuse of drugs is not a new phenomenon. Victorian authors such as Wilkie Collins used cocaine-based laudanum and Conan Doyle's Sherlock Holmes also used this drug. The growth of recreational drug taking since the 1960s has created an illegal industry concerned with the importation, distribution and some-times the growth and manufacture of drugs like heroin, cocaine, amphetamines and cannabis. Those with addictions have often contributed very significantly to the amount of income-generating crime committed. Gangs who formerly resorted to armed robbery turned to the lucrative business of illegal drugs.

DATE:
Undated

EXHIBIT:
Scales used by a dealer for illegal drug transactions

The Crime Museum has a number of interesting examples of how drugs have been concealed, but in truth, the task of detection is an ever-changing process of trying to thwart the imaginations of drugs importers, who develop new methods of hiding their illegal but lucrative cargoes.

The Commissioner's Annual Report for 1924 made note of a decrease in drugs cases. Although drugs crime reports are invariably initiated by the police rather than by the public, the 1923 statistics were quoted as 103 cases with seventy-two prosecutions. The 1924 picture was twenty-six and nineteen respectively. The commissioner put the decrease down to the deterrent effect of heavy sentences – some of penal servitude – that had been made possible by the provisions of the Dangerous Drugs and Poisons (Amendment) Act 1923. Over ninety years later, we can reflect on the changes in society and attitudes that have taken place since then, but would be only too grateful if an Act of Parliament could possibly achieve such an impact today.

Imitation Firearm

THE POWER OF a firearm is often the threat that it represents, and this imitation firearm is no different in its power to intimidate. This example was made of balsa wood in a prison, the result of much skill and ingenuity by a man intent on creating a threat to prison officers.

The Crime Museum has a collection of weapons ranging from various kinds of knives, swords, clubs, knuckledusters and adapted tools that can cause immense injury. Some are sword sticks, others are disguised as umbrellas. One recent addition is a Washbear 3D-printed gun made of plastic, but capable of firing .22 ammunition with a metal tube lining its barrel.

The fact that some items are in fact deadly weapons that look innocent, and apparently harmless items can be lethal, does not make the patrolling officer's job any easier. The number of calls to firearms incidents are numbered in their thousands in London each year, and officers need to attend them equipped with firearms in case the guns are used against the public or the police. It is not, therefore, surprising that incidents sometimes occur when a police officer makes a split-second decision to use a police firearm against a suspect who turns out either to have been armed with an imitation gun, or an object that looks like a gun but is not in fact a firearm. Sometimes inquests and inquiries have spent hours examining these decisions to reach conclusions many years later.

DATE:
Undated

EXHIBIT:
A balsa wood pistol and bullet made in a prison

97 Sword

SWORDS ARE OFTEN regarded as of historical interest and ornamental curiosities, but they have been involved in modern-day crime too. This sword was part of a collection owned by 34-year-old Gunter Wiora who was living with Shirley Allen, a model, aged 22. Allen would pose naked for photographers. Wiora, an insanely jealous man, attacked her on 4 May 1957 when he became convinced that she was involved with pornography and having an affair with another man. She ran, wounded, to a neighbour in an adjoining flat for help, where a woman offered her shelter and ran for help. Wiora then attacked the neighbour, causing severe injuries, and, before the police could arrive, killed Shirley Allen with the sword, the force of his blows bending the weapon as it struck her spine. The police had to break down the door of Wiora's flat where they found him with cut wrists and the gas turned on. Wiora was sentenced to twelve years' imprisonment for manslaughter at the Central Criminal Court on 25 July 1957 and was sent to Broadmoor Hospital.

DATE:
1957

EXHIBIT:
The bent sword used by Gunter Wiora

Detective Sergeant Bob Windows faced a samurai sword when he went to a house in October 1992 in Tottenham. The house belonged to the parents of a Peter Gilchrist and Windows had gone there to investigate a complaint of assault made by Gilchrist's former wife. The officer's hand was completely severed when Gilchrist, who had been suffering from a depressive illness, attacked him with the sword. He was convicted of causing grievous bodily harm with intent and was sentenced to five years' imprisonment.

Another sword in the Crime Museum's collection was used in 1999 by Eden Strang, who was suffering from a mental illness. His wife found him sitting naked at home, with the sword across his lap, hoping to defend the family from evil demons. On 28 November 1999, in a tormented state, he attacked members of the congregation at St Andrew's church, Thornton Heath, believing that they were demons; he injured an elderly nun and ten other worshippers, some very seriously. He was overpowered and was sent to Broadmoor Hospital, until he was released under medical supervision in March 2002.

Swordsticks, originally designed to act as walking sticks for respectable gentlemen, contain concealed thin-bladed swords for which the walking stick exteriors act as scabbards, and have been found more recently in the possession of less reputable men.

Knives, sometimes of frightening length, are a feature of the weapons carried on the streets, and the effect of them being used in fights can lead to a high rate of murders and serious assaults. Legislation prohibits the carrying of bladed articles, but firm policing measures are needed to ensure that the law is observed on the streets.

98 Observation Photograph

THESE OBSERVATION PHOTOGRAPHS were evidence in a prolonged operation to catch a serial rapist.

When a night-time attack on an elderly woman in her home in Croydon took place on 13 October 1992, the local police investigated the rape but were unable to trace the perpetrator. Further similar sexual assaults took place and, eventually, over the next eighteen years, there were to be over 203 linked offences: the victims being both men and women and aged between 68 and 93, spread over most south London boroughs and into Surrey, and occurring on random days of the week. The offender typically removed windowpanes to gain entry into the houses and cut telephone lines or, towards the end of his reign of terror, disabled mobile telephones. He would remove light bulbs from the bedroom and shine a torch into his victims' faces so that he

DATE:
2009

EXHIBIT:
Observation photograph from Operation Minstead

could not be identified. He made sure that his hands were covered with gloves or socks to avoid leaving finger marks.

Remains of the offender's semen had been left behind, however. As DNA technology improved, more samples from crime scenes were analysed, but there was no match on the DNA database. It was apparent that the offender would stalk his victims prior to the crime to ensure that they lived alone. In some cases the offender would show tenderness by kissing them on the cheek, but also great violence, like in the case of one victim, in 1999, who was raped twice and left bleeding from a perforated bowel – the injuries sustained on this occasion were almost fatal.

In 1998, the linked investigations were taken over by the Serious Crime Group at Lewisham under the name of Operation Minstead. Each crime scene suspected of being in the series of rapes was carefully re-examined by officers on the team, with a view to extracting the best quality evidence available, particularly details that may have been overlooked on the initial investigation. One item, now on display in the Crime Museum, was a glove that was found in a bush no less than seventeen houses away from an attack in an elderly lady's bedroom in September 2004 in Bromley, Kent. A widespread specialist search had found a vital clue far away from a normal crime scene search area. DNA traces on that glove linked it to the rapist.

Advanced DNA analysis indicated that the offender appeared to have originated from the Caribbean. Thousands of black men in south London voluntarily provided DNA samples so that they could be eliminated from the inquiry and help trace the offender. Hundreds of potential suspects were identified during the HOLMES (Home Office Large Major Enquiry System) computer-based enquiries and eliminated. One very grainy CCTV image established that the suspect might have been driving a Vauxhall Zafira car. But the potential for resolving the investigation was limited because of no clear geographical focus for making further intense inquiries. The sporadic nature of the offences sometimes had gaps of months or years between incidents.

In 2009, the offences started to occur more frequently, however, and a proactive operation became more viable. Under the leadership of Detective Superintendents Simon Morgan, and later Colin Sutton, over 150 officers were deployed on a nightly basis, with 100 undertaking observations and fifty doing follow-up inquiries. The staffing of an operation on this scale was a considerable strain on resources. On 15 November 2009, when this operation had been in progress for three weeks, an officer on observation duty saw a man running and then drive off in a Vauxhall Zafira, which had already been spotted parked several hours prior earlier. The officers reported the incident and the car was stopped by the police in Penge, some distance away. A crowbar was found in the boot, which made marks that matched those found at the scene of a crime in the series committed a month before, on 19 October 2009. A cagoule matched that shown on CCTV footage when the suspect had withdrawn money from cash machines using victims' credit cards, and a hat and fleece matched other similar images. The suspect, Delroy Grant, was then charged with twenty-six offences from fourteen crime scenes that were selected because of the strength of evidence, including matches of the prisoner's DNA profile. When Grant, who had become known as the 'Night Stalker', appeared at Woolwich Crown Court on 1 March 2011, he claimed that his ex-wife had collected and stored his DNA and given it to her boyfriend to plant at the various crime scenes. On 24 March he was convicted on a majority verdict and sentenced to life imprisonment with a minimum tariff of twenty-seven years.

A series of murders of prostitutes, linked with two similar murders in 1959 and 1963, took place in the Hammersmith area between 1964 and 1965. Thirty-year-old Hannah Tailford was found dead on the foreshore of the River Thames on 2 February 1964 near Hammersmith Bridge. She had apparently been strangled. Several of her teeth were missing and underwear had been forced down her throat. Six victims – all prostitutes that were found naked and dead – made up the series of unsolved murders. Detective Superintendent John du Rose took charge of the inquiry into what became known as the 'Hammersmith Nude Murders'. Two months later, Irene Lockwood, 26 years old, was found dead on the shore of the River Thames, on 8 April 1964, not far from where Hannah Tailford had been found, and the investigations were linked. Within three weeks, a caretaker, Kenneth Archibald, had confessed to the crime, but his account was not consistent with some known facts, and he was dismissed as being untruthful, particularly because another victim was then found on 22 April 1964 in Brentford – Helen Barthelemy (22). The police found flecks of motor vehicle spray paint at the scene and they started to concentrate their attention on paint-spraying business premises nearby.

Ten weeks later, on 14 July, 30-year-old Mary Fleming's body was found in the street in Chiswick. Paint traces were again found on the body, and neighbours had heard the sound of a car reversing down the street just before the body was found. On 25 November, Frances Brown (alias Margaret McGowan) was found under some rubble in a car park off Hornton Street, Kensington. Frances Brown had given evidence in the trial of Stephen Ward, a figure involved in the Profumo scandal. A witness, Kim Taylor, had been on the streets working with Frances Brown when Brown had been picked up by a man a month before, on 23 October 1964, when she was last seen alive. Kim Taylor provided the police with an Identikit picture of the man and a description of his car – a Ford Zephyr or Zodiac – but this did not yield any positive result. The sixth victim, Bridget ('Bridie') O'Hara, aged 28, was found in a storage shed in West Acton, her body again bearing traces of paint. The paint matched a transformer near to where she had been found and was consistent with her body having been kept warm for a period before it was discovered, so the location of the storage place for the bodies was finally identified.

John du Rose's team interviewed no fewer than 7,000 men in the area, but without obtaining sufficient evidence to prosecute anybody. He did, however, announce that he was 'whittling down the suspects' in an attempt to force the killer into unplanned action that might incriminate him, but this was unsuccessful. Du Rose wrote in his autobiography that his prime suspect committed suicide before the police had obtained sufficient evidence to confirm or disprove his involvement, but withheld the identity from public knowledge.

Because these were murders of prostitutes, there were some similarities with the Whitechapel murders. The suspect became known as 'Jack the Stripper' and there has been similar speculation by various authors about the identity of the killer.

From 1983 to 1989, a series of rapes of nine women over six years occurred in the west London area, the offender becoming known as the 'Notting Hill Rapist' who typically attacked women living in ground-floor or basement flats. He would threaten his victims at knifepoint, then tie, blindfold and gag them, assuring them, falsely, that his intention was only to steal property. There had been no finger marks left at the scenes and no victim was able to identify her attacker. The offences occurred within a relatively small area bounded by Ladbroke Grove, Lansdowne Road, Clarenden Road and Elgin Crescent. During some of the period, another rapist had been committing offences in South Kensington and it was not entirely clear whether they were a separate series or not.

The police, under the leadership of Detective Superintendent James Hutchinson, mounted a series of observations and patrols, and there were a number of occasions when a suspect slipped through the net and escaped. A four-year gap occurred at one point before the next offence took place, in May 1987. PC Graham Hamilton stopped Tony Mclean and had a hunch about him. Mclean, like many other local men, had given a blood sample to eliminate him from inquiries, but due to a slip of the finger, his blood group had been recorded as O secretor rather than the 0 (zero) secretor that had been traced to the offender. Another typographical error had wrongly recorded Mclean's date of release from prison, thus providing him falsely with an alibi for one of the crimes. When Graham Hamilton double-checked and revealed both of these errors, Mclean became the prime suspect. By this time, DNA profiling had been discovered and this enabled Mclean to be identified as the rapist for two of the crimes with certainty. He had lived just off Clarenden Road, was convicted in April 1989 and sentenced to life imprisonment.

Between 1989 and 1994, a series of rapes and sexual attacks occurred in and around the Plumstead area and nearby parts of south London. These amounted to an eventual total of about seventy offences, and became known as the work of the 'Green Chain Walk Rapist', the locations being loosely linked to the Green Chain long-distance footpath through that part of London. In November 1993, 27-year-old Samantha Bisset was viciously murdered in Plumstead. Bisset had been walking around in her home in a state of undress when an intruder had entered and attacked her; she was stabbed to death. Her 4-year-old daughter Jazmine was also murdered. The offender mutilated Bisset's body and took away parts of her internal organs as trophies. It was a grisly scene that was traumatic to see, not least on the part of the police photographer who was badly affected for a long time afterwards. A finger mark found at the scene led to the arrest and prosecution of Robert Napper in May 1994. He was convicted, and also admitted two rapes and two attempted rapes that were linked to the Green Chain Walk offences.

Napper had earlier been eliminated from the Green Chain inquiries by virtue of the fact that he was deemed to be too tall – at 6ft 2in – to fit the description of the offender. He was sent to Broadmoor in October 1995. In October 1989, Napper's mother had made a telephone call to the police indicating that he had confessed to a rape that had taken place in Plumstead, but this did not lead to Napper's arrest, possibly because the officer concerned was unable to identify the report of the crime concerned, and thereby corroborate this confession.

On 15 July 1992, Rachel Nickell was stabbed multiple times and murdered in front of her young son Alex, aged 2, on Wimbledon Common whilst they were out walking their dog. The police conducted a prolonged and controversial investigation that included interviewing thirty suspects, but centred around Colin Stagg, a man known to visit the common. In the absence of usable forensic evidence at the time, the police investigation focused on using an undercover female officer to befriend Stagg with a series of letters that progressively became more explicit, so that Stagg would be lured into making an admission that he had committed the murder. The operation resulted in the Crown Prosecution Service charging Colin Stagg, but at his trial the police technique – about which a psychologist, Paul Britton, had been consulted – was severely criticised by the trial judge as a 'honeytrap' and the case was dismissed. Stagg had spent fourteen months in custody and was paid substantial compensation after his wrongful detention. In December 1995, Robert Napper was questioned about Rachel Nickell's death but he denied any involvement. By 2002, DNA recovery technology had made further advances, and the case was reviewed using the original forensic evidence gathered with extreme thoroughness at the time. Minute fibres were then found that indicated that the chances of this residue not being from Napper were 1 in 23 million.

Napper was duly charged with killing Rachel Nickell and pleaded guilty to manslaughter on the morning that his trial was due to start. He was sentenced to be detained at Broadmoor without time limit.

Many lessons were learned from the Rachel Nickell case, which had no witness or usable forensic evidence at the time. Napper had managed to evade attending a police station to provide a DNA sample when he was one of many suspects for the earlier Green Chain Walk rapes and had later been eliminated on the criterion of his height. The psychological profiling and the honey-trap techniques both led to false conclusions in this case.

99 Roulette Wheel

THE ROULETTE WHEEL has been adapted so that it gives a greater chance of some numbers than others and was reputedly seized from Barnet Fair in 1885.

Casinos use more sophisticated roulette wheels than this particular example, but the gaming industry relies upon an enormous turnover of stake money that changes hands many times during the course of a session, and a roulette wheel will be operated many times. A slight change in the apparent odds can therefore have enormous implications for the casino operation and may not be apparent, even to the assiduous observer, of the operation of equipment that should give out results by random chance.

The most recent acquisition for the Crime Museum (2015) was a set of playing cards that Mihai Lacatos from Romania had used when playing poker, making very slight marks and bends on the cards to improve his chances and thereby fraudulently winning money from casinos in various parts of the country over a six-year period. The Playboy Club in Mayfair lost over £43,000 in one week, for instance. He had been banned from a number of casinos but had started to use false identities and was arrested at Luton Airport on 20 November 2014. He admitted fourteen offences and was the first person to be prosecuted for the specific offence of card marking.

DATE:
c. 1885

EXHIBIT:
Roulette wheel with cover (lifted to reveal ball location)

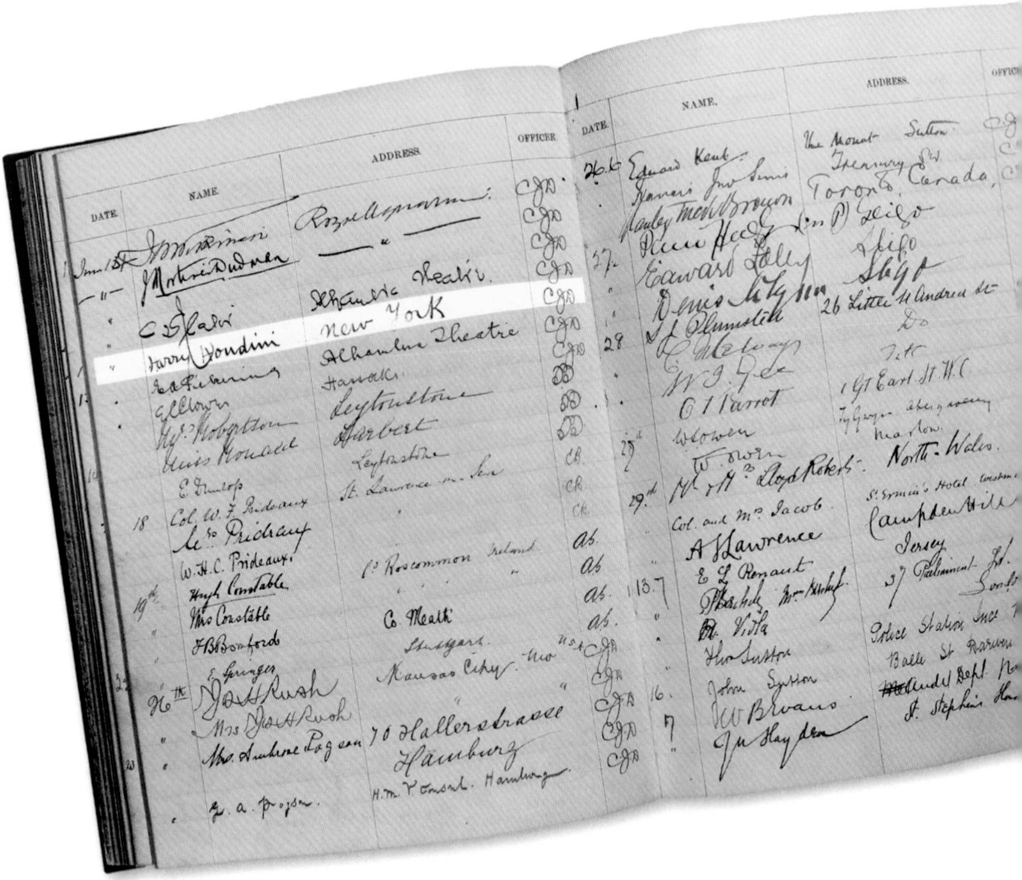

DATE	NAME	ADDRESS	OFFICER
	J. Morrison	Rozel Aynorm	CJD
	Mortris Rudner		CJD
	C. Blair	Atlantic Theatre	CJD
"	Harry Houdini	New York	CJD
	E. A. Reaums	Alhambra Theatre	BB
	E. Glover	Hawall	BB
	H. S. Robyston	Leytonstone	SD
	Miss Ronald	Herbert	CB
	C. Dunlop	Leytonstone	CR
18	Col. W. E. Prideaux	St. Lawrence on See	CR
	M.S. Prideaux		
	W. H. C. Prideaux	Co. Roscommon Ireland	AS
	Hugh Constable		AS
19th	Miss Constable	Co. Meath	AS
	F. B. Bomford	Stuttgart	AS
22	26th E. Springer	Kansas City Mo.	CJA
	Mrs. J. L. Rush		CJA
	Mrs. Andrew Pagan	70 Hallerstrasse Hamburg	CJD
		H. M. Consul. Hamburg	CJD
	G. A. Pagan		

DATE	NAME	ADDRESS	OFFICER
26.6	Edward Kent	The Mount Sutton	
	Francis Jno Sims	Treasury St	
	Hanley Men Brongon	Toronto Canada	
27	Nicw Healy	Sligo	
	Edward Jolly	Sligo	
	Denis Lilynn	26 Little St Andrew St	
	S. S. Olmstich	Do	
28	E. Meleay		
	W. G. Lee	161 Earl St W. C.	
	C. I. Parrot		
	W. Owen	Marlow	
29	W. Owen	North Wales	
29th	Mr. & Mrs. Lloyd Roberts	Campden Hill	
	Col. and Mrs. Jacob	Jersey	
	A. Lawrence	37 Parliament St London	
	E. L. Renant		
13.7	Blanche Mr. Mich	Police Station Inns	
	Br. Vida	Belle St Railway	
	Thos Sutton	St. Stephen Har	
16	John Sutton		
7	W. Brvans		
	Jno Hayden		

100

Visitors' Books

ONCE SCOTLAND YARD'S Crime Museum had been established, it rapidly became a popular place to visit for those both within and outside the Metropolitan Police. Because it has always been a private museum located within the secure perimeter of the Scotland Yard building, there have invariably been difficulties in granting all the requests to visit, even for some police officers. However, distinguished and famous people have visited and recorded their names in the Visitors' Book.

Several members of the Royal Family have seen the museum, such as the Prince of Wales, later King Edward VII, Princess Diana, and most recently, the Duke of Cambridge. The King and Queen of Belgium both signed the book. Arthur Conan Doyle no doubt gained more inspiration for his Sherlock Holmes stories than did Gilbert and Sullivan for their light operas. The museum was, in fact, mentioned in passing in 'The Adventure of the Empty House' published in *The Strand* magazine, in October 1903, when Holmes concludes the case by saying, 'The famous airgun of Von Herder will embellish the Scotland Yard museum.' Jerome K. Jerome attended with E.W. Hornung, who later published tales of the cracksman Raffles. Laurel and Hardy and the 1893 visiting Australian cricket team are recorded. One entry, in 1913, simply states 'The Man Who Knows', perhaps the famous mentalist Claude Alexander. Lloyd George gave his address as No. 11 Downing Street, whilst Stanley Baldwin simply wrote

DATE:
1900

EXHIBIT:
The Crime Museum Visitor Book signed by Harry Houdini

his address as Stourport. The signatures of famous barristers and judges appear, including the famous Travis Humphreys, who was involved in the cases of Dr Crippen, John Haigh and Oscar Wilde.

Perhaps, however, the most intriguing signature is that of Harry Houdini, the famous escapologist who would no doubt have been intrigued by the handcuffs on display. William Melville, the distinguished head of Special Branch, hosted Houdini's visit to Scotland Yard in 1900. Houdini was apparently handcuffed in Melville's office and given the prospect of joining his hosts for lunch if he could escape from his manacles in time. There is no doubt that courtesy and hospitality eventually prevailed for the lunchtime appointment, but the truth of whether Houdini had been able to escape from the handcuffs is now pure speculation. One interpretation of the incident, set out in *The Secret Life of Houdini* by William Kalush and Larry Sloman, was that the incident had been Melville's way of testing Houdini's character prior to his becoming an informant. Houdini travelled widely, spoke German and mixed with a wide variety of characters on an international basis. Being able to record 'Scotland Yard's astonishment' about his ability to escape from custody created great publicity for Houdini's career, and perhaps there was reciprocal assistance in Houdini providing information to Scotland Yard. If true, Houdini's visit was not merely for his entertainment.

Around 1890, an officer involved with the museum wrote a report about its importance to the training of police officers, but the surviving page of the handwritten report breaks off in the middle of a lament:

> The object of its original formation was for the purpose of instructing young constables as to the appearance of burgling tools, but it has since degenerated into a –

One may speculate about what the details of the unknown officer's complaint would have been, but it may have been connected with the museum becoming part of the itinerary for important and influential visitors to New Scotland Yard's fine new headquarters, such as the well-dressed ladies shown in one contemporary drawing. The issues about public access would have been the same as they are today and have also been taken into account in the production of this book.

In his annual report for 1951, Commissioner Sir Harold Scott stated:

> Applications from members of the public for permission to visit Scotland Yard have always been numerous. A drawing in one of the illustrated weekly papers of the eighties shows a number of fashionably dressed ladies enjoying the sights of the 'Black Museum'. But it has for many years been necessary to restrict visits almost entirely to police officers or other persons with a professional interest in police work.

The public have an interest in crime and it is important to understand what happens on the streets and how the police deal with it, but the museum needs to ensure that it is not feeding interests that may be merely prurient. Neither does it wish to create any inspiration whatsoever for those intent on illegal activities or to recreate the trauma suffered by victims of crime.

Authors' Note

THE 100 OBJECTS we have featured, and the cases we describe, reflect controversies, including the death penalty, how women have been treated, and awful things done by those who may have been mad, bad or both. We hope that they shine a light on the way in which Metropolitan Police and other detectives have tackled crime over the years, and the difficulties faced by police officers. Sometimes the police have solved the cases quickly; sometimes inquiries were only closed after a prolonged period, or not at all. This is not an official book published by the Metropolitan Police Service, so we as authors take full responsibility for any mistakes or misinterpretations.

We had many discussions about the best sequence for the objects, some of which come in a natural, broad chronological order. We let the object itself lead into some of the important associated cases we describe rather than attempt to adhere strictly to subject headings.

Some readers may find some of this book disturbing, but the material does reflect the nature of crime from which the police do their best to protect us. The police seek justice for victims and their families, and we hope that the book leaves us all with renewed concern for those who suffer the effects of crime.

Curators of the Crime Museum

INSPECTOR PERCY NEAME was primarily responsible for organising the establishment of the museum, assisted by Police Constable George Randall. Randall retired in 1900 and after that relatively few exhibits were added to the collection, and it was closed during the First World War. In 1921, a new committee was formed to take the collection forward and a sergeant in the Criminal Records Office was given part-time responsibility for maintaining the collection. It was redesigned in 1936, but then closed during the Second World War. In 1951 some exhibits were transferred to the Detective Training School at Hendon, and these have since been returned. A 1981 refurbishment has since been followed by other reorganisations.

In 1954, Alexander Hannay, a principal grade member of the civil staff, retired, and then became the museum's full-time curator. He was followed by a series of retired detectives:

1955	George Somerset
1957	Charles Dawson
1970	James Mackle
1976	Thomas McMacken
1981	William Waddell
1993	John Ross
2005	Alan McCormick
2011	Dave Thompson
2012	Paul Bickley

The Courtroom Sketches of William Hartley

WILLIAM HARTLEY (1862–1937) was an early Fleet Street photographer whose fame was achieved not with his camera, but from courtroom sketches at the Old Bailey, Bow Street, and other famous courts. Because photography inside the court precincts was not allowed, Hartley had to resort to his drawing skills to provide newspaper readers with images of the people taking centre stage in the dramatic trials for murder and other crimes that enthralled the nation. He was soon renowned for the speed, accuracy and the quality of his drawings. He became a famous exponent of what became an art form in its own right. In terms of quality, his drawings speak for themselves.

Six volumes of his original sketches were donated to the Crime Museum. The material covers the period from 1893 to 1919 when many classic murder cases took place. In an age when photography was not as common as today, Hartley's sketches often provided the public with their only images of notorious crimi-nals in their last public appearance before their death on the scaffold, interesting characters who acted as witnesses, and the often high-profile lawyers involved. Many of the images appeared in *The Morning Leader* or *The Star* newspapers.

There are approximately ninety-one cases covered by the sketches, not all of them positively identified. They include: famous murderer Dr Crippen; Samuel Dougal, who stole money from Camille Holland and was convicted on early ballistics evidence; George Chapman, alias Severin Klosowski, who poisoned his three 'wives' and was a suspect in the Jack the Ripper murders; Adolf Beck, twice the victim of a notorious case of mistaken identity for stealing jewellery from women; the Stratton brothers, the first to be convicted of murder on fingerprint evidence; Horatio Bottomley MP, convicted of fraud by the issue of Victory bonds; Emmeline Pankhurst, the suffragette; and many more. A list of some of the cases featured is shown below:

Year	Case	Details
1893	Charles Wells	Convicted of fraud at the Old Bailey on 6 March 1893, known as one of the men who broke the bank at Monte Carlo
1897	Elizabeth Camp	Murder on a train in SW London
1897	Richard Prince	Murder of William Terriss, the famous actor-manager
1898	Alfred Monson	Death of 18-year-old Cecil Hambrough. Monson tried to defraud the family of an inheritance
1898	William Horsford	Hanged for the murder of cousin Annie Holmes
1898	William Johnson (alias 'Harry the Valet') and Moss Lipman	Jewel theft of Mary Blair, Dowager Duchess of Sutherland. Convicted of £30,000 theft
1898	John Schneider	The St Pancras oven murder
1899	Mary Ann Ansell	Poisoned her sister Caroline for £11 life insurance
1899	Bertha Peterson	Daughter of the rector of Biddenden and killer John Whibley
1900	Louise Masset	A half-French governess who murdered her own child
1900	Ada Chard Williams	A baby farmer who killed children entrusted to her care
1900	Herbert John Bennett	Strangled his wife on a Yarmouth beach
1901	Ralph & Caroline Dyer	Took part in a murder to avenge the alleged rape of Caroline
1901	Ernest Walter Wickham	Murdered Amy Russell

1901	Maud Eddington	Shot herself in front of her lover John Bellis
1901	Horos Scandal	Swami Laura Horos was a fake medium put on trial with her husband for rape and fraud
1902	Kitty Byron	The Lombard Street murder
1902	Thomas Goudie	Defrauded Bank of Liverpool of £160,000
1902	George Woolfe	The Tottenham murder
1903	Samuel Dougal	Murder of Camille Holland at Moat Farm where he lived with her, and notable case for ballistics evidence
1903	William Gardiner	The Peasenhall Mystery murder of Rose Harsent
1903	Amelia Sach & Annie Walters	The Finchley baby farmers
1903	Nurse Sampson	Nurse Sampson murder – Kensal Rise
1903	George A. Crossman	Suicide case 23 January 1903
1903	Charles Jeremiah Slowe	Executed 10 November 1903 for the murder of Martha Jane Hardwick
1903	Edgar Edwards	Murder of John Darby
1903	George Chapman or Severin Klosowski	Poisoned three 'wives' and has been regarded as a suspect for the Whitechapel Murders and Jack the Ripper
1904	Adolf Beck	Notorious miscarriage of justice
1904	Joseph Stewart	Murdered his brother William Stewart in a drunken domestic quarrel
1904	Conrad Donovan & Charles Wade	Murdered shop keeper Emily Farmer
1904	Charles & Martha Stephenson	Prosecuted for deception by acting as 'Keiro Palmists'
1904	William Hoffman	Witness in a deception case involving Lewis Solomon
1904	Ernest T. Hooley & Henry Lawson	Once one of the richest men in England, Hooley was later made bankrupt. In 1904 he was acquitted of fraud, but Lawson was convicted
1904	James Whitaker Wright	A wealthy mine owner who was convicted of fraud and committed suicide afterwards

1905	Arthur Devereux	Murdered his wife and two of his children
1905	Hugh Watt former MP	MP for Camlachie 1885–92, convicted of attempting to procure the murder of his wife in 1905
1905	Rebecca Margaret Gregory	Charged with murder at the Old Bailey 14 January 1905
1905	Alfred & Albert Stratton	Convicted of murder of Thomas and Ann Farrow in the first British murder case to be decided on fingerprint evidence
1906	Matilda Stanley	Criminal libel case heard at the Old Bailey brought by Lady Gwendolen Cecil, about allegations that the chaplain at Hatfield House had fathered a child by her
1907	Robert Wood	The Camden Town murder, linked to a famous picture by Walter Sickert, and a proposed connection with Jack the Ripper by crime author Patricia Cornwell
1907	Richard Clifford Brinkley	Poisoned Johanna Blume after tricking her into signing a will in his favour
1907	John Edward Wyatt	Murder of Florence Wakeling by shooting her with his revolver
1907	Arthur Parker Hawkins	Stabbed his sister, Mary Alpe, to death after arguments about money
1907	Mary Ann Dearman	Costermonger who shot her abusive husband under provocation
1907	Charles Smith & May Vivienne Churchill (Chicago May)	On trial for attempted murder of Edward Guerin, appearing at Clerkenwell
1907	Millicent Marsh	19-year-old nursemaid prosecuted for perjury resulting in wrongful conviction for passing a forged cheque
1907	James Albert Jones	19-year-old baker's assistant who stabbed his wife to death
1907	Emilie Foucault	Threw sulphuric acid at Andre Delombre with whom she had been having an affair
1908	Franz von Veltheim	Blackmail case, demanding money from Solomon Joel, of Barnato Bros, bankers and Africa merchants
1908	Horatio Bottomley MP	Liberal MP who started the John Bull savings scheme, which was fraudulent

1908	George Woolf	Robbery case tried at the Old Bailey, 15 April 1908
1909	Oscar Slater	Controversial murder case brought against the German Jew Oscar Slater who was championed by Arthur Conan Doyle and eventually released from prison in 1928
1909	Davitt Stanley Windell	Appeared at the Old Bailey on 26 June
1909	Lillian Templeton	Featured at Brixton
1910	Dr Hawley Crippen	Infamous murder case
1911	Sidney Street Siege	The prosecution of surviving defendants after the famous Sidney Street siege
1911	Stinie Morrison	Controversially convicted of murder of Leon Beron
1911	Harry Bridge	Lambeth Police Court, 24 November
1911	Francisco Carlos Godhino	Murder of Alice Brewster on SS *China* on the high seas between Colombo and Aden
1912	Frederick Seddon	Poisoned his lodger Eliza Barrow with arsenic, and made an unsuccessful attempt to sway the trial judge with an appeal about freemasonry
1912	John Williams	Murdered Inspector Arthur Walls at Eastbourne. Notable ballistics case
1912	Albert George Bowes	Shot Police Commissioner Sir Edward Henry in an attempted murder case
1912	Emmeline Pankhurst	Famous Suffragette
1914	Karl Gustav Ernst	Islington hairdresser who acted as a communication link for espionage during the First World War
1918	Louis Voisin	Identified as a murder suspect by means of distinctive hand writing

Appendix III

Death Masks

THE CRIME MUSEUM'S collection of death masks comprises the following cases:

1767 Elizabeth Brownrigg

A death mask is speculatively attributed to Elizabeth Brownrigg, an apparently respected midwife who had opened a small private hospital and offered to take in parish apprentices to teach them the duties of household service. On this basis the London Foundling Hospital gave several female children into her care. But Brownrigg transpired to be an abusive employer who routinely beat, starved and chained her charges to wooden beams, making them sleep in a coal cellar. Mary Clifford, a 16-year-old employee, escaped back to the Foundling Hospital, but died of her injuries in St Bartholomew's Hospital. Elizabeth Brownrigg was convicted of her murder and executed at Tyburn, amid bitter expressions of indignation amongst the watching mob.

1817 John Nuttall

On Sunday, 23 June 1817 the marriage banns of the pregnant 23-year-old Ann White were due to be read in church, but then her strangled body was found in a well at a farm in Lancashire. John Nuttall, the 20-year-old father of the unborn child, was found guilty of her murder, to which he confessed to a fellow prisoner whilst awaiting execution. He was hanged at Lancaster on 6 September 1817 and his body given to a medical school.

1824   John Thurtell

John Thurtell, the son of a mayor of Norwich, owed £300 (then a very large amount of money) to solicitor William Weare through gambling losses. Thurtell thought he had been cheated, but invited Weare to join him and two friends, Joseph Hunt and William Probert, for a further gambling session at Probert's cottage at Radlett on 4 October 1823. The men travelled from London in Thurtell's horse-drawn gig, but just short of their destination, Thurtell shot Weare in the face with a pistol, but this did not kill him. Weare escaped from the gig, but Thurtell ensured his death by cutting his throat with a knife and ramming the pistol into Weare's brain.

The men hid Weare's body in a nearby pond, but then transferred it to another pond in Elstree. The two murder weapons were found at the scene. Thurtell was later found in possession of a pistol, one of a pair that matched the other found at the scene. The case was known as the Radlett, or Elstree, murder and gained great publicity both at the time and subsequently through books and songs about the case.

Probert turned King's evidence and testified against the other two men. Thurtell was convicted and executed at Hertford on 9 January 1824, but not before the trial judge, Mr Justice Park, had complained about unfair publicity given to the case, and indeed the gallows being erected before the verdict. Thurtell is reported to have said that he did not want a cast to be taken of his head in case a bust should be made, which might be seen by members of his family. The snuffbox, reputed to be the one from which he took a last pinch before his execution, is in the Crime Museum.

Joseph Hunt was reprieved and transported to Australia where he became rehabilitated. He married and later became a police constable. William Probert was not punished for the murder but became an outcast unable to find work, and was hanged in 1825 for stealing a horse worth £25 from a relative.

1837   James Greenacre

James Greenacre was hanged for the murder of Hannah Brown as described earlier in this book (see p. 29).

1841   Robert Blakesley

The 27-year-old Robert Blakesley set out on the morning of 21 September 1841 to murder his estranged wife but inadvertently ended up killing James Burdon, the landlord of the King's Head public house, Eastcheap, who had intervened to protect Mrs Blakesley from his attacks with a butcher's knife. Robert Blakesley was executed outside Newgate prison on 15 November 1841.

1842   Daniel Good

Executed outside Newgate on 23 May 1842, seven weeks after the murder of his common-law wife Jane. Good's case was the catalyst for the formation of Scotland Yard's Detective Branch, as described earlier in this book (see p. 39).

1843   Samuel Bonsall, William Bland and John Hulme

These three casts arose from the hanging at Derby, on 31 March 1843, of the three men who had committed a robbery of two wealthy spinster sisters, Martha and Sarah Goddard, at their home in Stanley Hall, near Derby. Both sisters had been savagely attacked, with Martha dying from her injuries. A £200 reward was offered for information, and the promise of a pardon, except for the person who had committed the murder. Bonsall, Bland and Hulme separated to try and avoid police inquiries, but one of them inadvertently admitted his involvement in the crime and mentioned the names of his accomplices to a neighbour. This led to the police being informed and to the arrest of the three men. There was no doubt that all three had been involved in the robbery, but each blamed the others for the murder. The prosecution relied upon the legal principle that all were equally guilty of murder if they had gone out on their criminal enterprise prepared to use violence to overcome resistance. The jury took fifteen minutes to agree to their conviction, and the executions took place with a crowd of 40,000 and a 'carnival' atmosphere.

1845   Thomas Hocker

When Police Constable John Baldock discovered the body of James De La Rue at Hampstead on a bitterly cold night, 21 February 1845, he was approached by Thomas Hocker, an acquaintance of the dead man, who offered the police officer some brandy (refused) and a shilling (accepted). Because of Hocker's suspicious behaviour he was arrested, and incriminating evidence was found in the form of bloodstained clothing. A letter in De La Rue's pocket also helped to convict Hocker, whose defence, written out on many pages, was rejected by the jury as falsehoods. He was executed at Newgate on 28 April 1845.

A feature of Victorian executions were the broadsheet ballads that appeared shortly afterwards, this example entitled 'The Lamentation of Thomas H. Hocker':

Farewell! Vain world; a long farewell
For I'm in Newgate's dismal cell;
For death I'm cast, alas 'tis true,
For murdering poor James de la Rue.

Alas! I own, with grief and shame,
Thomas Henry Hocker is my name.
Sweet innocence once filled my breast,
But now with guilt I am oppressed

While gaping thousands round appear,
And none for me will shed a tear,
Cut off in youth, no pitying friend
Will weep or mourn the murderer's end.

Young men, all take this warning pray
And don't by guilt be led astray;
Theft and murder always shun,
Think of the cruel deed I have done.

1846   Martha Browning

Martha Browning was a 23-year-old domestic servant, who murdered Mrs Elizabeth Mundell, aged 60, on 1 December 1845. Martha Browning shared a room in Westminster with Mundell and, whilst Mundell was asleep, twisted a knotted cord around her neck twice and then arranged the body so as to make it appear that she had committed suicide by self-strangulation. She then stole two £5 notes which led to her arrest and conviction. The executioner at Newgate on 5 January 1846 did not do his job well, and she was reported to have died after 'prolonged suffering'.

1846   Thomas Wicks

Thomas Wicks was an apprentice gas fitter who shot his employer, James Bostock, through the head at 6 a.m. on 16 February 1846, at a house in Drury Lane in apparent retaliation for bad treatment. Thomas Wicks is notable for his indifference which he demonstrated by whistling and singing through the Bow Street court proceedings. He was executed at Newgate at 8 a.m. on 30 March 1846. The case of Wicks contradicted any argument that public executions were a deterrent to crime. It was believed that Wicks had attended most of the recent executions there and had even paid half a crown for a seat in a room opposite the gallows to witness the execution of Martha Browning six weeks before he committed his own offence.

1847   John Platts

John Platts, a butcher, was executed at Derby prison on 1 April 1847 in front of a crowd of 20,000 people. The *Chambers Journal* of 25 April 1885 recounted a visit to the museum and described this death mask as 'a big heavy head, ticketed as that of John Platts', with the rope that was used for the execution being looped over a gas pendant in the middle of the room.

1848   Thomas Sale

Thomas Sale (25) was convicted of the murder of 57-year-old John Bellchambers who had been attacked and robbed by a gang of thieves a few yards from his Westminster home. Sale made a full and open confession of his guilt before his execution at Newgate on 10 January 1848.

1848   William Hewson

William Hewson had served nine months of a two-year sentence at Cold Bath Fields House of Correction for incest with his daughter and concealing the birth of a child from that relationship when, suffering from a grievance that made him wish to kill the prison governor, he attacked, stabbed and killed William Woodhouse, a prison officer. The only regret that Hewson expressed was that he had been unable to kill the prison governor himself. Executed at 8 a.m. on 10 June 1848, at Newgate, the newspapers noted that 'the attendance of persons to witness the scene was not great'.

1853   Alfred Waddington

Alfred Waddington (20) was executed at York Castle on Saturday, 8 January 1853 for murdering his illegitimate baby in Sheffield by cutting off her head, and then attempting to murder the mother. An unsuccessful petition to Queen Victoria sought mitigation of the sentence because Waddington had injured his head by falling down steps at the age of 8, after which, 'under excitement or sudden impulses' he became temporarily insane and unable to discriminate between right and wrong. A crowd of 10,000 attended York castle to witness the execution.

1853   James Barbour

One week later, on 15 January 1853, 21-year-old James Barbour was executed at York Castle for the murder of a hawker named Robinson at Sheffield, admitting his guilt an hour before his execution, and being so terrified that officials completed proceedings in the shortest possible time. *The Times* commented that only 3,000–4,000 people attended on a cold, wet morning and that 'there was no exhibition of feeling of any kind on the part of the spectators'.

1855 Luigi Buranelli

Luigi Buranelli, an Italian tailor, shot his landlord Joseph Lambert dead in a case that the newspapers described as the Foley Place murder. Lambert ran a boarding house in Marylebone but objected to his tenants having affairs with one another, notwithstanding that he himself went to bed with one of his female tenants. When Lambert found that Buranelli had started an affair with Jane Williamson, who had the room next to Buranelli, Lambert gave them immediate notice to quit. Buranelli duly left the premises but returned with a gun the next day and shot both Lambert and the tenant sharing the bed with her landlord. Lambert died, but his mistress was only wounded. Buranelli then shot himself but survived the injuries to be hanged outside Newgate prison on 30 April 1855.

1856 Robert Marley

Robert Marley attempted to rob a jeweller's shop in Parliament Street when the brave intervention of a young man, Richard Cope, thwarted his attempt, but at the expense of losing his life from a brutal attack at Marley's hands. Marley, hanged outside Newgate on 15 December 1856, was described as a fine young man in appearance, nearly 6ft tall, and appearing younger than his age of 39 years.

1860 James Mullins

When Mary Elmsley, a wealthy widow of 70 years who rented out a number of properties but lived in an untidy and neglected home, was found battered to death in her house in Stepney, east London, a reward was offered for information leading to the arrest of the offender. The investigating officers were Inspector Stephen Thornton, assisted by sergeants William Thomas and Richard Tanner (who later investigated the murder of Thomas Briggs by Franz Müller). Mullins was a former officer who had been dismissed by the Metropolitan Police, and had undertaken decorating work for Mrs Elmsley. Mullins visited Richard Tanner at his home in Westminster and told Tanner that he had seen a man, Walter Emm, at 5 a.m. carrying a suspicious parcel which Emm had left in a ruined building in a nearby brickyard. Mullins promised

'If this goes off all right, I'll take care of you' meaning that Mullins would have shared part of the £300 reward with Tanner.

The officers went with Mullins to the brickyard where the officers searched the building and Emm's cottage without success. When they returned to Mullins with this news, Mullins berated them for not searching properly, and then went straight to the ruined building where he asked them to pull down a stone slab. Under the slab was a parcel with a number of spoons and a £10 cheque connected to Mrs Elmsley's house. Emm was arrested and charged, but so also was Mullins on the basis that he had demonstrated knowledge of the location of the parcel of spoons that he could not have known about had his story of observing Emm from the exterior of the premises been true. The implication was that Mullins was so keen to claim the reward, and to divert suspicion from himself, that he was prepared to 'frame' Emm for the murder. In Mullins' lodgings was a hair-strewn plasterer's hammer that was consistent with a head injury sustained by the victim, some tape similar to that used to tie up the parcel, and, in lodgings where Mullins had stayed with his wife, a spoon that matched others contained in the incriminating parcel. The Mullins' landlady had found a boot thrown out of their window that had a pattern on the sole that matched a bloody boot mark at the dead woman's house.

Mullins was convicted of the murder and sentenced to death, protesting his innocence to the end. In a statement handed to prison officials before his execution on 19 November 1860, however, he did state that he believed Walter Emm to be innocent. The original letter from the Governor of Newgate prison to the Commissioner of Police of the City of London recording Mullins' death is an exhibit in the Crime Museum. A phrenological report by Cornelius Donovan, the Principal of the London School of Phrenology, was composed directly after the execution.

1864 Franz Müller

Franz Müller was convicted of the railway murder of Thomas Briggs (see p. 43). He was executed at Newgate on 14 November 1864.

1892 Frederick Deeming

Frederick Deeming was born in 1853 in Leicestershire, ran away to sea at the age of 16, but then began a life of crime, mostly theft and obtaining money by false pretences. He married Marie and had four children. In 1891, after being released from his latest spell in prison, he took out a lease on a house, Dinham Villa, in the Rainhill area near Liverpool, supposedly on behalf of a Colonel Brookes. He then started a relationship with Emily Lydia Mather, and, when his wife and children visited, introduced them as his sister and her children. Shortly after this visit, Deeming complained that work needed to be done on the drains and the kitchen floor replaced. He took care to closely supervise the work.

He married Emily and immigrated to Australia where they lived for a while in a rented house in Andrew Street, Windsor, New South Wales. On 3 March 1892, the new tenant complained of a nasty smell in one of the bedrooms, and, when the hearthstone was lifted, the body of Emily was found. Her skull had been fractured and her throat had been cut. Deeming was arrested, tried and convicted of Emily's murder, despite a plea of insanity. The discovery of Emily's body prompted the police to examine the new floor at the Rainhill property, and this led to the discovery of the bodies of Marie and the four children. Deeming was also convicted in Australia for these murders, and executed on 23 May 1892.

As with some other horrific murders, there was press speculation that Deeming may have been in London at the relevant time to have committed some of the Whitechapel Murders of Jack the Ripper. He was reported to have admitted 'the last two' of the Whitechapel murders, but this confession was strenuously denied by his solicitor. The head cast was made in Australia and sent to London to assist with potential identification by witnesses of the Jack the Ripper crimes.

1945   Heinrich Himmler

Heinrich Himmler was a principal assistant to Hitler in the Second World War and was captured by British forces. This cast is unusual both in being much later than the others, and in the fact that Himmler was not executed, but poisoned himself in custody prior to appearing in the Nuremberg war trials. A British detective brought the cast back to London, apparently as confirmation of his death, so this death mask is not really part of the series taken for phrenological reasons.

Remembering the Fallen

LISTED BELOW IS part of the Metropolitan Police Roll of Honour of officers who have been killed on duty by criminal conduct. The Police Roll of Honour Trust, incorporated by Royal Charter, contains details of officers who have died on duty for any reason on a national basis, regardless of whether a physical memorial exists: policememorial.org.uk.

1830 **PC Joseph Grantham**
Kicked in the head whilst attempting to arrest a drunken man at a disturbance in Somers Town.

1830 **PC John Long**
Stabbed to death when he challenged three suspects near Gray's Inn Road.

1833 **PC Robert Culley**
Stabbed to death during the Coldbath Fields riot.

1839 **PC William Aldridge**
Died from a fractured skull after being stoned by a mob during an arrest at Deptford.

1841 **PC James Carroll**
Attacked by a mob and struck with his own truncheon whilst making an arrest in Shoreditch.

1842 **PC Timothy Daly**
Shot dead attempting to arrest a man for highway robbery at Highbury.

1846 **PC James Hastie**
Died from injuries after being assaulted by several men at a street disturbance at Deptford.

1846 PC George Clark
Brutally beaten and stabbed to death whilst on night duty at Dagenham amid suspicions of collusion by fellow officers. An unsolved mystery.

1848 PC Daniel Monk
Struck with his own truncheon by a man trying to free a prisoner at St Giles.

1850 PC Alexander Scott
Died during hospital operation to an injury received during an affray at Deptford.

1851 PC Henry Chaplin
Attacked and struck with bricks by a disorderly crowd at Vauxhall Walk.

1858 PC Henry Morgan
Died from injuries received during an affray.

1863 PC William Davey
Shot through the head on his doorstep by a man whom he was investigating for a crime at Acton.

1864 PC Daniel Langford
Died after being assaulted in 1862.

1866 PC William Fitzgerald
Violently assaulted by a drunken prisoner in Drury Lane.

1866 PC Thomas Baker
Died from effects of assault in 1863 when apprehending two men for burglary.

1867 PC Dennis Clarke
Died from effects of assault on duty in 1864.

1868 Inspector Daniel Bradstock
Stabbed by insane prisoner in custody at King Street police station.

1868 PC Joseph Eite
Died from injuries after being kicked by a drunken man.

1870 PC James Nice
Died from injuries after being kicked on duty in 1869.

1870 PC George Waring
Died after being kicked by drunken prisoner in Shoreditch.

1873 PC Alfred Bennett
Died following injuries received after being assaulted during an arrest.

1881 **PC Frederick Atkins**
Shot three times and fatally wounded at Kingston Hill when he disturbed a burglar who was never traced. This case was the only unsolved murder of a Metropolitan Police officer between those of PC George Clark (1846) and DC James Morrison (1991).

1882 **PC George Cole**
Shot whilst attempting to arrest Thomas Orrock in Dalston, in an early ballistics case.

1887 **Sergeant David Groombridge**
Died after being beaten and kicked by two men during an arrest at King's Cross, in 1886.

1892 **DS Joseph Joyce**
Shot twice when arresting a burglar at Charing Cross Road.

1898 **PC James Baldwin**
Stabbed when arresting a man for creating a disturbance at Hoxton.

1900 **PC Ernest Thompson**
Stabbed in the neck by a man he had moved on after a disturbance in Whitechapel.

1908 **PC Joseph Williamson**
Kicked in the head whilst arresting a violent drunken man in 1907.

1909 **PC William Tyler KPM**
Shot in the head whilst pursuing armed robber Paul Hefeld during the Tottenham Outrage.

1915 **DC Alfred Young KPM**
Shot dead in Hampstead by Richard Gorges during an attempted arrest for fraud.

1918 **PC George Judge**
Fatally injured at Cricklewood by a motorcar that failed to stop.

1918 **PC Herbert Berry**
Assaulted whilst making an arrest in Euston Road.

1919 **Station Sergeant Thomas Green**
Struck on head by a Canadian soldier in the Epsom police station siege.

1919 **PC Frank Bryant KPM**
Died from injuries received after rescuing dangerous person with mental health problems from drowning in 1918.

1919 **Thomas Rowland**
Died from a fractured skull after being assaulted whilst attempting an arrest at Walworth.

1920 **PC James Kelly**
Shot three times whilst pursuing a burglar at Acton.

1921 **PC William Hallett**
Killed on patrol in Drury Lane by car driven by drunken driver.

1929 **PC John Self**
Violently attacked by man he was questioning in Golders Green.

1930 **PC Arthur Lawes**
Deliberately struck by hit-and-run driver in an unlit car in Tooting.

1938 **PC George Shepherd**
Thrown from running board of car whose driver he was seeking to stop.

1940 **War Reserve Jack Avery**
Stabbed by a man sketching gun emplacements in Hyde Park.

1948 **PC Nathaneal Edgar**
Shot whilst on plain-clothes patrol questioning suspect burglar in Southgate.

1952 **PC Sidney Miles KPFSM**
Shot on a Croydon rooftop whilst attempting to arrest Christopher Craig and Derek Bentley.

1956 **PC Leonard Demmon QPM**
Shot by terrorists whilst serving with the British police unit in Cyprus.

1958 **PC Raymond Summers**
Stabbed whilst breaking up a gang fight in Seven Sisters Road, Holloway.

1959 **DS Raymond Purdy**
Shot by Günther Podola who was escaping arrest in South Kensington.

1960 **PC Leslie Meehan**
Thrown from car by driver he was questioning into the path of another car.

1961 **Station Sergeant George Hutchins QPM and Inspector Philip Pawsey QPM**
Shot by man escaping from questioning in West Ham police station.

1966 **DS Christopher Head, PC Geoffrey Fox and TDC David Wombwell**
Members of a Q-car crew shot near Wormwood Scrubs prison.

1969 **PC Michael Davies**
Stabbed whilst off duty after identifying himself as a police officer to deal with man who had accosted him.

1973 **PC Michael Whiting QPM**
Killed after clinging to car which had driven off whilst he was questioning occupants in Charing Cross Road.

1975 **PC Stephen Tibble QPM**
Shot whilst off duty pursuing suspected terrorist who was later arrested after the Balcombe Street siege.

1975 **Captain Roger Goad GC BEM**
Explosives Officer killed whilst dealing with PIRA bomb in Kensington.

1980 **PC Francis O'Neill QGM**
Stabbed by suspect attempting to obtain drugs from chemist in Lambeth.

1981 **Kenneth Howorth GM**
Explosives Officer killed whilst dealing with a PIRA bomb in Oxford Street.

1983 **Inspector Stephen Dodd, Sergeant Noel Lane and PC Jane Arbuthnot**
Killed by the PIRA Harrods bomb.

1984 **PC Stephen Jones**
Run down attempting to stop drunken drivers racing down Seven Sisters Road, Holloway.

1984 **PC Yvonne Fletcher**
Killed by gunfire from the Libyan People's Bureau.

1985 **PC Keith Blakelock QGM**
Murdered during the Broadwater Farm riot.

1985 **DC John Fordham**
Stabbed to death whilst keeping surveillance on a suspected stolen gold bullion receiver at West Kingsdown, Kent.

1987 **PC Ronan McCloskey**
Killed whilst clinging to a car that drove off after the officer tried to administer a breath test to the driver.

1990 **PC Laurence Brown**
Killed by suspect with a sawn-off shotgun in Hackney.

1991 **PC Robert Gladwell**
Killed by blow to the head whilst making an arrest on Harrow Road division.

1991 **Sergeant Alan King**
Stabbed by a suspect he stopped in Chingford.

1991 **DC James Morrison QGM**
Stabbed to death when chasing a suspect at
Aldwych whilst off duty.

1993 **PC Patrick Dunne**
Shot when responding to reports of gunfire in
Clapham.

1994 **Sergeant Derek Robertson QGM**
Stabbed when intercepting three armed robbers
leaving a post office at New Addington.

1995 **PC Philip Walters**
Shot when dealing with three men for causing a
disturbance in Ilford.

1997 **PC Nina McKay**
Stabbed during the course of attempting to detain
a man known to be violent towards the police at
Forest Gate.

2013 **PC Andrew Duncan**
Killed in Sutton by the driver of a speeding car who
struck him to avoid being stopped by traffic patrol
officers.

2017 **PC Keith Palmer GM**
Stabbed by an Islamic terrorist who killed pedes-
trians on Westminster Bridge with a car and then
attacked the precincts of the Houses of Parliament.

2020 **Sergeant Matt Ratana**
Shot in a custody suite at Croydon by a handcuffed
prisoner who had a concealed firearm.

The National
Police Memorial,
St James's Park,
London

Acknowledgements

WE COULD NOT have written a book like this without a great deal of help from many people, but our thanks go first and foremost to Paul Bickley, the curator of the Crime Museum, who has given unstintingly of his time, advice and judgement to help this book emerge. He has continued to use his expertise and knowledge to help us enhance this edition with the most recent developments at the museum. Lindsay Siviter, a diligent historian, as well as a volunteer at the Crime Museum, has also greatly assisted us with research and corrections. Jonathan Oates is a recognised authority on some of the cases dealt with in this book, and we have been most grateful for his advice and corrections based on primary sources.

We are grateful to other Metropolitan Police staff, including Barry Nicholson and DC Mat Wake; and Neil Paterson, Phillip Barnes-Warden and Simon Littlejohn from the Heritage Centre. Kyri Georgiou, Faye Robinson, Donald Poyser and Laura Wooders have helped with the process of the agreement to reproduce images in the book. There have been other people who have provided information and their expertise to confirm details of the stories behind some of the cases like Zeb Micic, Stuart Douglas, Maurice Garvie, Tim Richardson, A.J. Griffiths-Jones, Carol Ann Lee, DS Lauren Brady, DC Laura Welham, DC Sophie Hayes and John Murray, but not least Dick Kirby, whose own research into some of the cases mentioned here has resulted in excellent books, as quoted in our bibliography. Jackie Kiely, Julia Hoffbrand, and Zey Kussan, hard at work preparing *The Crime Museum Uncovered* exhibition at the Museum of London, have also given valuable assistance to clarify details of some cases of mutual interest. Ken Butler did invaluable research on the William Hartley collection. We would also like to acknowledge the work, help and advice from Joan Lock, Stewart Evans, Kevin Coombes, Sandy Kaye, Stewart McLaughlin, Honorary Curator, Wandsworth Prison Museum, Adam Wood, Linda Moss, Coral Atkins, Alan White, Bruce Robinson, Monty Marwood, Mike Bennett, Peter Lovesey, Clive Dawson and Beverley Edwards BEM.

We appreciate the enormous support from Cate Ludlow, Sophie Bradshaw, Chrissy McMorris and Alex Boulton from The History Press, without whose faith this project could not have taken place, and their colleagues Juanita Hall and Naomi Reynolds. The layout was designed by Jemma Cox and the images prepared by Martin Latham, whose excellent work is there for all to see. Our endlessly patient literary agent Robert Smith has always been at our side in times of need.

The assistance of others has helped us, we hope, to keep our mistakes to a minimum, but we take full responsibility for any errors we have made.

All images in the book have been reproduced by kind permission of the Metropolitan Police Service apart from those on pp. 392 and 397, which are the authors' own.

We hope, above all, that this book will shine an interesting and fascinating light on previously little-known aspects of the world of Scotland Yard and its excellent detectives.

Bibliography

Adam, Hargrave L., *The Police Encyclopaedia* (Blackfriars, 1920)

Allason, Rupert, *The Branch: A History of the Metropolitan Police Special Branch: 1883–1983* (Secker & Warburg, 1983)

Begg, Paul, Fido, Martin and Skinner, Keith, *The Complete Jack the Ripper A to Z* (John Blake, 2010)

Borowitz, Albert, *The Bermondsey Horror* (Robson Books, 1989)

Cameron, J.M., 'R vs Payne' in *Medico-Legal Journal Proceedings* of 10 June 1971

Charles, Keith and Shuff, Derek, *Psychic Cop* (Blake, 1995)

Cherrill, Frederick R., *The Finger Print System at Scotland Yard* (HMSO, 1954)

Clarkson, Charles T. and Richardson, J., *Police! A General Account of the Work of the Police in England & Wales* (Field & Tuer, Leadenhall Press, 1889)

Du Rose, John, *Murder Was My Business* (W.H. Allen, 1971)

Fido, Martin and Skinner, Keith, *The Official Encyclopedia of Scotland Yard* (Virgin, 1999)

Field, Katherine, *Margaret Waters: A Convenient Villain: Infanticide, Baby Farming and the Status of Women in Victorian England* (NEH Seminar for School Teachers, 2012)

Gaute, J.H.H. and Odell, Robin, *The Murderer's Who's Who* (Pan Books, 1980)

Goodman, Jonathan and Waddell, Bill, *The Black Museum: Scotland Yard's Chamber Of Crime* (Harrap, 1987)

Griffiths-Jones, A.J., *Prisoner 4374* (Austin Macauley Publishers, 2015)

Herber, Mark, *Criminal London* (Phillimore, 2002)

Honeycombe, Gordon, *More Murders of the Black Museum 1835–1985* (Hutchinson, 1993)

Honeycombe, Gordon, *The Murders of the Black Museum 1870–1970* (Hutchinson, 1981)

Kalush, William and Sloman, Larry, *The Secret Life of Houdini* (Pocketbooks, 2006)

Kelland, Gilbert, *Crime in London* (Grafton, 1987)

Kirby, Dick, *Death on the Beat* (Pen & Sword, 2012)

Kirby, Dick, *The Brave Blue Line* (Pen & Sword, 2011)

Lane, Brian, *The Encyclopedia of Forensic Science* (BCA, 1992)

Lee, Carol Ann, *A Fine Day For A Hanging: The Real Ruth Ellis Story* (Mainstream Publishing, 2012)

Linnane, Fergus, *The Encyclopedia of London Crime and Vice* (Sutton, 2003)

Lock, Joan, *Scotland Yard's First Cases* (Robert Hale, 2011)

McBride, William, 'Mysteries My Camera Has Solved' in *The People's Journal and Angus Herald* (9 February 1935)

Marston, Edward, *John Christie* (The National Archives, 2007)

Moss, Alan and Skinner, Keith, *The Scotland Yard Files: Milestones in Crime Detection* (National Archives, 2006)

Moysey, Steven P., *The Road to Balcombe Street* (Haworth Press, 2008)

Oates, Jonathan, *Chesney: The Middle Class Murderer* (Mango Books, 2016)

Oates, Jonathan, *John Christie of Rillington Place* (Wharncliffe True Crime, 2012)

Oates, Jonathan, *John George Haigh: The Acid-Bath Murderer* (Pen & Sword True Crime, 2014)

O'Connor Sean, *Handsome Brute: The Story of a Ladykiller* (Simon & Schuster 2013)

Simpson, Professor Keith, *Forty Years of Murder* (Harrap, 1983)

Waddell, Bill, *The Black Museum: New Scotland Yard* (Little, Brown and Company, 1993)

Wensley, Frederick Porter, *Forty Years of Scotland Yard* (Doubleday, Doran & Co., 1931)

Williams, Guy, R., *The Black Treasures of Scotland Yard* (Hamish Hamilton, 1973)

Wilson, Colin and Wilson, Damon, *Written in Blood* (Constable & Robinson, 2003)

Opposite: Memorial to the victims of the 7 July 2005 attacks, Hyde Park

7 JULY 2005
08·50
KING'S CROSS
7 JULY 2005
08·50
KING'S CROSS
7 JULY 2005
08·50
KING'S CROSS

Index